Copyright

All private information disclosed in this book is done so in the interest of public awareness, and of which disclosures are crucial for the writer to tell his story. For it is written:

"Thus saith the Lord; Execute ye judgment and righteousness, and deliver the spoiled out of the hand of the oppressor: and do no wrong, do no violence to the stranger, the fatherless, nor the widow, neither shed innocent blood in this place."
(Jeremiah 22:3)

"And have no fellowship with the unfruitful works of darkness, but rather reprove *them*. For it is a shame even to speak of those things which are done of them in secret. But all things that are reproved are made manifest by the light: for whatsoever doth make manifest is light."
(Ephesians 5:11-13)

"Congress shall make no law respecting an establishment of religion, or prohibiting the free exercise thereof; or abridging the freedom of speech, or of the press; or of the right of the people peaceably to assemble, and to petition the government for a redress of grievances."
- Amendment 1, Constitution of the United States

Most scripture quoted from the Authorized King James Version.

Copyright © 2016 by Joseph John Kacin

All rights reserved.

This book or any portion thereof may not be reproduced or used in any manner whatsoever without the express written permission of the author except in the case of brief quotations embodied in critical reviews and certain other noncommercial uses permitted by copyright law.

ISBN: 978-0-692-03268-8

The names of some of the characters have been changed.

THE PART ABOUT THE SERPENT

Contents

1. Field of Vision 5
2. Surrender, I love you!..............................15
3. The Price of Having Dreams....................69
4. Jo Jo the Dog-Faced Boy.........................98
5. Losing Touch..123
6. Down Time...131
7. Born Into the Hands of the Devil.............169
8. Sacrilege...187
9. The End Motel Room................................201
10. After Dark...207
11. Hard Stuff..228
12. Kindling... 294
13. Fire-breathing..347
14. Hindsight...367

THE PART ABOUT THE SERPENT

For those who were and are still being robbed.

THE PART ABOUT THE SERPENT

"Now the serpent was more subtle
subtle than any beasts of the field the
Lord God had made."
(Genesis 3:1)

THE PART ABOUT THE SERPENT

Field of Vision

"OH, GIVE-EM' A DIR-DY LOOK!" my mother always tried inciting me, as if she felt entitled to employ the endowments of my own personal characteristics for her own good pleasure, such as when passing an offending motorist, or to a group of ignorant people who were unworthy of all other forms of intelligible communication, who we referred to as "low-lifes." But dirty looks were never anything I could be instigated to give on behalf of someone *else's* wrath!...

THE PART ABOUT THE SERPENT

Born on November 13th, 1969, my mother always said I was born with a "reeeal meeean" look in my eye. In that very sentence you're looking at a visually orientated observation about vision of a visually oriented person speaking in terms of seeing. Not to mention, the age of Aquarius, the sign of the scorpion, the rock-hippie cult, widespread panic, the devil's favorite number, a spellbound mother, and a few superstitious stories.

My mother also marveled for years that I turned 13 on Friday the 13th. While after 15 years of drifting as an adult, and losing valuable things such as birth certificates and friends, I managed to salvage one photograph of myself at birth, and the photo confirms what my mother was referring to. I had thin golden-blonde hair, chubby cheeks, a tiny chin with a dimple in it, and my eyes are enormously huge, wide, and blue; eyes with an attitude! They look as if they were meant for some old, wise-man's head, but rather got stuck in a baby's head instead __...

I learned I could use my eyes authoritatively, and storytelling, my mother depicted a time when I was in a carrier at a shopping center. While she must have been getting the car closed up, two women stopped to give me attention, and although my mother could not see my face because my head was facing away from her, she knew by the, "Oh my" impression and nervous laughter from the ladies that I was scowling at them. And she said, "and you *were* too!"

THE PART ABOUT THE SERPENT

My first visual memory is fuzzy Christmas lights, up close, as if someone was holding me up so I could appreciate them. And this concurs with other memories of my mother's behavior, such as setting me on the smooth stones of a shallow delta in a beautiful river on one occasion, and witnessing her walking around the house after retirement with her cat upside down in her arms so the cat could decipher fascinating objects upside-down for fun.

We pretty much had the same lights put up the same way each year. I can almost remember where in the house I first saw those fuzzy lights, and that would be over the once white/now black mantle in the living room atop of the deco-style fireplace with the fake logs in it that would probably burn the house down if you actually tried to light a fire in there. There was a wide mirror over the mantle and the lights - always buried in dark, green pine branches and evergreen, were refreshingly, false...

Mrs. O'Brien, our elder neighbor across the street - who owned O'Brien's Party Store downtown along with her husband, gave us a glossy, ceramic Christmas tree she made about 14" high that was hollow, with perfect little plastic lights on it that would all faintly light up by one electric bulb inside the hollow part. All these fuzzy electric lights - dark orange, bright red, frosted green, unreal blue - essentially they had no business adorning natural foliage, there was no realistic communion there. Even a more natural light such as a flame from a candle surrounded by pine needles to suit a special occasion appears authentic (for someone), however that is a fire hazard.

These glass bulbs we were using back then were the hot type that would singe your fingers when you touched them, they smoked chemicals when they broke, the paint chipped off, and they left broken jagged glass wherever you handled them or stored them. And no, I'm not an environmentalist or anything like that. But if the real thing couldn't work, we painstakingly created these imitation lights strung along on 110 volt wires (thanks in part to the delirium of Thomas Edison), the wires themselves being green-colored as if to pass as co-habitable with human beings who were sentimental to nature and decided to bring assimilated frondescence into the home and set it ablaze. Why did we have to force these traditions and extravagant luxuries together when it is so obvious that it is not even safe?

See, when your cat or your puppy chews on your Christmas tree lights and gets his hide volted, you've failed as a reliable source of paternal provisions for that thing and have long-since moved into the realm of selfish endangerment. Do you think I'm kidding? It may make a funny story to share for some time: the cat didn't die, and the dog will not chew on wires ever again, however, those are the very kinds of tritely hazardous instances that we became immune to in our culture and likely find humorous because we ourselves have handled electric current enough to know how *not* to handle it. Enough that it downright disturbs us when *we* get electrocuted, save it is not life-threatening. Then

THE PART ABOUT THE SERPENT

moments later when the sweat dries off our chest, we resume our drama, only more cautiously; amazed at both our resilience, and our stupidity.

We can handle a good deal of external power, but not our own cruelty.

And what to make of this huge sandstone fireplace that was hollow in the center, supported by plywood (not to be mistaken with real boards), made not of brick, but decorated with sandstone-faced tile-like things with sparkly flecks in them that were spot glued on the back with black tar stuff to stick to the plywood (though they always fell off); and electric logs in the fireplace that we could never use because the electric motor in the imitation logs itself had a short in it?

What's more, all the standing plants in our house were lustrous plastic, as well as the fruit laid out to tempt the guests, which had to be dusted on Saturdays - the day my mom's hair was in pink and sea-foam-green plastic curlers and it was in your best interest to avoid her! ... Pink and sea-foam-green plastic curlers being a laborious undertaking to misrepresent long wavy hair that probably looked fantastic just the way it was!

And ceramic replicas of *real* trees that people chop down to drag into their homes to adorn with live wires were treasured, and dusted!

I remember doing allot of thinking on a chair on the front porch, which was an addition to our house prior to our obtaining it, waiting for my dad to come and pick me up for visitations. My mother divorced my dad when I was four years old, which would have been 1973. My mom hung cedar shake on the wall that entered into main part of the house around a large picture window, and like the back porch, it was lined with jalousie windows that were too un-air-tight to heat during the winter. I still remember what it tasted like having dared to lick one of the metal screens containing dust and pollen in the holes after watching a squirrel hike the power line one day: "Many years of human development and nature gone wrong!…and maybe rabies!"

My mother upholstered all her furniture herself: orange corduroy, flowered prints, and lots and lots of vinyl with gold and Gothic-black thumbtacks. It would be two weeks since I've seen my dad as appointments were bi-weekly, and some years before visitations were ever instated following the divorce. He lived in Royal Oak and sometimes I would begin waiting for him, if I recall correctly, around 11:00 AM on Saturday, as scheduled. Sometimes I would wait several hours and when scheduling changed for him to pick me up on Friday nights after work, which was more convenient for him, I remember he often didn't come until very late, more like 11:00PM.

I remember trying to exact his position on route in my mind and would envision him in the driver's seat from an aerial view of the driver's window ... passing cars and taking all the curves around the lake as he was

THE PART ABOUT THE SERPENT

approaching to come and get me, even pausing patiently for all the red lights, stops and left-hand turns it took him to get off the main roads... But it seemed the more intensely I anticipated the time of his arrival, the longer it would take him. I was never even close. And I remember when I understood how all the horrible fatalities caused on the road were due to cars opposing each other on the same slice of byway, I could never understand why we allow it... In my mind, if you want to drive a car safely in one direction, you pave a road for that direction, period, no exceptions. Maybe I was thinking of a one-way only, which could be a big loop and perhaps many different loops, all one way - no more head on collisions. But that might mean if you wanted to drive two blocks south you would have to jump on heading north for many miles until you came back around (which would be foolish), and if you missed your stop you'd have to complete the loop again. I don't even think I ever cared to finish that thought until just now, but I could see that if you organized the traffic with two semi-parallel roads - each heading the opposite direction - the only chance for a head on collision would be for the bizarre maniac who took all the drugs he could get his hands on in one afternoon and was hell bent on crossing the prairie into oncoming traffic.

Years later my mother told me that it would be too costly to design roads like that, but I could see that men did sometimes create one-way roads, and also started putting concrete barriers between expressways with the intention of keeping the head on collisions down. Now,

THE PART ABOUT THE SERPENT

however, you had to take a right hand exit to eventually get to your destination on the left, which requires a massive amount of roadwork, and confusion, because the answer came as an affix and appeasement to an ugly situation. Which therefore leaves it unfinished work, and an ugly situation, glorified.

Lake Orion, where I grew up, is close to Detroit and lots of my neighbors worked for Sea Ray and The Big Three. We called cars a "necessary evil" and if you have to truck fruits and vegetables from the southern states to the northern to prevent nutritional deficiencies like scurvy and rickets, fine, however I am the only one I know of in my entire family that has ever driven a commercial vehicle for the sake of nutrition. Everyone was so eager to have his own private luxury vehicle that he forsook safety and calls it a risk he must take so he can get to his job at the factory to assemble artificial Christmas tree lights (reflecting his industrialized education), and to get the beer store to pretend none of it is really happening.

It was clear that we spent an exceeding amount of time, technology, sweat, and money into providing everybody a horribly violent and destructive device with a thin shiny veneer; decked with carpeting in it that will be replaced by a new one, ten times over (and plenty of coffins), before a fraction of that intelligence is spent on wisely designing and maintaining one semi-permanent road and protecting man from *un*-necessary risk. Rather, we authorize such risks by antagonizing him

THE PART ABOUT THE SERPENT

with discontent and fear of failing to perform his duties should he not.

I'm not exacting an argument on the cost of road design and it isn't worth the ink and paper to go on about it. I will, however, exact an argument on morality and give you a standard example of how I thought about everything growing up: our values and priorities were not what we said they were. Nothing in my culture was genuine to begin with; we valued phony things and sacrificed the meaningful things to have them, and then when we tragically lost the meaningful things we ought not to have sacrificed, we justified our inadequacies, because if we didn't, we might stand out! It's like giving up and going with the flow that is headed straight for a pit rather than desisting to spare the life your family, because our priorities are such that we'd rather die than to draw attention to ourselves. We are so preoccupied with our concerns of what other people might think of us (which is intentional on their part, and a pathetic weakness on ours) that we forfeited our ability to make any sense.

...

So, to close with the thoughts that began with my mouth wetting the back of the orange corduroy chair, I could never understand it… "We desperately wanted to protect lives and save every one of them at all cost, right?"… "My dad was just as excited and eager to

THE PART ABOUT THE SERPENT

come and see me as I was about seeing him, right?"... Then to see my dad arrive in the rain at night, backing his van over the neighbor's fence, knowing he was intoxicated, robbed the joy and merit of the entire effort. Where is the honor in senselessly dying in order to demonstrate a sense of compassion to persons other than the individual who would then bear the guilt of it and live on to hear the hales of their loving sacrifice - perpetuating that guilt; not to mention, putting *their* lives at risk on top of it? My friend, that is a manifold insanity: one, on the half-effort of the party who shrinks back and lets the sand fall where it may who continues to throw worth on it; two, on the respected parties admitting no knowledge of deception; three, that this kind of behavior has gone on uncontested so long in our lives that it's become normal; and four, on the part of the so-thought-to-be beneficiary who deceives himself for the protection from all parties named. Are you seeing it yet?

THE PART ABOUT THE SERPENT

Surrender, I love you!

MY MOTHER TOLD ME on more than one occasion, after I was an adult, that my father refused to hold me in the hospital when I was born. I thought on that for some years before getting back with her, dwelling on the word, "refused." That meant he " would not" as opposed to "did not" or "never did." I told her, "*that must have been weird*", meaning, awkward. I have very select few memories in tact from my childhood, especially those of my dad, but one was an evening when he must have been rather frustrated. I was just getting around on my own and I was studying how my dad drank his beer in his favorite black-vinyl recliner pointed toward the RCA floor-model, possibly like every other night.

Repetitiously, he would sip it and then set it down with precision, balancing it on the arched wooden arm to his right that was only half as wide as the can, swallowing delectably with his lips pursed, his head tilted away from the can, stretching the distance between his eyes and the can which were fixed to it, confirming it wouldn't fall, (and its value) and would then cock his head back to the right to contemplate as if he were now prepared to testify with greater confidence. I think the brand was Pabst's Blue Ribbon. But I was going to demonstrate to my dad this evening that I could do what he did, just like he did. I got up and toddled over to his chair, and grabbed his beer with both hands attempting to tip the can back to drink out of it but he then mean-spiritedly shoved me to the floor - retrieving his beer all in one transaction. I was impressed that he could execute such a hostile maneuver and still remain seated. It was like his right arm could reach across the living room floor if he wanted it to when leaning into the side of the recliner, as if he were a zoologist leaning way out of a rowboat with one arm and only one chance to fetch an injured waterfowl while coasting by...

Then there are the photos where, assuming my mom, would dress me up like a hobo, slurping a can of beer with a woman's cigarette in my hand - my eyes rolled back in my head insinuating intoxication.

My father having jet-black hair - I was told that I screamed any time I saw a man in public with dark hair, and I fail to find anything normal about that. My mother explained to me, in other words, what it was like laying in bed at night listening to the sound of my dad trying to make it up our spiral stairwell when he was smashed, to come to bed; trying repeatedly, somersaulting back down the stairs, pleading in peril

THE PART ABOUT THE SERPENT

from the bottom of the steps for her to come down and help him up.

She pointed out to me where she found a black heel mark on one occasion from the sole of his work-shoe on the stairwell ceiling that was so high that he would have had to have been violently airborne. And I am not using the word "violent'" here as a state of mind, but rather an abnormal amount of contortion and force, given the circumstances, that were beyond physical possibility. After becoming an adult however, I actually understood my dad better, pondering that heal mark in my heart.

It wasn't until I was 30 that I faintly remembered my dad throwing me off our dock when I was just a little boy, before I knew how to swim - to entertain his buddies who were all laughing. In the memory, I remember deadening my weight on the dock and pleading with him not to, while he dragged me toward the end... Truthfully, I don't remember going into the water and if it was after our basement was dug out, it would have been only waist deep for a little boy, if that, at the end of our dock, because rather than haul the dirt out, we unloaded it in the lake. I must pause at this point to tell you that if you are sensing denial by my rationalizing things with many words after sharing something appalling, that is how lies work; they take enormous amounts of energy to protect rather than to admit something was unbearable. I will be expounding upon that theme throughout the remainder of this book due to the fact that lies are the principle nature of the devil.

THE PART ABOUT THE SERPENT

My mother said she didn't remember my father throwing me off the dock, plus she added, "knowing the way your father was with you, I never would have left you alone with him in the first place." However discomforting it is to acknowledge the words, "knowing the way your father was with you, I would never have left you alone with him in the first place", my mother's claim to supervise me for 24 hours a day, seven days a week, for even one year without giving my father a chance to be alone with me would require a severely over-protective mother. Or perhaps a mother's overly-protected reputation was at work. Furthermore, when I tried to describe to my mother the time when my father shoved me down after trying to drink from his beer, she covered it with a hollow and well-worn "Oh, I let him have it over *that* one!" However, my mother was covering herself in a memory she didn't have…so you can sense what futile distance was presented for any such consolation.

Therefore, concerning my dad throwing me off the end of the dock, I have been hesitant to validate that memory as gospel. Objective voices work to diminish truth as well. I do remember clearly however, going alone with my dad during visitations to the Detroit Zoo, and he held me up over a couple hippos that were probably 20 feet down and I started screaming and kicking. He laughed a genuine public laugh after I got everyone's attention. So, characteristically, yeah, he had that spirit...

THE PART ABOUT THE SERPENT

The only memory I have of my whole family being together (four of us) would be camping in Munising in the Michigan Upper Peninsula. All I could see in the dark was my dad standing in the smokey light of either the firelight, or possibly a lantern, as if he were on stage - facing my direction with a stick under his knee grasped with both hands to break it. And when the stick broke, he fell, and we all roared laughing!... It stands out as the most wholesome memory of my family, although my dad was probably good and looped. I don't remember seeing anybody, just my dad, and then hearing the laughter between us all. It was like the best night of my life, actually. We were healthily camping, it told me my mom was well inside, it mitigated my half-brother's need for autonomy, and I could tell that my own laughter was contributing to the mix....

I also remember eating wild blueberry pancakes on a picnic table in the cold morning rain under a Visqueen shelter that my mom made off the back of my dad's camper in view of Lake Superior. I remember it was always my mom's thoughtfulness, innovation, and instinctive haste to make due that would justify the unpleasantness of such situations so that one memory of eating wild blueberry pancakes outdoors in the wet grass made unworthy any formal dining experience men pathetically try and market. Like the day I must have imagined Crystal Gayle in Rita Coolidge's blue jeans...Woe!

THE PART ABOUT THE SERPENT

My dad had a modest-man's ski boat, and I remember some of us out on the water afloat with the engine off after docking to get some ice cream. And I remember dropping my chocolate-cream-colored-looking-thing right in the lake, watching it being taken away in the bass-smelling drift without a prayer, crying at the top of my lungs like there will never be another tomorrow, invoking consoling voices, even my dad's.

My mom drove the boat while my dad skied behind it and he was known for skiing with a beer in one hand and a cigarette in his mouth, and he used to start by being yanked off the dock! Knowing personally, how much power and force it takes to get up on two skis being tugged through the water, it was no doubt that our back yard was a stunt scene.

I heard stories, like the time my mom was backing their Z-28 to launch the boat off a ramp, and when my dad yelled, "take it" after the boat was afloat, my mother stepped on the gas and proceeded to back the car into the lake! And the time that my dad was tangled up in the ski-rope trying to undo it, and yelled, "kill it!" meaning, "Kill the engine" she, thinking he said, "Hit it!" thrust the throttle forward!

We had a friend of the family, Larry, a character like my dad who had a cottage on the Island, and on one particular evening he and Larry were out drinking in Larry's brand new Sea Ray. They were on the longest stretch of lake where they could open it up. At one end of that stretch, visible just off the bridge was Squaw

THE PART ABOUT THE SERPENT

Island - that was just a mound of bushes and sand with an old, beaten down metal break-wall around it, assuming the island supported a structure at one time. Larry and my dad had the boat at top end, screaming across the water, but their heads were buried below the dash watching the speedometer when they hit Squaw Island - tearing the bottom of the boat off. I imagine they then swam ashore leaving the boat to the Boat Graveyard of Lake Orion, because reporting it at that point would be very costly. Nevertheless, Larry had other new ski boats, and beer was distributed in semi-trailers...

...

Before I can remember, and before the basement was dug out, we had pet geese in the back yard, and I heard stories of them going out onto the thin ice and not knowing what to do. They would squat, and then we and the neighbors would have to throw pebbles at them to keep them moving back toward shore so their feathers wouldn't stick to the ice. We had to get rid of them because they hated my guts and my parents were afraid they might do me bodily harm. We also had a black cat named Tiger that craved fish so - that if one fell in the water between the boat and the dock, the cat would jump in the water after the fish! We also had a yellow bird named Tweety (I think), and I heard that we had a cat that would always jump in the bathtub when my bother was taking a bath, and then my brother would get yelled at for it until one day my mom saw it. Apparently the cat was walking the edge of the tub and my mother warned him, "Steve! don't you touch that cat!" And he said, "No, no mom I won't touch the cat!" and then the cat leaped in the tub and then jumped right back out because he actually hated it!

My mother made any accommodation I needed to save injured and rejected baby birds - to try and keep them alive, and we even put Tweety's old birdcage and feeders to use for the effort. One bird in particular - so traumatized and sick that he would have been better off dead - we put in the cage on the back porch to calm him down and keep him protected. We may have put warm linen around him and administered human stuff no bird would ever eat in an ear-dropper. The memory I had to retrieve from the Vault of Unbearables was walking my chubby butt out onto the back porch in the pre-dawn light before school to check on him, and hearing a piercing squeaky sound and then looking down to see his curled up tongue jetting out of his mouth at an alarming length and his eye bugged out, because he'd managed to get himself toward the door during the night and I was standing on him...

Despite our best efforts, not one of those baby birds ever lived. My mother even told me as an adult, "No baby bird that has been rejected by its mother stands a chance."...

One day there were Canadian geese in our next-door neighbors' back yard and I tried to approach the

THE PART ABOUT THE SERPENT

goslings after slipping between the fence, and every adult turned on me hissing at me with black tongues and I yelled, "snake! snake!" ducking back though the fence!

At one time, an old bald neighbor who lived within the island, but not on the water, shot a mother duck and all her ducklings were scattered across the island in terror while all the neighbors were scrambling to try and rescue them, and fathom what could provoke some old man to do such a thing. And those kinds of things drove me from tears to action.

…

There was no hiding the fact that I was unlike the other kids and the treatment I received growing up. It is still just as intense today after many different changes in me, and in others, and all the different complexities that alter along with them. Today it is more understandable, but the bottom line is, it hurts. Sometimes it appeared as if I was being given favor but it was usually for the wrong reasons, and then it always backfired. Most of the other kids took their aggression out on me openly. It was apparent to everyone that my mother favored me though she was relentlessly hostile toward me in spite of that. A severe cruelty buried the conspicuous favoritism and I continued receiving low-level punishment from my brother in a familiar way I received it from my mom. Everywhere I went I was drawing far too much attention and I hated it. Ninety-eight percent of it was injurious and accusatory and I remained silent because of what was going on in our home. I was confounded; I didn't instigate it, I couldn't change it if I knew what it was, I was not provoking people to take their abuse out on me, but I could not even hide from it.

I disturbingly remember what was probably the first day of school, or first few days of school, at the bus stop one year. I freakishly, though synchronously almost cannot allow myself to remember Brian O'Million catching someone's gray and black, striped house cat, swinging it around by its tail with both hands while it was screaming, and letting it soar up onto the grass above a stone break-wall, which happened to be the yard of the old bald neighbor who shot the mother duck.

All the older kids, like him, including the younger kids with darkness in their hearts, laughed what seemed like a secret inflected laugh the moment it was over. Like all of their teeth suddenly turned yellow at the same time and were trying to hide it. It was first, horrifying, then sinister. I did not know them. I think I actually fainted in my mind, and for years told myself it was a nightmare that never happened...

And if the boldness of Brian's act (being a daredevil that did 360's off the wooden ski jump he constructed in his back yard) astonished the other kids, they still kept their hands in their pockets and made no protest in

THE PART ABOUT THE SERPENT

their minds…which Brian was almost antagonizing them to do, and came to a consensus that evil really is kind of cool when it is obscene like that.

The Older-Kids-Group on my bus, remaining stationary to the island (many of whom eventually graduated to the earlier bus heading to junior high and high school) consisted of Jeff Jacobs, Steve Stucky, Terry Smith, Brian O'Million, Pat Lapaort, Laura Laport, Jimmy Kondash, Karen Kondash, and Chuck and Charley Skylas. I know I am missing others, but that was basically the adult line-up. On the bus we sang marching songs always conducted by one of the older kids who would shout out the verse like a drill sergeant, while the rest of the bus would repeat it:

> "A yellow bird (a yellow bird)
> With a yellow bill (a yellow bill)
> Sitting on (sitting on)
> My windowsill (my windowsill)
> I led him in (led him in)
> With crumbs of bread (crumbs of bread)
> And then I crushed (then I crushed)
> His fucking head (his fucking head)…!"

And we paraphrased the Doors song, Hello, into something too profane to write.

Additionally, if we were good all week, our school bus driver would crank her eight-track cassette of AC/DC Back in Black, featuring Highway to Hell, on Fridays, where we knew every word, every strike of the strings, by heart.

And I remember Danny Brown fist fighting me before the bus arrived during the confusion. Danny, a sparky jock, was younger and smaller than I was though it was nothing to him to fight me - he was proud of himself; he was taught this type of aggression was right. I remember lowering my head and looking up under my eyebrows to try and hide the tears welling up in my eyes, pretending to stand in a fighting stance. I remember seeing the blurry vision of the cold morning light behind Danny, veiled through my eyebrows, which looked like reeds magnified through a glass of water. But I honestly could not understand what was happening...

…

At home, Steve and I were taught never to resist my mother's assaults; not physically, not verbally. My mother would get a medium-heel shoe (or whatever was the closest semblance to one), command me to lie down on the couch or wrestle me to it, face up, and then she would straddle me at my waist, pinning me down with her weight while she would take her rage out on me, beating me with the heels of her shoes. If I resisted by blocking the blows with my hands or clinging to one of her wrists, she would threaten me, "Don't you use your hands!" "Don't you use your hands!" "Sit on your hands!" "Sit on your goddamn hands!" because if I did, she would increase the intensity of the violence twofold. Resistance was a trigger that sent her wild. I remember feeling my thin, staticy hair stuck all over my burning hot, sweaty face, rolling my head from side to side, begging her with a broken, "no-ho, no-ho!"... It was as if she was preaching, or forcing a message out on me, pounding me with each syllable to spread her energy out and to solidify what she was conveying. Her eyes were full of blazing hatred and her lips curled up showing all her teeth in blind rage. It's a look I've never been able to forget. Like when people pretend to be Frankenstein and they put 1,000 watts of rage into a face that can only handle 100 watts. She was out of her mind. There was no stopping her and she wouldn't let up until she was exhausted. She would be gasping for breath like she just ran down a train; her breasts rising and lowering, cursing at me between each breath, all her teeth showing and sheer hatred in her voice.

It was as if she found what it was that ruined her life, destroyed her family and all the good she ever loved and stood for, and was now determined to avenge herself upon it.

And I very much believed I was it...

The only option was compliance, and the only hope to try to cut the power source between violent episodes was making ourselves scarce and keeping our mouths shut. We were required to do normal chores like clean house, do our own laundry, yard work, painting, and pulling the weeds out of the lake with a rake to dry them on the dock and then bag them, which many of us in the bays and no-wake areas had to do. Otherwise you would wind up having a personal bog in your back yard, complete with dead fish and a Styrofoam cup in it.

But we were guilted into scratching my mother's back, rubbing and scratching her feet, and getting her up for work with her coffee ready by dramatizing her pain and suffering in guilt-provoking fashion; syndromatically repeating how everybody treated her like shit. That, reared by a subtle continuum of reminders of how much she has done for us, the times we hurt her and how much we did so, followed with "…and I just don't need that."…

We always had to fight with her to get her out of bed and all our clocks were set 20 minutes fast which created a lifestyle of always being late, angry for being late, missing appointments entirely, and if her coffee was cold, we would be reprimanded - having to reheat it, being instant coffee with cream and sugar. And we were not using microwaves back then, at least not in our house.

…

I always took to organizing and sweeping out the storage part of our basement on my own accord, usually getting in trouble for it, but which was always the worst

THE PART ABOUT THE SERPENT

part of our house, and I would kick up dust that I could smell was many years old. It was both solitude and purpose for me, and a chance to play in my dad's old one-man submarine that he designed and partially completed which he never came back for...

I would annually take a shop-broom to the three way intersection of our street in front of our house, under the street light, so all the neighbors could benefit, which meant: digging the dirt out of the man-hole cover, pounding the broom down to push out the moist soil and hatching chestnuts, and staying out past dark until I was all dewy and out of energy. I usually stacked all the spare blocks from the basement on the side of the house in some new order, and since we had little money and not a man of the house around - we built a makeshift black-Visqueen lean-to off the side of the house which was always water logged, noisy, and unsightly; housing rusty bikes, moldy boat cushions, and garbage.

Being that we were supposed to store our bikes on that side of the house, you could ride right over the broken concrete sidewalk and shoot your bike between the house and the neighbor's stockade fence (of which its very construction was likely necessitated by our unsightly junk) and run in the house without actually stopping to park the bike. One day my handlebar went through the basement window and I don't even think I stopped to attend to it, thinking maybe no one would ever know, or, if and when they did, my bike would not be suspect, though I knew that because the window had an aluminum frame that was special for a basement, it would be costly and hard for people like us to find.

Weeks later, my mom found the window and knew exactly what happened. I was so careless and destructive. I remember I often carried around a palm-full of garlic salt because I liked to lick it, and one day when I'd had too much - as I was walking out the door - I dropped the leftovers in my mom's outdoor plant, potted in a standing wicker basket, making the organic connection "garlic" and "plant" not thinking it would hurt anything, but failing to observe that "salt" could damage a plant topically. My mother found that too, and knew it was garlic salt that I had dumped there, though I never told her why. I just let her yell at me.

As we got older, we were told not to come into the house after school until she came home from work, which was usually around six in the evening, though we got out of school around 3:15 in broad daylight. Other times she would lock us out through the chain on the front porch door, which was typically how we locked the house when going away - by slipping her slim wrist through from the outside - not having a key for the deadbolt we locked ourselves in with at night.

That feeling of being locked out is hard to describe: the slice I could see of the interior of the house now looked different; it was now private property and she didn't want me in it, and the atmosphere - even the carpet on the floor - had increased in value and admiration without me welcoming myself in to fuck it up, while

THE PART ABOUT THE SERPENT

searching thoughts came about what hardhearted old neighbor or cruel babysitter I might orphan myself to - who could take in a broken kid without damaging their sustainability and who would not betray my mom. It would have to be someone who already knew her and sensed that the situation was hopeless...

In essence my mother was telling me, "You're on your own *now*!"

My brother once taught me how to climb the tree by the master bedroom, and I could sit my butt on the corner of the roof, let go of the tree, stand up, and walk to the window and get in. My brother and I were never in the house together like this, and when done eating and watching cartoons, we would cover our tracks - climb back down the tree off the roof, and resume our nomadic roaming.

There were late nights I remember my mother, being overworked - would be on her hands and knees in the kitchen, searching the cupboards for a can of something to eat in tears - shouting and shaming me for eating "everything in the house", while I stood there with my head down and my heart bleeding in remorse.

...

I tried to forget the names my mother used to call me, and some of them I forbid allowance for the sake of self-preservation for so many years that the place where they were may still exist as phantoms, but they have been defaced. It usually started with a familiar monologue; "You-god-damn-sonofabitch…!" Or, How dare You! You In-credibly! Selfish! Egotistical! Pig-headed-Bastard…!" Or, she'd say "Yesss your High-nesss!" She'd use adverbs like "You chauvinistic…!" or, "You macho…!" and, "You asinine…! however, I was just a little boy - obviously taking the brunt of someone else's punishment. Or maybe many someone elses'…

Once, I saw my mother whip my brother over the head with a wire coat hanger in one strike so sharply that my brother grabbed his head with both hands, almost dropping to his knees, asking her what she hit him with. I could tell it hurt him like nothing he was used to being hit with by her, and couldn't see it in her hand against the dark, calico shag carpeting as she stood there condemning him with her arms straight down and behind. He was asking her out of curiosity what the object was she hit him with rather than telling her not to hit him, because that he would never do. In *our* minds, we deserved it…

I dearly loved my brother and I tell you, I hated my mother for that.

Following such a senseless memory, necessitating such a destructive conclusion within me, I could no longer tolerate anyone harming my bother; not physically, not verbally. My brother was the kind of brother that when

THE PART ABOUT THE SERPENT

he and I were both on a rope swing, coming back fast for a tree with the weight of both of us on the same rope, he maneuvered himself so that he would take the tree, and not me, splitting his head open, and then riding home erratically with me on his handlebars while trying not to get overly upset and ditch me.

There was also a group of guys in a car that stopped and beat him up while he was walking home from town one evening when he was a teenager. I remember him lying in bed in the daytime with his face all scraped up, and they broke his horned-rimmed glasses, which dubbed him the name, Poindexter, at school. Allegedly, there was a man who pulled his car over to the side of the road that night while these guys where kicking the crap out of him and yelled, "Get in!" My mother told me years later that if that man would not have stopped, "they'd-a-killed him."

The violence my mother took out on my brother I did not often see, she, privatizing the abuse between us; which meant that my brother and I were afforded more protection when we were together. And having a different temperament than me, my brother, in essence told my mother "I don't *need* you" and would rehearse smart-ass remarks he'd gleaned from an Argumentation and Persuasion class offered by the high school - in defense of her attacks - that were so shocking to her that she would have to back down, though her very next thoughts were reconnoitering a way to get rid of him.

THE PART ABOUT THE SERPENT

And since my brother knew my mother was going through his things when he was gone, he once left a note on top of his dirty laundry under the lid of the hamper in his room, presumably in his, I'm-this-way-I'm-not-gonna-change illegible, cryptic left-handed writing with a faint blue Bic that said, "NOPE, NOT IN HERE!" and she never was the same... You could tell she had a pot-belly stove deep inside her that was busting in flames with a devil dancing in it, and a look in her eye now - cast off to the side in suspicion, trying to anchor in the near distance, while sensing some of the floorboards she'd been standing on had been removed...

There was a resolute period where my mother tried to enforce us to make our beds though she may have not been able to sustain that practice herself, plus Steve, not tempered to engaged himself in mechanical things, would lay his thin, suede bedspread over his wrinkled under-blankets on a 17 degree angle that looked worse than if he'd never touched it. By the looks of it, I could not tell who was suffering worse, him or her. It seems the sight of it disturbed my mother into relinquishing the idea out of sympathy, while on the other hand, I think that was how my brother practiced defiance against her.

However, there were a number of years that my brother remained alarmingly quiet and introverted; he wouldn't smile and many of his close friends and people he looked up to died within close proximity of one another, regarding time. He became ghostly white, even sickly, his hair turned red and things just happened to him, all of which he internalized. One particular photograph after the three of us - me, my mom, and my brother - went Christmas shopping at Montgomery Ward in Pontiac, as we did every year, shows my brother's shame after getting caught trying to steal a wooden mug from a shop in the mall. You could see that he was robbed in life, ashamed of being robbed, and now ashamed of robbing…

Comparing our lamentations for validity as adults - the times my mother physically beat us - when she would not let up; questioning if that was normal behavior in a home - my brother told me in a solemn tone that once he punched my mother in the jaw and knocked her out. "I felt *no* emotion," he said. I could almost pinpoint in my mind the time that may have happened by remembering the duration of hostility and mutual silence between the two...

I vividly remember my mother walking away off the back porch after shoving me - my back landing against the seat of a chair - knocking the wind out of me without a second thought; while I gasped for air, thinking I was going to die. However, noticing at that point, even though my mother may not have known she knocked the wind out of me, the empathic chord from her to me did not exist on these terms. Just as the times she would scream at me to shut up when I was crying after she wailed on me.

THE PART ABOUT THE SERPENT

I could see that the spirit in her that unscrupulously shoved me to the chair and then switched face to resume her daily business of keeping her hair perfect and presenting herself to the world were working together, like passing pitons, and she was becoming less concerned about exposure and more confident in violence. It spooked me, for one: because I didn't know her and I felt abandoned with her - knowing it was going to be a very long road ahead, and two; I could tell that that was not a true life-giving spirit but an animated force that was reaping corruption. Still in that vision, I could see her costume now - which was covering cysts, tumors, strange growths, and surgeries she'd been acquiring that no one knew about, including false teeth though she was only in her mid thirties. And that "covering" and need of it, seemed correlative to her guilt-devices and violent behavior...

My mother was taking psych classes now and she had long-time been leaning into Medicine, even undergoing hypnosis for smoking cessation unsuccessfully. I remember the high-volume anatomy and physiology assignments she used to show me out of anxiousness. I believe we tested the validity of all the fad medical claims, such as magnetic healing properties and copper on the body, by personal experimentation; judging the type of consumer attracted to whatever claim, and how long consumers clung to them. We had mood rings and worry stones all over the house, fish and frog ceramics, and my mother was always explaining in a lamentable feminist's voice - pleading for Peace and Reason - the effects the gravitational pull of the moon and the earth's

THE PART ABOUT THE SERPENT

tide had on human behavior. And she noted the discoveries of psychic ability in crime investigation often enough that she resembled something herself a psychic, other than she was too calculative, personally; and she never acquired that little witch's laugh or the swollen eyes.

These types of endeavors seemed to be generating a spirit in my mother that was over-driven and out of character.

My mother explained to me that Lake Orion (pronounced Or-e'on) was once an Indian lake that were many small lakes combined into one larger lake after installing the damn (whether that was true or not), so there were plenty of small islands and bays to explore that made it heaven for kids like me. And the Indian connotation, I think, inspired us both - that we were living in a territory worthy of a people who prized the beauty of natural resources and used such areas as a means of spiritual grounding and respite. It seemed to lengthen the willows over the water, add grace and romance to the swans, and deepen the tranquility of the sunsets, regardless the race-boats and the rock and roll.

To us it was as if the Indians were some kind of apes driven to extinction, and every outing, every picnic, every blue heron we saw - demanded, it seemed - a moment of remorseful silence. While all our neighbors were sold on cheap thrills, Budweiser, and the color red; we took camping trips to the Upper Peninsula and visited every scenic place we could find. We preferred two tracks over paved roads, we collected rocks and driftwood, and anything Indian inspired awe.

When my mom and her short-lived boyfriend, Tom, a TV repair man from Oxford, heard a leak that an Indian burial ground was uncovered in Oxford where some development was in the early stages, she and Tom went there for an evening and my mom brought back pieces of what appeared to be skull and rocks that were all clay colored. One rock, she almost insisted was a piece of clay held in an Indian's hand who squeezed it; our hands fitting perfectly around it, our fingers resting in the furrows. Those artifacts took temporary possession of the places we normally kept our beloved décor in the house. Truthfully, something was wrong with my mother's going there no matter what her sentimentalities. She was intoxicated by it, and it was a lingering binge. It gave her new life and she ridiculed the newspaper and the developers over the ongoing story as if she were a private investigator who discovered it. So, I think the word denoting the Indian attraction was "sacred", though we never used those kinds of words in our home.

In actuality, we really wanted the Indians' state of mind, otherwise we wouldn't have preserved so much of what he had. And if he was as intelligent as I believe he was, he knew for certain that no white man, abusive as he is, could ever acquire the appreciation needed to cultivate the land we were now ruining, taken by brute force.

THE PART ABOUT THE SERPENT

...

We lived in a very, odd old three-story house at 16 Highland. I remember the number from Bell: 693-2466. In occult language we're looking at the infamous 6 with an inverted 6 suggesting sexual impropriety, and then two individuals all for it. I faintly remember getting milk delivered and the gas meter man used to have to come into our kitchen and open the bottom cupboard to read our meter. I heard the queer old man living there before us was a Howard Hughes type who was apparently dirt poor, even bathing in the lake, but when he died, some of the old-timers in the neighborhood said they witnessed a lot of business going on with people removing unlikely items such as paintings carried out by one of the judges who handled the estate. There were rumors that he was actually quite wealthy and my mother believed the paintings came from under the once white/now black mantle in the artificial fireplace.

The spiral staircase was carpeted and at the bottom of the steps was a landing and louvered closet door. And in the floor of the closet, under a mass of my mother's old vinyl purses and shoes, was a wooden door that you could lift up and then there was about a two-foot deep storage space. My mother used to keep her sewing things in there and when I was home alone I used to investigate and would find things, such as a baby-blue jewelry box with an airbrushed ballerina on it. It opened to a miniature dance studio with a mirror adhered to the lid, and there were all kinds of broken pieces of silver jewelry in felt-lined slots and tiny drawers; even a whole silver-studded ballerina crown built for a little girl's head that was heavy and actually bent too easy like precious metal does. And I remember a shiny shawl of some kind. I'd never heard about where these things came from and because I found them by snooping, I was always afraid to talk about them. Like the day I saw my mother put on her white figure skates with the fake white fur on them. We shoveled a rink in the floodlights every year on the lake but I'd never known her to skate. This year the ice was bare with only cloudy patches of snow leaving it wide open for losing hockey pucks and fish shanties in the wind, and when my mom launched off on those skates my mouth dropped wide open!...

She reversed her direction and started pumping momentum backward with fluidity - her rear end navigating - letting off power to stand erect and coast at the precise moment, like you see when a figure skater relaxes with their arms swinging while zooming along effortlessly just before they do a triple axle. She was a veteran! Her figure, widened hips, her bone structure, the length and color of her hair, and instance upon her appearance all came together and made perfect sense to me in a way that I'd never imagined of her before.

My mother revealed something to me, she never did it again, but she won my devotion even if I never spoke it; she became beautiful to me. It is said in psych literature that no matter how abusive a parent is to a child - that child will always seek approval from that parent. Whether or not that is true - I cannot validate, though it does seem that there are times when an abusive parent seeks approval from the object of their brutality…

When my father was remodeling and digging the basement, he found the housing for a listening device on the back porch of the main floor that ran up to the master bedroom. They believed the master bedroom had been bugged at one time. This room had heavy, white plush carpeting and a bay window overlooking the water; but not a real bay window you could sit in, no, a fake bay window you could only look at. It was obvious that this room got more elaborate attention than the rest of the house. I believe the walls in this room received wiring to provide luxury lighting on them before my dad re-paneled it, and this home was lucky if it had overhead lighting wired in for safety or any other reason!

Of rumors and stories gathered from the neighbors, my mother told me that the old man was known for having young boys over and my mother believed he would take them upstairs into the master bedroom and then go downstairs and listen to their conversations... Such dark psychological narratives were typical of my mother who empathized with criminologists like Vincent Bugliosi and Ann Rule.

The bathroom said it all about this man, and the times: pea-green sink, pea-green tub, pea-green toilet with two-tone purple plastic tile halfway up the walls. It had a three-fold beauty mirror over the vanity, hence the word, "vain" that was lighted by long, vertical fluorescent bulbs that were hard to get started, and the overhead light switch was on the outside of the door. Later, being it a more reasonable sacrifice for us to redecorate what we could not remodel, my mother installed purple shag, to the bathroom! The whole place was weird, the behavior of the people living around us was weird, and it was a very peculiar time to grow up in this world. More about that later...

My mother pet named me Bump when I was little because I whacked my big head into stuff, and everyone knew that it was a mistake to give me SpaghettiOs in a bowl because I would wear it on my head. We had a dark, wooden coffee table, grounded well in the shag by the weight of two granite panels set in the top, which had dangerously sharp corners on it at one time, though over the years the paint rubbed off the corners and had become rounded, and I think it was because of my head!

I remember my mom coming from the kitchen wearing her huge, fuzzy, red K-mart bathrobe with a mug of coffee where I sat in her throne which was always more comfortable and accommodated than my dad's old vinyl recliner, and she'd say, "scootch" and we'd share the chair... It was preferable to claim the chair pre-warmed. There were always sketch pads and pens and a magnifying glass to the right, on a simulated-wood coffee table supporting a massive ceramic lamp she painted 70's gold and brown, and to the right of that - a homemade bookcase stocked to the ceiling, including my brother's mystery-series books depicting a black gargoyle powering his hands over a beaming light between his knees on each binder of the series which were color-coded, and not too loudly as one might think, the color scheme likely adhering to the content-nature. My books were a mammoth color photo book of wild animals that my grandpa Kacin gave me along with a childhood subscription of Ranger Rick magazines, and I had a velvet-like Edgar Allen Poe compilation that I took places. My mother read an uncountable amount of true-crime paperbacks. There were so many of them that we could use them for handy needs around the house, such as shimming up the corner of an appliance, or taking down a hornet's nest, for example, and no one would miss any of them. Today, my brother and I could play Name That Criminal, recalling all the creepy, disfigured mug shots lying around the house staring at us when we were growing up.

On her sketchpads were doodles of squares, most of which she drew while talking on the phone. Many squares made with strictly, straight, aggressive lines over and over until the ink bled through the paper and the pen ripped it. She knew the doodling type, different types of doodling, and why they do it. She said that John F. Kennedy who she very much admired, was a doodler. She knew handwriting analysis, or graphology, as they call it, we used to have a book on it and she used to teach me stuff, as she did out of all her subjects. Funny, it seems I became so self-conscious of my own signature that I never was comfortable creating it and settled for, "I-wanted-to-set-myself-apart-once-but-now-I-don't-have-that-kind-of-confidence-so-here; this-sucks!" and would literally fight my right hand over the years to try and enlarge the capital letters of my name as if I were fighting an accuser for my dignity. Interestingly, I lost the ability to write in cursive, including my signature, probably in my teens, preferring the orderliness and laboriousness of printing in death-heavy ink and have been questioned only once about the validity of my printed signature by a northern Michigan post man who happened to be the Secret Signature Police for the day - noticing that my printed and signed names were identical, regardless that an x is considered a legal signature.

My mother and I talked science, we talked universe, we talked physics, we talked behavior, we talked animals, we talked architecture, we talked royal lineage, we talked dark ages, we talked sociology, we talked Crystal Gayle, we talked Curt Douglas, and everything in between.

Reflecting on those talks during intervals of synchronicity between her and I throughout the years, she often reminded me that I always asked her the deepest, most drawn out, impossible questions that would take her forever to answer. And I tell you it means everything to me that she took the time to answer each one as best she could. We talked there in that chair so many late nights together that it made positive, enduring memories for both of us.

THE PART ABOUT THE SERPENT

Or could it have actually only been one or two positive experiences out of many bad?...

I also remember my mother would make me sit in my dad's recliner to show her friends and neighbors how I could read the newspaper aloud. I don't know how old I was, all I remember is that physically the paper was way to too big and unmanageable to handle, as it still is; and knowing me, it was probably more important for me to look like an adult than to care about what I was actually reading, especially a dumb newspaper, as it still is...

Possibly due to my mother's single-mother work schedule, I was forced into kindergarten early and I have lots of unpleasant memories of being dropped off at strangers' homes to baby-sit me. I don't think I ever told anyone other than my mother once, but I used to hold my breath when people of inferior stateliness, such as shabby looking box-store shoppers who infrequently washed their hair would pass me in the store until I was certain that all traces of their wind was off of me and well on its way to the place where toxins gather under the ozone where I didn't have to think about it anymore. I would be lightheaded and need to dash for air. Like seeing an endangered fish in a dirty fishbowl, dwelling in the bottom right-hand corner of the bowl - diagonally opposed to the mysterious gray lather with pepper flakes in it forming over the upper left. He is ever mindful of it and if he determines that its growth is inevitable and might start causing him behavioral problems, he might choose to die by his own hand and leap out on the carpet! Likewise, the disgusting odor of human denial in some of the homes of these babysitters still registers in my memory. Yeah, while they were cooking lunch! The key words that prevail are, "homes" and "lunch" that give me no real right to complain. However, it was like they all had a certain brain center, the amygdala - which causes one to think and feel - that was either broken, veiled, or missing entirely. I could not determine if it was the result of abuse, neglect, retardation, laziness, or just plain ignorance...

In a tone of lament though, when taking it all in, these people get up every morning unwillingly by the demands of systematic solutions so promised to be the most viable means necessary for the future of their world, knowing the course of man's directives hasn't reaped anything other than bizarre chaos and destruction, and the mat next to their bed that used to spell "hope" on it, is yanked out from under them before their feet even hit the floor. Sub-sequentially the question that makes all the phonetically identifiable wrinkles in their forehead you see on the way to the coffee pot is, "why?" That starting position is the foundation that will make the biggest determination as to the amount of effort they will be willing to sacrifice to win the fight for that day. *If* they fight, that is. Furthermore, hope is the missing element in their world. No hope, no discipline, no drive, no improvements. "We'll raise our American flag, wear our "I'm With Stupid" T-shirt, and we'll just pretend we're living and maybe we can sneak through undetected, and to hell with sit-ups and books and scrubbing floors!"

Such depreciation was going on when I was growing up, it was like everyone was on drugs! Furthermore, if man was not so bent on inventing catastrophic devices like automobiles to ease his burdens, sit-ups would not be such a burden to him either. And I didn't want their lunch...

I remember the Layland's babysitting me from time to time (not attributing the above mentioned dispositions) who had two girls, Tara, who was a touch older than I was, and Ricky, who was a touch younger. Tara was more reserved and careful toward me, as if she could be trusted, or wanted to be trusted, and seemed to be enduring something around me which resembled formality that exceeded that of her parents. She never engaged her attention to me or with me unless I was fully consenting of it, but more often at me, or about me, peripherally. Tara just seemed to me very well behaved. Ricky, other hand, was very outspoken, upfront, and physically abusive toward me.

The Layland's had an older boy babysit a group of us at the Layland's house one day and he held us all hostage in the upstairs bathroom. He sat on the edge of the tub with his shirt off, filling a squirt gun, while taunting us. He made a demand on one little girl, threatening to squirt her with his squirt gun, but she quipped, "I can't, I'm allergic to water." What then must have gone through the brute's brain was,

THE PART ABOUT THE SERPENT

"Oh/allergies/reaction/parents finding out/intake records/busted!..."

Then he turned to me, "then *you!*" And I said, "I can't, I'm allergic to water too." However benign it may sound (a squirt gun), the boy was bigger than us and terrorizing us in criminal fashion. What I remember noteworthy was how much power the other little girl's lie had on him, how instantly it enforced... But I probably remember it most by how stupid she must have thought I was to repeat it...

And I remember one strange sunny afternoon that Mrs. Layland came over to our house, maybe for payment or cigarettes - I don't remember, where my mom didn't quite invite her in, but trusted her enough to let her study me with a look of concern on her face before she said to me, "Well Joey, if you ever get bored you are welcome to come over!" My mom stood aside at that and let it pass though it was more direct attention than I was accustomed to getting from an adult. I later had to ask my mom what the word "bored" meant, and although she never commented on Mrs. Layland's invitation to me, it seems my mother had already grasped her gesture as a means of diverting attention from the real reason she came over...

...

THE PART ABOUT THE SERPENT

My mother worked as a bookkeeper for Patterson's pharmacy in Oxford. She used to clean the building on Sunday nights and employed my brother and I to help with it when I got older. I was enrolled at Elizabeth Street Elementary School and immediately I started facing problems. Assigned to a work "cell", I recall a huge round, dark wooden table, badly in need of refinishing, and there were a few different tables in the room with other cells seated at them. In my cell there was me, a dark haired handsome boy with dimples when he smiled named Donny; and one girl who sat right next to him. Donny and this girl may have been readily acquainted; maybe they knew each other outside school or rode the same bus, I don't know, however, these types of learning cells make a child's academic development (or records of academic development) dependent upon factors like their level of skill and camaraderie with the other kids in the cell. As if all diverse social backgrounds, preferred learning styles, particular biologies, values, beliefs, character qualities, spiritual histories and conditions, developmental gaps or accelerations in learning, and therefore individual strivings within the above could all be homogenized.

I remember sitting diametrically opposed to Donny and the girl at this huge table that could easily seat five kids and it was like being on a double-date with smooching lovers without having a date for yourself. They controlled all the material, their eyes never lifting to me, and I never demanded to see it. For one, I was terrified of asserting myself due to the oppression at home. Second, it seemed that if I did, I would be

THE PART ABOUT THE SERPENT

interrupting some kind of honeymoon and it would go from them never talking to me to begin with, to them having a valid reason not to talk to me. Third, it wasn't worth it to me. And fourthly, I should not have had to.

Soon I remember placement in special groups for things like speech therapy and garbage I was not even aware I ever had. There was a photograph of me after the first day of school getting off the kiddy bus at some stranger's house wearing a huge name-tag around my neck, tied with 70's-colored yarn that said, "JOEY" on it, and you could tell from my ghostly white head to my toes that I was mortified.

Still required to live and breathe as the other kids, I remember passionately loving school materials and office supplies, as it is this day. Globes, calendars, charts, graphs, neatly cut paper, organizers, sharp pencils, et cetera... I liked all that smart information-handling stuff and wherever it was the money was coming from to fund it because it told me that someone had to care somewhere, or had... We used to have these 3' high blow up characters representing the letters in the alphabet such as Mr. T who was probably shaped in the head and arms area as a T, and if I remember correctly he had Tall white Teeth and was brushing them with a Toothbrush, better associating the letters in commonality. These great people were teaching us how to care for ourselves, like proper oral hygiene; treatments where they gave us red, chew-able die to see where our brush had missed. I was not getting this education at home, and all the adult women on my mother's side of the family had lost their natural teeth. I was madly in love with Mr. T and remember asking one of teacher's aids if she knew how I could get one of them. Her response was so vague I don't remember it, I had forgotten all about it. She came to me sometime later in the year with an educator's supply catalog pressed down firmly to the pages with the Mr. Alphabet Blow Up Guys on them that had an order form attached within the displays. She handed it to me privately and said hesitantly, something very introverted about what it would take to get one, perhaps lacking confidence I would understand and follow through, and then she withdrew to the non-existent adult presence in the room she had always been, for the remainder of the year.

I took the catalog home and examined it in our half-finished basement where I could find solitude and open the windows of my mind. But these blow up guys were very expensive and would require a check and series' of multiple blanks had to be filled in with digits and letters that would have to come from somewhere important... and I only wanted one for a toy. None of that would ever fly with my mom.

It was both strange and humbling to me that the aid actually remembered and followed through to give me premature materials like that as if she didn't know I was a little boy that was going to drag Mr. T around in the dirt with me and eventually puncture him with a big nail! I'm sure she did. But she took me seriously. She didn't sugar-coat anything. Any other adult would have said, "No no, those are for teachers only," et cetera et cetera... However, she made no excuses and she didn't deny that it was possible. She didn't blow me off. She found the actual path and she taught me the actual path like a real teacher, whether I was worthy of the information or not. That was special to me. She remembered me. What she did was validate rather than discriminate. It was probably normal for her to pass out papers, hold her arms over the students' shoulders at their seat to demonstrate with her hands in front of them, blowing noses, and tying lots of shoes on the wrong foot. Here, however, she pursued this overzealous request I had of her, which, if not directly related to student curriculum, would be done in her private time...

...

Elizabeth Street had a massive playground with a giant hill that eventually afforded a 40 foot slide with a dip in the middle to modify the ride. After the fresh raw thrill of riding the bare metal wore out, we heaped snow on it in a brigade, riding a black plastic trash bag! Our playground was the rave of all playgrounds. The top of the hill was black top and it even had monkey bars on the pavement. You often heard shouts of astonishment, "she got her head split open!" Which seemed either a way of victimizing an accident for the sake of congeniality, or that someone was behind manufacturing our injuries and we were ever calculating the death toll. If you asked her, she would

THE PART ABOUT THE SERPENT

say, "I split my head open on the monkey bars at school." No one says, "my arm got broken" unless he was unconscious when it happened or was objectifying the blame because it was totally involuntary like you would expect him to say when talking to his insurance company. Besides, if he said, "my arm got broken" as if it happened "to" him - to all the overly sympathetic who cannot help themselves but to glorify tragedy and expose such things in conversation - knowing they would maul him with a litany of interrogative questions when the embarrassment is felt long before the noticing becomes verbal - it's just easier to wear the blame.

Moreover, whatever it was that split her head open came *to* her, not *from* her, and she, in her mind, must rationalize everything even if she swore to herself she had everything under control but something bizarre happened to her that didn't really make sense. Over time, the many things that don't make sense get categorized as "me" or "my fault" and we stop questioning those mysteries. More about that later…

Around the perimeter of the playground was a chain-link fence and looking at comments online in 2010 posted from other students, they recalled there were giant tree roots we used to play in, which were at the top of the hill close to the fence by the road. The school was four stories high of red brick and a massive smoke stack. It had large molten–like rocks littering the playground that seemed they would break your ankle if you stepped on one while running. Our scientific minds as kids assumed the rocks spilled out of the smokestack which came from the boiler. Mrs. Pain and Mrs. Burger were the aids on the playground - one took the upper portion and one the lower. And no, Mrs. "Pain" never threw us to the ground and put us in a scissors lock to make us beg for mercy! They only passively intervened and blew their whistle when there was something serious, or when the boys would body-pile Jessica Clouse or Missy Hickman just to kiss their head; relentlessly groping them while they missed all their precious outdoor-time.

We were a rebellious bunch of foul-mouthed juvenile delinquents who grew up listening to the rock and roll powered out of Detroit through the 70's. Everywhere around the lake you heard WLLZ, WRIF, or WABX. Arthur Penthowel was the deep signature rock DJ voice of WRIF famous for his impassioned "BABY!" that later became bumper sticker material I still see on rare occasion. RIF was your more personality-oriented rock station, while WEELZ was harder driven and less thought-provocative for the *unscrupulous* drug addict. There was no static within these stations, and at night, they would play programs like The King Biscuit Flower Hour and other psychedelic cult arrangements. It was like, our food.

It seems years went by while my brother listened to his earphones and his albums making no other attempts at human contact, all the while growing his hair and consuming a large amount of "eye-glass papers" to clean his glasses, so he told me!...

THE PART ABOUT THE SERPENT

At one point, I remember going to Sunday school with one of my neighbors and I must have gone more than once. I remember things like a small upright piano that sounded like the proverbial Piano in the Basement, and visuals on the walls and in books - mostly colored with dark purple and gold - of robed men wearing sandals in the dessert with camels... I remember sitting uncomfortably in close proximity with others for long periods, so that means there were lessons, plus we did crafts.

I also remember a small group of us kids at Elizabeth Street, gathered outside on the playground singing, "He's Got the Whole World in His Hands" which we may have learned in Music class. We had a little fever going that was so gentle, innocent, and trusting opposed to the destructive influences all around though I don't think we sang it more than once that day and our group disbanded like a mist. I remember feeling vulnerable because of that song, maybe even embarrassed...

In dark contrast to those thoughts at the time, I remember hearing collaborations of rock titles put together for albums, movies, and cult specials such as Night Flicks or Night Flight, which would feature just the minor suggestion of the choruses of what are considered today - ordinary ballads like Night Moves from Bob Seger, which would be Am-G-F. I could tell that if I followed these ways, these images of these artists, if I went after it, I would premature expediently and my religion would become misery, just like theirs.

THE PART ABOUT THE SERPENT

Carefree for a season, pay for a lifetime. Why would they expect *me* to want it?

It was long hair and dark power. I remember hearing the Immigrant Song by Led Zeppelin on the radio and it used to scare me. I thought to myself, "Whatever those guys are into that cause them to do that is not good!"... I knew by the vivid dreams in my heart and through imitationism that feats of that nature required abnormal spirit. And if those words seem prematurely descriptive for my age at the time, they are, it took me 32 years just to begin equating them.

...

My mother was dating Less Perkins, the chief of police, when I was in the first grade which would have immediately followed my mother's divorcing my dad, and Mrs. Candy was my teacher. Chief Perkins was tall and thin, black-haired and wore dark-rimmed glasses just like my dad. He kind of reminded me of Sonny Bono because he was almost dopey, but a great portion of that could have been attributed to his sense of humor. In the beginning of the year, Mrs. Candy wrote on the blackboard both her maiden and her soon-to-be married name to clarify the transition to us. I believe it was Ms. Rameers/Mrs. Candy, the maiden not certain, but a nice transition. There was some identification between her and my mother in the community - the dead giveaway, Mrs. Candy didn't flunk me.

THE PART ABOUT THE SERPENT

My mother may have conveyed to me years later that my mother's relationship to the chief of police had some impact on Mrs. Candy's treatment of me, but my mother was not aware of Mrs. Candy's treatment of me and may have been speaking vanity. Routinely, Mrs. Candy would stop the class to order me to stand up next to my desk which was a heavy tabletop with an open hole or drawer beneath to store your books, supported by a bunch of tan-colored steel tubing with little kids' gross on them. She would have intuitively selected one of the prettiest, smartest, straight A students I most admired, who brushed three times a day and flossed, who sat up straight and wore sweaters like someone cared about her, to assist her. And while I stood in mortification to the right of my desk, she would ask her assistant to come and sit at it. Fully aware now what a proper student looked like to me sitting at my desk, she would instruct her assistant to pull out every unfinished assignment one by one, to un-crinkle it, and then to place it on top of my desk in a stack while the whole class counted along… and they did so loudly, knowing there was 32 of the fricken things in there! I was paralyzed, and I was too insecure of a kid to raise my hand in class for any reason to begin with. There was no outwardly resisting a mob like that, though over time I became able to tolerate that kind of thing, I had no choice. Like an automaton who though appearing stoic and aloof is in truth wroughting internal wars against dragons and winning by the sweat of his brow for the sheer justice of his cause just to keep from passing out...

THE PART ABOUT THE SERPENT

...

Around Lake Orion there was an old homeless Indian named Chief Pontiac who you would see hanging on a park bench with a bag of tobacco if he was not long-distance walking. Geographically, Pontiac Michigan is about 20 miles south of Lake Orion and you would see Chief Pontiac anywhere in between, taking M-24. My mother, taking after her mother, taught us to be kind to people like Chief Pontiac. I do not remember ever talking to him and I doubt that my mom would herself, but we thought well of him in our sentiments and estimations. He belonged as much as we did, if not more. And in truth, more. Moreover, one day before school, the kids started a rumor that they saw Chief Pontiac stab someone with a knife outside the chain-link fence. Mr. Sawicki, a power driven principle, known for whacking kids with a perforated paddle named Big Bertha, made a hasty visit to Mrs. Candy's class to interrogate us about the rumor. He was tempered because many of us, if not all of those he asked, said we saw it; too afraid to say we didn't. For one, he was overly aggressive and frightening us, and secondly, we were terrified of being different and standing out which could mean ridicule and lasting difficulties (mentality strangely akin to that of our parents!). He was ready to storm out the door and he turned to me at the last second. He looked at me startlingly with his huge, threatening eyes; his straight dark hair combed from one ear to the other was fallen jagged over his forehead due to quick movements and stress like Adolf Hitler"s, then he drilled me, "Did *you* see it?" as if he were expecting a different answer from me, and I said, "Yes." Then he left the room more disturbed than before he entered.

I remember noticing Regina in Mrs. Candy's class who was very tall and thin with long light brown hair that was sometimes done in a braid. She was pretty, I could tell her parents took good care of her, and because she was in a higher socioeconomic class than I was, I never dared talk to her. She never spoke one word outside on the playground to anyone, nor ever a word inside. She sat by the windows and all I remember is this lifeless haze about her, never moving.... But then everyday in class she would throw up. Then there would be a serious stir out in the hallway and I remember listening with my eyes widened and my heart in my mouth while Regina cried and choked on her tears in dying agony of some kind; an adult agony. More of an emotional infirmity, something psychosomatic. All those hours of silence, she was restraining it and suffering. You can only hold something like that back for so long until it gets let go. Otherwise, as it remains internalized it becomes self-destructive. It ferments and multiplies. One way or another it will manifest itself.

She never would come back in the classroom and soon someone would be notified to come and pick her up. I must explain to you that by rule, I am only romantically attracted to extroverts and it doesn't work any other way. This was not a romantic noticing. It was perhaps a *re*-cognizing. Something you knew personally and can perceive in others. I felt quite strongly some kind of identification, like a deep sympathetic bend toward Regina that would forever remain a secret...

Looking back, there were certain points of dread in my life and one was the realization that it had been so long that Regina hadn't come back to school that I knew she probably never would. And she never did. Over 36 years later, I continue to dread that memory. I have drilled myself, coaching myself - that I should have gone up and talked to her no matter what!... That no social barriers created by default of man's ignorance or pathetic childish insecurities of mine should have prevented me from trying, because now that chance is gone... While still yet a kid, I thought in hindsight, *and* foresight, "Maybe if I'd married her then she wouldn't be so sick ...I would just take care of her!"... Simultaneously encompassing that thought is a vast expanse of emptiness that gets groped at for meaning when assessing the cost of being brutally traumatized year after year with the profit of a piss-poor public education I wasn't getting anyway. As for Regina, I did not see some introversive young girl walking around with tapeworms in her gut for half the school year that needed medical attention; I saw a very beautiful, gentle, sensitive and mature young lady responding in silent martyrdom to the inescapable violations of her surroundings...

THE PART ABOUT THE SERPENT

Consequently and fittingly, Regina is the only student I can cognitively recall in the first grade.

At Christmas, we were to put on an after-school play for the adults in the auditorium of *Rudolph the Red Nosed Reindeer*. We'd been going over the lessons in music class with the Piano in the Basement and the songs we all knew by heart, from tradition. However, while preparing us and choreographing the night of the play, it was evident that Mrs. Candy had already picked me to be the star, no questions asked, nor opportunities given to the other students who actually did their work. Here, there was no merit of quality student, good attendance, or audition for which the determination settled. She got out her lipstick and walked over to me, screwing the bottom of the stick to raise up the makeup part, and totally painted my nose with hot, smelly, red lipstick that almost made my eyes water; because I could see it shining on my nose, and my skin couldn't breathe. Then she stood back and examined me with hawk-eyes. The lipstick wasn't even red; it was like dark, fancy sex-red with silver in it. I felt something criminal; I was despised to begin with, but now I was suddenly worth something, and after I got done being used, I would go back to being despised. It was shame. It made me feel wrong and I already felt wrong. It was inappropriate and what did that say to the other students commanded to shout out every number of unfinished assignments I had crammed in my desk all year?

Furthermore, this wasn't likable favor, it was something else. She wasn't even nice to my nose when she handled it. I was a burden to this woman. She wasn't telling *me* she liked me and was promoting *me*, she never once expressed that. And it wasn't the kind of thing where my mother insisted to this woman that her son be the star of a play or given stature of some kind. My mother was too humble for that. And besides, even though my mother may have promoted me in her mind, she would not promote me outwardly because then she would have to let me go as I gained independence. You cannot keep something that you send. Moreover, any complements I ever shared from outside sources with my mother, she promptly extinguished, and it always felt like a dark stranger slipping his arm around my head to smother my face with a rag saturated in chloroform, while my heart continually dismissed it, supposing a loving mother… Like discretely placing a wet towel over a sparkler to conceal it, though occasionally it would be so obvious and unthinkably cruel that I would have to contest it. Because if I didn't, it would be like telling a bad snake he was doing a good job at being a bad snake, when he was really a bad snake doing a poor job at being a bad snake. And then the veil would lift and my mother's eyes would open just enough to tell herself she needed to be more covert because her tactics were showing! I didn't know which was worse - the obvious stuff can be fought and won quickly because you have evidence of the weapon, however, the sneaky garbage comes in malignantly over long periods; leaving you weaker with a re-opened wound, and a repeat suspect...

THE PART ABOUT THE SERPENT

The night of the play, my dear brother Steve came to watch though my mom may have had to work late. All I remember about the entire evening was being abandoned on the stage at the end of the play standing over a dark, musty auditorium full of unhealthy old adults wearing fake fur lapels, artificial wool-lined coats; and vinyl boots, applauding. I had no idea what happened, how I got there, why everyone around me was gone, and what they were applauding for, because whatever it was, I didn't do it. Likely out of the intense pressure and sheer immaturity I crossed my eyes. I recalled to myself years later how Rudolph in the TV specials was cross-eyed, possibly trying to acquit myself from the shame of it. Aware of only the end of the play and not one iota of rehearsals or anything leading up to it was similar to an experience I had sleepwalking when I was very small. Due to money being scarce in our home, undergarments and socks were not high priority, and I remember waking up out in the street in the early morning fog in pink fuzzy underwear. I saw a Back Hoe bobbing my way down the road and it frightened me to wakefulness and to running back into the house...

Today I wonder if it is possible that Mrs. Candy picked me to be the star of the play solely because of her witnessing my ability to keep my composure under the inhumane pressure she judicially enforced upon me while standing at my desk-side in a stoic blackout when all her students were shouting out my failures. And is it possible that she did not flunk me out of selfish reasons, such as it being too much of a burden to face me another year, which might add to some complexities of hers? or was I a threat? Because unless a teacher is oblivious, careless, inadequate, or compensated, a child who does not do any of the work should not graduate any of the grades...

I believe Mrs. Candy knew that I was perfectly capable of doing any of the schoolwork but that I was resisting its authority. No woman, no female human being with any trace of empathy would make a public show of humiliation of a little boy because he was special needs, or dumb, or lacking in intelligence in an era of hypersensitivity to anti-discrimination, would they?

Nevertheless, my second grade teacher with the chopped-off hair *did* flunk me, but my third grade teacher, Mrs. Acton, was like a beacon of light to my capabilities, who simply read to us an entire series of Laura Ingalls Wilder books. I still read those books today, even gleaning recipes from them, such as how to make Ginger Water (for dehydration), and other practical ideas for when things are tight. I identify with Laura as a "seer" who had been through a thing or two and could cut through the rhetoric. There are three different types of learners: Auditory, Visual, and Kinesthetic. Or in non-rhetorical language: Hearers, Seers, and Doers. So if you were a student in Mrs. Wilder's class, you would hear, "...so you see...and if you look at it this way..." and "now it appears..." all terms of seeing. Now, if you happened to be, or should I say created to be an Auditory or Kinesthetic learner in the predominately Visual Mrs. Wilder's classroom, you might not be able to identify with her, and digress. And if you were being taught that way less than a century later in the public education system, having industrialized its approach, sadly focusing on five base subjects, you would be regarded as having learning disabilities. Contrary to common sense, a student with an Intelligence Quotient of 140 wastes half his time in school, and a student with an Intelligence Quotient of 170 wastes almost all of his time in school. Thomas Jefferson said, "Nothing is so unequal as the equal treatment of unequals." *I* know it to be abuse!

I remember reading *Jonathan Livingston Seagull*, and creating a wax seagull to explain the book during Show &Tell. I was so moved by the book, I told my mother, "Mom, that's the best book I've ever read!" To which she retorted, "That's the *only* book you've ever read!"

Subsequently, a friend of mine, Bucky Stimpson and I won scholarships – scoring among the highest in science and something else, though I never followed though with my scholarship; and I never did any of my schoolwork, period...

...

Mr. and Mrs. Reichert next door were very loving and safe toward me, and on occasion, they would have their granddaughters over who were both closer to my brother's age, who was eight years older than me; Shelly and Wendy. They were healthy, attractive and gregarious. One had long blonde hair and the other long dark hair, same length. There was no inequality between them, meaning, they were the same height, same size, and they both wanted the same things and were both content receiving the same things. One did not think separately from the other. If Shelly was standing in the yard, facing east, troubled about what someone had said; Wendy was right beside her in the yard, facing east, troubled about what someone had said. If Wendy was kneeling down on the break wall admiring the water, thinking about Back-to-School, Shelly was kneeling right beside her on the break wall admiring the water, thinking about Back-to-School. If Shelly was eating a hot dog, Wendy was eating a hot dog. You did not think of Shelly to address Shelly as an individual, nor did you talk to Wendy privately. There was no Shelly and there was no Wendy, it was always Shelly and Wendy.

They were one in agreement. Even their names had two syllables, each beginning with attractive consonants followed by a neutral sound in the vowel, and then both wrapped up with a pretty "y" at the end, leaving a pretty ring in the hearer's ear, which also makes them almost descriptive names. It's personalized. Wendy is short for Gwendolyn which means "white browed"; and Shelly must be Michelle, a derivative of the masculine, "Michael".

THE PART ABOUT THE SERPENT

All names to me are automatically assigned a color of one or more since I was a little boy. My mom used to ask me who's name was what color as if she were pointing her finger from person to person, slightly fascinated, but also testing them for some kind of psychic understanding. She even remembered the color of her own name, brown for Ruth, in later years but she under-esteemed her own name for other reasons and failed to understand that the colors I assign to names have nothing to do with the popularity of the color. Although she didn't express it, I knew it stood out in her memory as an unconsciously-exposed negative judgment I had of her. Truthfully, brown has to do with pretty hair, books, and power.

Primarily, the name scheme has to do with the letters. Shelly is a nice one of multiple colors, more complicated though: the "S" is dark, like royal blue behind black, "H" is always green, and the "elly" is yellow. Wendy is gray or silver because of the "W" and "endy" looks like yellow, black, burgundy, and yellow again. That's the articulate description, which is too impractical. Basically, Shelly is a very dark Blue that is hard to understand, and Wendy is Grey.

Moving along, I heard that my brother tried selling Shelly and Wendy Cheerios in a baggie when they were little, telling them they were doughnut seeds! It also seemed that my brother and his best friend Irv were always physically available when they were around, acting like adults, probably enticing them with knowledge of adult things. That would have required

THE PART ABOUT THE SERPENT

my brother to either notify Irv somehow, or perhaps there was some admirer leaks that led to communication before they arrived. In spite of that, when Shelly and Wendy came out the door, look out! Because they spent all their energy chasing me around and shouting at me with passionate threats, and when they caught me they would not stop hugging me and kissing me and tickling me, telling me that they couldn't wait until I grew up so they can marry me! Now I have to admit that *this* type of attention wasn't so bad, and today I'd like to know what ever happened to Shelly and Wendy!

While although that appeared to be a positive reinforcing experience (actually kind of overexposing and over-stimulating for someone like me), it would be a long day in hell before I would come across any other open attention like that. And what did that say to my older brother who already took second place to our mother?... Because in our culture, if he wasn't romantically inclined to at least one of them, something was wrong with him as a normal teenager.

See, Shelly and Wendy were brave souls who were getting their information about me from somewhere other than where everyone else gets theirs. I didn't make *them* nervous. They had no fear of me. And that was *all* the difference, and a time-tested indicator of who is, or who is not, reading me appropriately.

Those girls could disarm me today in an instant! "Surrender, I love you!"

THE PART ABOUT THE SERPENT

The Price of Having Dreams

MRS. REICHERT FELT SORRY for my mom - watching a single mother of two, working two jobs, trying to maintain a three-story home and a car, verbalizing it on one occasion after witnessing my mom washing windows past midnight standing on a chair while the curtains were in the washer. When we had mechanical failure or our hot-water tank went out, Mr. Reichert would come over and I remember him lying on his side for hours by our hot water tank in the strange closet of our bathroom, while Mrs. Reichert talked with my mom. She sat on the seat of the couch nearest my mom who was to her left, though her body was almost deliberately kept in proportion to the direction of the couch as if to declare her propriety, so she always looked like a stranger in our house, even after many years. Her voice was loud enough to send out an awareness that she was a woman of convictions and not easily persuaded, so she appeared to be a really big lady, however, her heart was so soft that it tilted her head and drew her chin inward in awe of you, and you could tell she was praising you, even when you were doing something bad and she didn't know it!

The Reicherts' had a small collie named Frisky and of all things they gave him/her sliced up Snickers bars that made me jealous to be their dog. They owned the proverbial goldfish that were too big for the fishbowl, who's eyeballs outweighed the rest of their bodies.

Mrs. Reichert used to take me for walks around the island when I was so small that I had to take sitting breaks on things like a guardrail, or on the huge boundary stone at the base of Long Pointe Drive. She and my mother both walked me around the island on one occasion after I got into my mother's tranquilizers, which were in her purse, but not surprisingly, I don't remember it. My mother purported that the advice came from a nurse upon calling the doctor's office. It always seemed like fountains of amber-colored pill bottles of all different height, width, and value, were emanating from my mom's purses - like towers laying in ruins; and there were prescription bottles all around the house, lining the kitchen windowsill, loose pills here and there in her old purses, down under the couch, and stuck down in the sides of chairs...

Dr. Williams was looked up to by my mother as if he were the father-figure in our home, though himself married, and deploying his paternal care from the doctor's office with a sense of indignation at her predicament, which recurrently impelled my mother to seek him when there was trouble.

He was the image of the Big Boy of Elias Bros.: boxy build, wearing plaid, and his head was always sweaty from a combination of being unhealthy, overweight, likely being over 50, and a subtle freneticism at the prevalence of all the infirmities around him. Kind of like a beekeeper who keeps stirring up the bees, insisting to the minds around him that the manufacture of honey outweighs every sting, though he himself doesn't eat the stuff. His shirt pocket was full of pens and he was so cushioned in his practice that the pen that he used to depress your tongue was very likely the same pen he used to depress your tongue during your last visit ... including every sickly, feverish, contagious tongue in the interim.

Dr. Williams knew enough about medicine and my mother's physical complaints that he could treat her, but not enough about pathology and the truth to know he shouldn't. Often my mother would sleep to the point of neglect and you couldn't get her up. I used to call them Coma Sleeps. I remember trying different ways of pleading with her to rouse her - like saying her first name on the fourth of July when she was sleeping outside all day on the deck in a full-length lounge chair after I had dinner cooked on the grill. She'd been sleeping there through the vandalistic myriad of fireworks throughout the day, including the race-boats that nailed their throttle toward the open water just off our dock. Saying her first name worked, but she only got up because she thought it was someone to respect - which was my intention - however, she was so uncomfortable getting up and disturbed by what I said that I never did it again.

I remember on that occasion I unintentionally got lighter fluid on her hamburger, and I regret that I tried to serve it to her, hers always being charred by preference, where there was neither time, burger, nor coals enough to make another one. My mother didn't want to get up that evening, she didn't want to eat, and she definitely did not want to eat a toxic burger!

For the most part, we let her sleep. She would lay down upstairs in the afternoon and I would come home late to the house void of life - the windows open upstairs in the dark, the curtains filtering the street lights from outside, and an eerie dread as if I could tell her lair had been under spiritual siege, diligently advanced upon during every hour she lay unprotected without watch or alert. Something akin to the blood-quickening surprise you get when you see a little kid's sucker covered with thriving ants in the summertime - not knowing where they came from or how so many could be dispatched so effectively...

I remember running up to the landing of the stairs to shout up to My mother that John Lennon had been shot the night the news aired on the 11:00 program. She said, "Oh no…oh no…" but just went back to sleep.

THE PART ABOUT THE SERPENT

I could talk to her; it was like she was hypnotized. I would gently plead with her, every word a question, summoning her up while probing her. There was enough willingness in her responses that I could tell she loved me and acknowledged that I felt sympathy for her, like you would when you baby-talk to a kitten until it cannot refuse but to swing its head at you to look you directly in the eyes, as if it dawned on him that you were a feeling thing. But it was like there was a thick, dark floor of static between us and we were both aware that she wouldn't come through it.

It seemed that if I drew her too close to the surface her breathing would shallow and she would stop responding and wait at that level - as if she were considering it... But the longer she considered it, the less air she got, the more uncomfortable it would be for her, and then she would eventually faint and faze out into another direction of coma-state again; now additionally traumatized.

So it was better to talk to Mom through the floor.

I remember being home alone the day a Detroit rock station aired a minute of silence in dedication to John Lennon, and I remember sitting on the floor with my back to the couch for the duration of that very long, intense one minute.

Scarcely, there were times in my life when I saw something unusual that stuck in my heart about an individual, or words that were spoken, that caused me to say to myself, "they have something going for them; that person knows something I want to know!" as if there was a reserve inside me, as if it were deep under my feet where I stood - a case I was gradually gathering that would nearly be barren until another impression would come, and then I could see a very clean reservoir that was increasing in clarity and value.

My mother took me to Meadowbrook Mall to see Matilda Dodge's old mansion, and what I remember most about the property was a partially opened bookcase that provided secret passage to a spiral staircase leading up to Mr. Dodge's private study. It was roped off at the time, but it has never been roped off from my imagination...

I filled up on *Mutual of Omaha's Wild Kingdom*, and in secret, I exalted myself above my surroundings with passionate dreams of someday being a major contributor to Public Broadcasting every time they aired a telethon. I remember the lingering aftermath of John F. Kennedy's assassination followed by scandal in the White House. I also remember a kaleidoscope of lamenting songs coming out of the late 60's, glimmering the reflection of a giant, hazy, golden sun that was driven to extinction - haunting my sympathetic soul no less disturbing than an image of a hand reaching out of a graveyard: I'm Leaving On a Jet Plane…Mrs. Robinson…Seasons in the Sun…

All of it provoked a dread within my spirit to peripherally epitomize, symbolically, what was going

THE PART ABOUT THE SERPENT

on around me. I vividly remember watching television after Jimmy Carter left the White House when I was 11. The Iranian hostages were freed that day, and I saw a passenger bus full of freshly released hostages being televised as they went by on their way to freedom. Peculiar to me was one ethnic-looking young gentleman near the rear of the bus holding a small cardboard sign out of the window that said, "Christ is the Road!" or "Jesus is the Road!" It was as if he'd come right out of Jerusalem after Christ's resurrection and hopped on that bus in 1980! He had had a desperate experience that proved his faith, rebuking thenceforth any fear of what people thought of him...

My mother had a lady friend on the island named Chic; a plump strawberry-blonde with swollen eyes, and glasses. She lived one house down on Long Pointe, which was a dead end, up on a hill, sandwiched between a very tall house that burned down and Mr. Barber's daughter's tar-paper shack, that Mr. Barber took over after his own house burned down next to it, which was on Belleview, three lots away from our house. Chic purported a faith and of the time she adopted it I do not know, moreover, she moved away when I was very little. But I was familiar with Chic enough to comfortably recognize her in years to come. She had a beloved daughter named Amy who was run over by the school bus. From what I was told, Amy's head swelled from the injuries and she died.

It seems a lingering trail of such devastations marked our neighborhood. Directly across the canal from Chic, a young blind boy fell in the water and drown. A black dog on the end of Long Pointe had only three legs because he got ran over by a motorcycle and went aggressive toward kids like me on their bikes. And all the abandoned lots where houses burned down became auxiliary playgrounds for us kids.

Pondering the incident Chic lived through, many years later, when my mother was trying to convey to me the love a mother has for her child (whatever her intention), my mother stated her amazement, in other words, at Chic's abnormal and extraordinary act - given the circumstances - that Chic would not rest before personally calling the school-bus driver who was driving the bus to tell them she did not hold them accountable. Any other mother would have been so focused on the loss of their child that not only would they never have considered that that driver was probably sitting in the dark believing he deserved punishment of hell, they would have channeled that energy into blaming him! Chic knew this, rose above herself, and intercepted it. Perhaps that was because Chic knew God.

I also wondered if Mrs. Reichert could be a Mrs. Robinson? because heaven was waiting for her if she prayed...

Brian O'Brien, Mr. and Mrs. O'Brien's grandson, from across the street and I were weekend buddies since we were very little. He was kind of short and pudgy, often making reference to his being left-handed, pigeon toed,

THE PART ABOUT THE SERPENT

and double-jointed, as if he were a circus freak, showing us what his shoulder looked like in the dislocated position, or how close he could get his purple sucker-drool to the ground before sucking it back up into his mouth. Brian submitted to befriending you by being so familiar with his own idiosyncrasies that it was impossible not to like him. He was very book-smart and he could handle an unusual amount of knowledge of stuff that no one else would make use of, unless they were some kind of specialist. He was like a giant flea market of knowledge of random items, complete with the chaos, and many items for which he deemed no value to himself, though he would if they were presented to him from someone else.

Consequently, his bedroom at home resembled a giant flea market of knowledge; complete with magazines from BMX bikes, to Guitars, to cars, to posters covering the walls, and sports equipment strewn about an unfinished, un-carpeted floor that looked almost Social Services-interventional. No amass of any of it would inspire him to think himself anything other than a hobbyist that was bored out of his mind, which caused it all to turn to junk before him. It was like he brought material in so he could examine and appraise it, and then after being exhausted by it all, roll over and take a nap on it.

Furthermore, I envied that Brian did his schoolwork, and on Sunday nights at his grandma's, both lights were on in he and his little sister's room, doing their homework while I was outside again till after dark -

wishing, on one hand, that Brian could come out and play, and on the other - that I was someone inside sitting at a desk in the comfortable lighting of a loving home doing my homework...

When me and Brian were small we were playing in the dirt in our front yard, probably when our basement was being dug out, and I remember I stupidly womped Brian with my giant bouncy-ball thing made of thick-heavy rubber that probably flattened him, and he, in turn, blasted me between the eyes with the bottom rim of coffee can full of dirt, blackening both my eyes. I remember my mother quickly taking me into the house without investigation, and I remember resting upstairs; seemingly the therapeutic protocol for bodily injuries in our home...

I never once questioned that I didn't deserve getting blasted with that can of dirt, though I remembered in hindsight the anger in Brain's spirit that warned me not to be so leisurely about playing Anything Goes.

Brian's mother's name was Jan and his little sister's, Megan. His father was a race car driver, or derby driver, or both. I remember they drove funny-cars out to the Island that looked like shinny go-carts with sparkly flecks in the fiberglass; sporting chrome mag wheels, with all the aruggah horns and perforated steering wheels. I couldn't help but to slide in the driver's seat and dream, making shifting noises.

THE PART ABOUT THE SERPENT

For some reason, Brian's dad reminds me of Elvis although I don't know if I should remember his appearance, which in my mind, is a stocky, sweaty, self-fulfilling, black haired guy that had problems, because while Brain was still little, his dad committed suicide.

There were a number of failed attempts where he would take a handful of pills after carefully negotiating the time Jan was supposed be home, so she would find him; both in time enough to save him, and create for himself a circus of attention. However, one evening Jan's plans had been rearranged outside of his knowledge and he expired before she got home. And I deliberately use the words, "got home" rather than, "got there" to differentiate to the reader that Jan had no obligation to dash home every night as if she lived at some crime scene.

So, Brain and his mom had a short, well-rehearsed formal defense, offering a generic philosophy as a banister in case the subject went to the second level, but no deeper, because the issue could never be totally avoided. It came with barbs, as it should, to thwart off nosy people, however, Brian's soccer photos depicted him throwing his head back to freshen his face with a forced smile, getting in enough enamel that no one could call it a Not-Smile, but it was congruent to their true attitude which was kind of spiteful of life. It was as if Brian's family were openly obliging to follow the Pursuit of Happiness for everyone else's sake; agreeing to dot all their I's and cross all their T's - to say hello, goodbye and thank you - but knowing full well it was

THE PART ABOUT THE SERPENT

all a crock of shit. And to those of us who were close to O'Brien's, we had no objection to such dispositions.

Mr. and Mrs. O'Brien employed Jan at the party store faithfully, and when my mom stopped in it would be hours that I would be playing outside while they talked, usually practicing my nunchukus.

Mrs. O'Brien was fairly snooty, never approving of me, fully, and I know it was that way with my mom, or maybe it was that way with everyone. And although she appeared to be unaffected by the loss of her son, it seems that by it, where once had been a hard embankment fully enforced around her, there remained only an imaginary girder around her now, and if she wanted to speak its effect, her humanity now prevented her. Kind of the way Less Nessman insisted people pretend to knock on the pretend door of his office; it wasn't that important...

...

I resisted ever coming into the house when my mom was home and would stay out past dark after all the other kids were accounted for. It seems that one out of every 10 homes in my neighborhood smoked pot in those days and there were a few times me and some of my friends were chased by cars and people we never saw before - sometimes confirmed by screwy reports in the news. One was an incident with a fillet knife and an unwanted homosexual advance in a parked car - I remember being chased by the previous night, and me and my friend David went to look for evidence. I remember bringing home what looked like a bloody molar from the scene.

And then there was a guy who attended Lake Orion High with my brother. Supposedly, while his mother was in a nursing home, his father was having an affair with another woman, when this guy visited the woman's home and proceeded to saw her head off with a hacksaw. A group of us biked it to the address mentioned on the news (to see the blood!) but all we saw was sand washed out across the driveway where the scene had been thoroughly hosed.

I was always viewing joints being distributed among the older kids and could smell its sweetness everywhere from my brother's friends' to my babysitters'. My mother's type of physical infirmities were then being touted alleviable with marijuana, and out of sympathy, I bought her a joint from some guy in a car I never saw before for .65 cents; who had a baggie under his steering column full of more pre-rolled joints than I have ever seen.

The dealer wasn't pushing dope on a little kid, he was dealing to the teenagers his age, but I stepped in and asked. I took it home and hid it outside beneath a concrete block within a stack of blocks on the side of our house, though I couldn't give it to her at that time because her temper made her unapproachable. I could sometimes tell by listening to my mother's voice while she was on the phone whether attempting to talk to her was wise or not. Usually, I could tell that if she cleared her throat politely, especially if no one was present, that meant that she was either in a grateful mood, or holding herself to a higher standard of some kind, or both, and that was the time to approach her.

I remember trying to teach her to smoke it, as if perhaps, she didn't know, but she could not co-ordinate holding her breath while the smoke was in her lungs and it would burst out of her with a choke. Then we used a bobby pin for a roach clip. However, it was uncomfortable for her and the benefits never met our expectations - outweighing the cost and the risks of its illegalness with the availability and social acceptance of prescription drugs.

David and I could buy cigarettes at Rick's party store with a note from our moms, and we did it so often that getting them for ourselves was no big risk. I remember stealing whole packs of Marlboro out of our china cabinet drawer and I remember getting grounded for trying to teach Candy, the girl next door, how to smoke, who couldn't grasp the concept, and continued blowing instead of sucking. And I also got a tiny, pearl covered jack-knife taken away from me that day that I showed to Candy - that I think I traded something worthwhile to get, and got in trouble for that as well.

I remember experimenting with a Salem after not having a cigarette for a long time, down by the dock of

THE PART ABOUT THE SERPENT

the boat launch at the end of our street, where the residence from Victoria Island kept their rowboats when heading inland. The funny thing was, it was like the most horrible tasting thing I could ever put in my mouth, and every bit of right in me repulsed it! Continuing to smoke beyond that very point meant that not only was I initially attracted to the cigarette by every thing other than its medicinal properties, I was forcing myself to feel sick in an attempt to gain them!

Oh how I loved wine! Especially red wine! How it was heavy and hugged the glass; elegant and strong! How it warmed my stomach… I could always have a glass after Thanksgiving dinner or other special occasions, where my mom seemed to be letting me in on a secret. "Drink it slow" she'd say. Next it would be, "I said, 'drink it SLOW!'"

My dad was gourmet oriented, taking after his mother and father, even having a garden himself. He made everything from the best pickles ever, to homemade horseradish, to smoking his own fish, to making his own sausage, to making wine; and it was good stuff! He would bring a gallon of it with us in the boat when he would take me and Steve out on Lake St. Clare for the day, when it was cold, during visitations. It was both a perfect opportunity for him to show off his talents and wisdom by offering us some, saying; "It'll warm you up" without violating propriety, and for me to put a little buzz-on. Then the cold steel seats and the vibration from the motor in my ears were almost bearable.

THE PART ABOUT THE SERPENT

My dad drank so much beer from the time he was cooking breakfast till bedtime that he slightly covered it by buying my all the pop I could drink during the weekends I was with him. "As long as everyone else is piling up empty cans I won't feel so awkward; besides, people need their comforts!..." Once he made a large batch of homemade root beer and this was one time when his homemade experiment failed though he didn't know it. I was the one who had to drink it all and I hadn't the heart to tell him it was in-consumable. There were cases of it, bottled professionally like his wine, and I think he may have mentioned how much of it there was to drink when I was asking for some store-bought pop. Therefore, every weekend *my* emptying bottles slowed down.

On my paper route were a couple that worked for a race-car driver, Della Woods. Never heard of him, or her, but they gave me a t-shirt of theirs that was printed on some kind of user-unfriendly cotton that just made you want to hang yourself when you wore it. They used to leave their house open and I would walk in and explore. One time I was in there stealing their marijuana roaches and trite valuables and I walked upstairs and someone was snoring away and I assumed it was both of them. I could see that although they were passively friendly they had no idea what was going on around them, like they were hung over at all times, hair all messed up, slouching. They lived on a peninsula so they parked across the road where their vehicles were on the water. One winter's day, when the ice was bare, the man's pickup truck, facing rear-end the lake, was spinning it's rear wheels, and I saw him dopily drag a sheet of plywood around the truck, place it under the back wheels, get in the cab and hit the gas, and that sheet of plywood shot out so far onto the ice you couldn't see it anymore! An when he got out to look under the truck, there was no more plywood under it, and it seemed that it never dawned on him that it was a half a mile out on the ice. He didn't even bother to look; he simply staggered on to another hopeless idea.

Just before school started, when the summer needed to be redeemed, knowing that this couple had two bottles of wine in their refrigerator, I took David with me and we stole them and then climbed up on top of Goat's Hill, which was very close to their property, to drink them. A red one and a green one. We got to the top of the hill and positioned ourselves so we could see the town over the lake and still be out of sight while we drank them. As if we were going to solve the world's problems over a drink, which was unusually somber for Dave and I.

After we unwrapped the black foil from the bottle tops, we found them corked, unlike the type of wine poor boys like us expected. We picked and scratched at the corks and weren't getting anywhere, then I told David authoritatively, possibly knowing the frequency the other neighbors had seen me at this house, "David, you have to go back down to that house and go into the kitchen and find a corkscrew." David was the kind of kid who was like a blood brother who wouldn't do anything bold like that without me, but I could see the sub servitude mixed with unwillingness in his eyes, but then he also trusted me and so promptly dispatched without complaint. We drank the entire contents of both those bottles while it was still daylight and laughed our asses off! We were so dunk we forfeited our need to conceal ourselves, so we could go home, and then staggered down the street in broad daylight throwing up along the way. All the kids on the Island gathered around us, like they had never seen anything like that before!

We were up on Flower's Hill now, semi-secluded and detained, and I remember them individually looking into my eyes and then looking into my eyes individually; sounding out to determine how far gone I was, and then I'd puke my guts out and they'd all jump back with their feet spread apart! I walked home with all the neighborhood kids following me that evening to my house because they wanted to see what I would get! I walked in the door, my mom was waiting, "Get to bed" she said, and that was that.

The next morning I had to deliver the Sunday Free-Press, the day the papers are the heaviest and the customers expect them early. Waking before my mom did, I was convicted enough that it motivated me out the door on that gloomy and foggy morning even though I felt like Death. Remembering my grandpa Kacin admonishing us in an old story of personal experience while in the military - never to get drunk on champagne - I found this applicable to red ones and

THE PART ABOUT THE SERPENT

green ones! And it took a long, long time for me to re-acquire a taste for wine.

We were back to school and one of the adults on the back of the bus who witnessed us on Flower's Hill, who may have been a foster kid who had seen his share of fucked up stuff - and too old to be on the bus - said to me with informative concern snaked across his forehead, "You're a drunk!" But I didn't care; further damage to my pre-damaged reputation meant nothing in comparison to the benefits of alcohol. Life was going to be good as long as there was booze around!...

On a snow-day one day, David and I went right at a fifth of cheep vodka that was nearly full, left over by one of his mother's guests, or by David's stepsisters who came on occasion. David taught me that it gets mixed with orange juice, against my thinking, and it seems it was only 11:00AM by the time we finished off the better portion of half the bottle and we were out naked, rolling in the snow laughing our asses off in broad daylight!

On the fourth of July, there was always so much unusual commotion and partying going on that David and I could simply stumble around the island after dusk helping ourselves to people's beer, and his next door neighbors had a cottage with a boathouse-type room under their house where we would scootch under the door to nab beer out of the fridge.

THE PART ABOUT THE SERPENT

I knew what I wanted to do with my life since I was a kid and I would race home from school before anyone got home, crank up the Detroit rock and roll and jump up and down on the couch jamming air guitar across the room from the giant mirror on the once white/now black mantle over the artificial fireplace until I was drenched in sweat, everyday! A photo of me the day I was given my own, real eight track/receiver, I was lying face down on the living room floor with my head between the speakers, under! My brother gave me Alice Cooper's Hallowed be Thy Name and Jefferson Airplane's Red Octopus. Somewhere I got a hold of John Denver's Greatest Hits and I sang along to it daily until I permanently inscribed every song in my memory. Then I got a hold of Alice Cooper's Greatest Hits.

My brother, I can never forget it, just before my birthday, we were walking back from town after he got a hair cut or got his glasses fixed or something, and fabricating some reason why I should wait for him at O'Brien's Party Store (having asked them to keep an eye on me) he covertly went back to Bailey's music shop and bought me a cream-colored recorder that came with its own sleeve and presented it to me on my birthday. Now, we were poor, he was just a teenager, he had no money of his own, and my brother was typically mean to me; but I cannot think of a better brother than that... In addition, my Uncle Richard on my mom's side brought me an old, jumbo western Kay Guitar with a Roy Clark beginner's book and had to leave it with a broken string upon tuning it for me. Though I had no idea of its tuning or of chording, I knew what to do with a guitar enough that I was wailing songs like Michael Row Your Boat Ashore the first night I got it, and I used to treat my mom's lady friends when she wasn't around.

I bought a deep burgundy, Gibson SG electric guitar with black and chrome hardware from the pawnshop with my paper route money - my mom having to take me there to get it - and my brother still tells people that I used to sleep with it.

Although my grandma Bezesky, a severely dispirited Jehovah's Witness on my mother's side, came to baby-sit my brother while I was born, my mother then refused to allow any contact between my grandmother and I for another three years… When I was home from the hospital after being born, I heard that while my grandmother was watching Steve - after sending him off for the school bus – he was so excited about it all that he was walking so that his steps went slower and slower until he missed the bus and turned around and came home for the day.

We often took trips up north to Houghton Lake on special occasions to visit my grandma, which always excluded the words "…and grandpa" who was a brutal atheist with a Nazi bend still referred to at family reunions by the old-timers as "The Meanest Bastard Anyone Ever Knew"; and often there were other aunts, uncles and cousins visiting, and beer.

THE PART ABOUT THE SERPENT

My grandpa ran a tiny resort named Stroup's Resort for his sister Jenny; and Roy Stroup, her husband. After Uncle Roy was put in a nursing home, Aunt Jenny was very isolated and alone with her hard liquor and we used to make fun of the way we could see her Coke-bottle glasses with the horned rims, peering out her kitchen window at us kids, around an old ash tree where our grandma tried to keep us hidden, like a cat. All you could see was the glare of her glasses and nothing else, and then you would see her glasses and a clear bottle of vodka going straight up over her head. So all you could see was a pair of mean-old lady glasses and a vodka bottle in action. And since my mother sympathized with her, living up to her given name, she was very loyal to my aunt Jenny and treated her with dignity. She would sit where she was asked to sit with her legs crossed like a lady for hours and hours smoking cigarettes with Aunt Jenny - inheriting the family legacy and getting the stories none of the rest of us cared to earn. When my mother found out that we were making fun of her along with Aunt Jenny - saying she was just like her - she packed up me and Steve in the car and then drove 130 miles back home without saying one word. As soon as we got in the door, she said to Steve, "Pack up your shit and get out!"

My mother was very sneaky and I could not admit it. She had sent me to the door to answer it so many times with the, "tell them I am laying down", or "tell them I am taking a bath" et cetera, that when she joked about dodging process servers with her neighbor-friends, she called it "dodging surveyors" because that is what she

THE PART ABOUT THE SERPENT

led me to believe she was doing... Men coming after six PM persistently to take random surveys and drill me on where my mother was!... I also remember we had a phone recording device and we were keen to turning it on before picking up the receiver...

Once, there was a time when Steve was still home I accidentally set the outside of the house on fire with a wax candle, and it may have been the same day that my mother noticed that a stack of concrete blocks on the side of the house had been pummeled... Then she noticed a small tear in the back screen door which may have given a tool access to the lock... But I was the active agent around our house...I stacked the bricks – I pummeled the bricks. I stole the cigarettes – I taught the neighbor girl how to smoke...But at that time, my mother was also parting ways with her TV mechanic boy friend, and maybe that very night, there was also a huge splash in the water behind our house. Our tenant, Steve, who rented our basement said that he came out and a drunken man said he was looking for his "lady friend"... The next morning a body was pulled out of Lake Orion and my mother was shaken by it. Although I did take responsibility for the fire, I did not take responsibility for the bricks, nor the back door (which I don't remember what happened there), so I let my mother incite a stalker incident where someone had climbed up the rear balcony, knocking the bricks down on their way up before coming to the screen door with a tool to unlock it. (Why they wouldn't have just taken the stairs, I don't know) But when the story rudely imposed itself as a possible reality, it was obvious my mother bore some responsibility, if not for the fictitious embellishments that feminists often employ against their exes.

I lived alone with my mother for many years after all outside connections and intimacies with family members were forbidden. I could see the haunting finality in every relationship that ended between my mother and other people. Looking back in summation, all I could see was my mother beating me with the heels of her shoes when there was no one in her life left to beat… Then she started taking me to see psychiatrists.

At one indefinite point, while standing alone in a place of strength, I made an inner vow: that I would never smile ever again … That woman will never see me smiling...

About that time, I started having severe asthma attacks. I remember while being home from school one day that I was so weak I had to crawl to the refrigerator to get something to eat to try to gain some strength. I doubt that I ever told anyone. Then I started getting rushed into emergency.

Strangely, even though I was very ill and at times my chest was the same width as my abdomen, it was as if whatever it was that made me sick had unwittingly afforded me temporary alone-time where I could process things without being threatened, and that was where I would become most creative; even excited.

THE PART ABOUT THE SERPENT

Asthma always worsened during the night while I was in bed. My mom learned to tune herself in to constantly evaluate the sound of my wheezing throughout the night while sleeping in close range. It is like becoming invisible while your eyes are wide open, but inside there is no alarm; it is too laborious to breathe to care about yourself. The alarm came from what was going on around me...

And revisiting now situations like Danny Brown fist fighting me at the bus stop, I could never understand why people where taking their violence out on me. People hated me but I don't know what I did to them. I didn't have it in me to fight them. *I* didn't hate *them*. I couldn't dream of harming *them*. Those things would not compute in my head...

...

Steve had a friend named Mark who lived by the tree with the rope where we had our accident about half a mile toward town and his family were giving away kittens. So Steve and I went there and took a female calico, naming her Killer, because Steve's chest and shoulders were all bloody after walking her home in the summer heat. Killer blended into our carpet in the living room so closely that you could hardly see her in photographs; just a carpet with a pair of female eyes, nestling. She usually got chased by Sainty, Joe and Debbie Schmidt's Saint Bernard, who had to prove she was a dog every now and then and make a full chase till Killer hit the giant tree in front of Mr. and Mrs. Riecherts' house.

Killer had several litters of kittens and there was a problem with the black ones, usually those with a white splotch on the front of their neck. They were born deformed with protruding chests and they usually suffocated within a few days or weeks. I was kind of alone now as Cat-Superintendent and I remember doing everything I could for the kittens panting in the summer heat, such as placing ice in front of a fan on low, upstairs where Killer fed them, and I remember burying a black one in the back yard under the deck, wrapped in a plastic bag.

We had no register cover over one of the heating ducts in the wall upstairs and one day I heard a kitten crying for help somewhere in the house. I went to the basement where the registers were overhead and I called the kitten, trying to mimic the sound that Killer made when she called them which said, "Where are you? I love you, I am your mother, I need you, I will help you, what do you want?" all in one uttering, but I couldn't get him to come. So I went and found Killer and took her to the basement, holding her up, and then she made that communication which brought the kitten to a register. There I unscrewed it and lifted it down, checking him for signs of red or cuts in his skin of which I found none. Just a shaken up kitten with really big eyes, and a grateful mother!

THE PART ABOUT THE SERPENT

We had one, gray striped juvenile that had a chubby belly, big enough that he was no longer a helpless kitten, but too small to be an adult. On a Saturday, when my mom's hair was in pink and sea-foam-green plastic curlers, doing an industrial cleaning upstairs, he was laying behind my dad's old vinyl recliner and I entertained the idea of stabbing his belly with a knife. I was excited at the risk of it, not thinking past that - such as what to do with the body and the blood; and I grabbed a plastic-handled, serrated steak knife from the kitchen. Getting down by him, actuating the scenario in my head, suddenly my mom started coming down the stairs. I got up and put the knife back, never telling anyone for so long that I almost forgot about it.

Dinky may have been one of the first black ones with the white splotch and we named him Dinky because he was the runt. But Dinky fought for his life and prevailed. There was obviously something mentally wrong with him because of his antics, however, he was not jovial. He liked carrots and sometimes he would mistake the food and water tray in the dining room for the litter box in the bathroom. He had diarrhea so - that the mosaic tile corner behind the door of the bathroom was usually covered in his splatter, and he was noisy about it. He used to bring ducks into the house and I often found him aggressively copulating with his mother, holding her neck down in submission with his teeth. I used be so mad at him that I would sling him off the end of our dock as far as I could every time I caught him doing it, and he would have to swim back all black and wet like a muskrat.

THE PART ABOUT THE SERPENT

We tried to take him the Humane Society but we couldn't keep him in a box, then when the Humane Society gave us a specific type of box - a thick, corrugated animal carrier with several, one inch air holes along the sides, I saw Dinky tear his way right out of one of those holes!

One night, while in bed, after Steve had moved out - my mom and I the only ones in the house - I heard someone pounding on the front door to the living room. It was so persistent and violent that I was frightened until I imagined it to be Steve... Thankful that he was coming home, I went downstairs to let him in but saw in the dark from the bottom of the stairs - Dinky's massive right arm, all of it, under the front door reaching straight up, black against white, shaking the whole solid front door between the jam and the deadbolt trying to get in! It was more disturbing than any wild animal scene I think I've ever seen - knowing the insurmountable odds this house cat had survived, fighting on so deathly hard for his life that he was now literally bent, unable to rest and unstoppable, probably even struggling in his sleep...

When no one was around, I used to lock myself in the bathroom with him. I had a white, homemade, woven jump-rope and I used to double it up and whip him with it where he couldn't get away from me. It was such that I could see thin, red, blood marks from the rope left on the walls from my back-swing left in different striking directions. He would leap in the porcelain sink and get

THE PART ABOUT THE SERPENT

down in it to protect himself and I could see his yellow eyes - not in terror of me - but fixed against the situation, and then I would turn the water on to show him what a stupid idea his getting in the sink for protection was. Then, to show him how merciful I was, I'd rip the door of that hot sweaty bathroom open and glare at him with my hand on the doorknob until he snuck passed.

THE PART ABOUT THE SERPENT

Jo Jo the Dog-Faced Boy

It seemed necessary that if it were not possible to rise above my circumstances physically - if a situation was utterly unbearable and I had no choice but to take it - I would bypass it with applied dreaming, and I started practicing it at the micro level so when the real bomb came I might endure it. It is basically the practice of resistance; denying one's impulses. It became like, my strength.

If I were eating a cookie, say, and in our home it was a reasonable sacrifice to shop quantity oriented over quality - I would have to exult this particular cookie that I planned to stick in my mouth by first studying it; imagining that it was some exclusive item imported from someplace important where important things get imported from... I think the mindset was, "We cannot possibly be poor!..."

THE PART ABOUT THE SERPENT

But, for some sad reason we insisted on being fancy, or fell for, or thought other people might fall for our settling for the next best thing, even if that was a counterfeit.

I remember Barclay cigarettes coming in the mailbox - hooking my mother to its low-tar/low-cost-but-fashionable sales pitch; and the cartons, including every individual package I saw for years to come, adorned an elegant printed band upon them that looked exactly like the simulated wood-grain, plastic dashboard of our LTD Wagon, complete with distorted ghoul-faces embedded in the design for the creative type, such as they do in the destructive marketing devices used in whiskey adds.

My mother also drank Sunny Delight which resembled orange juice (oranges now being the American symbol of health for the upper-class following the Depression; hearing someone testify that during the Depression a piece of fruit was considered a luxury), and at that time Sunny Delight held the same nutritional value as sugar and water, or, artificially flavored punch, and probably scoring a negative in health benefits due its dies and preservatives, not to mention being bottled on shelves in grocery stores next to real orange juice for desperate single-mothers to believe they might afford to provide their family something healthy. As if perhaps, the makers of Sunny Delight had developed an inexpensive fruit-processing technology alternative that could now compete with Florida; like maybe 60/40 with some sweetener added or something, or, "here I'll just get it.."

THE PART ABOUT THE SERPENT

It even kind of burned the back of your tongue with a slight citrus taste. Don't ask…

We drank out of jars at home and I recall vividly, being upstairs in my brother's room with a huge jar of Sunny Delight luking in my hands when his best friend Irv asked me if he could have a sip. Irv was Dope-smoking Hippy: numb lips under a scruffy mustache, and although I never allowed anyone to eat or drink from my food, I loved Irv and could not refuse him. I watched him take a couple Adam's apple slugs from my Sunny Delight and then he slowly passed the sticky jar back to me, obviously unaware of the horrendous drool still suspended from his lower lip to the rim of the jar blowing in the wind like a suspension bridge as he placed it back into my hands! I think I boycotted Sunny Delight on that day, and Irv, and jars!

Personally, I could not keep my hands off real butter, as it is this day. When I was still sitting in the grocery cart I would eat it out of the wax-paper wrapper before my mother could pay for it. I always heard my mother talk about sitting at the dinner table and seeing this tiny little hand go up over the side of the table, patting this way and that way for the butter dish, and then it would go "squish" and I would take it and eat it!

We were also using a lot of lard and Crisco in those days, and few people seem to delve into the fraud going on behind nutrition enough to know that Crisco was originally designed as a submarine lubricant for the military. If I did eat at all during the day as a kid, it might be a fried egg after school in all the salty lard and Crisco I could stomach. That was actually doing well for myself. Once, after spending the night at the O'Brien's I was so starved (not attributing any fault to the O'Briens) that when they made toast the next morning, I salted mine down to try and complete a meal.

I could not allow myself to spit the seeds out from oranges and watermelon when eating them, and in my mind - having the discipline to eat the strings, chords, and whites of such things was really to find its value and earn its strength-giving properties that other people who followed some non-compromising form of civility - who refused to eat nothing but the human-apportioned parts, lost. Additionally, I could not refuse to eat the fat off of meat, such as I saw other people trimming to the sides of their plates, and I even crunched down all the un-popped popcorn kernels in the bottom of a bowl of popcorn, then fingered the remaining salt and grease out of the bowl. My mother also noticed that I always broke my bread in pieces, but it was to make more...

I preferred the pulp and the dregs of things; that's where the substance was, nearer to the semblance of life; and the appreciation - although partly a form of defiance - somehow stood alone, disproportionately greater a health benefit than that of the object from which I was seeking it.

But to return plainly to my original point: in my heart I was in torment and terror of my mother. The very sound of her car approaching - whatever the location, whatever she was driving - always brought dread, and then nothing else mattered but to brace myself for what was coming, knowing if I appeared as such could trigger suspicion that would lead to an all-out explosion.

Individuals subtlety aware of their own abusive behavior, especially if it's bizarre, have a way of normalizing everything, which is a cover-up operation demanding of them a new level of energy: all of it! An easy one is the Joker, who's jokes are demeaning and hurtful. If you refute the Joker, rather than try and justify what he does, in an attempt to keep with a cloak of defense, he will try to *un*-justify *you*. He'll say "oh everybody does it!" or, "You do it too!" or the quickest slope to some version of "You suck!" which is still the same abuse, only on a deeper level spoken by a guy with a gravel in his hand.

In my mom's case it was a fully audible and exaggerated, "JJJowe!?" with the emphasis - her body language and the look of astonishment on her face, pressuring me on the spot to answer for myself, knowing that I wouldn't, because I was not in a place of guilt as an offender that would necessitate an answer and she knew it. It was as though if I couldn't see her, I wouldn't know what she was talking about... Then it would be, "What were you thinking?" to, "What in the Sam hell is the matter with you?!?"

THE PART ABOUT THE SERPENT

I learned that while in the same room with my mother, that if I could just manage to casually slip a blanket up over my head so I couldn't see her, even though I could still hear everything, it was like endorphins of relief would flood my body...

There were a few different psychiatrists my mother took me to see, and I believe it noteworthy to mention that I usually never saw any of them more than once, however, I remember seeing regularly, a thin, broken, victimized counselor of some kind, who would never be caught smiling, named Bonny Zimmerman, in Lake Orion. My dad's Blue Cross and Blue Shield covered all of these visits and I believe I may have felt shame toward my dad - assuming he had some notification somewhere that his insurance was frequently being tagged, and from where. And my mother would not have taken me to see anyone his insurance would not have covered.

One psychiatrist in particular I remember, had an office upstairs in his semi-new-age nest of a home that resembled a tree fort. The place was so rickety and the atmosphere so unprofessional that I knew my mother could hear from downstairs - if that was where she waited - and it was definitely in my mother's nature to eavesdrop. This day my mother looked exceptional, even tying the belt of her blue, suede-like coat with the white, artificial seal fur lining on it that matched both her eyes and her Ford Granada, uncomfortably around her waist. This guy was the beard-stroker: unclean, and the dull-gray color of his hair with his grave, magnified eye sockets deeply set behind his wide glasses told me that he had been unhealthy for a long time, unable for the life of him to understand why everyone else was so unhealthy! I remember he gave me inkblot tests and he sat behind his desk in the fashion of putting one leg upon the other, burying his elbow in his thigh to touch his face while peering at me in the silence. For the record: nothing could be more psychically derived than someone trying to make mental diagnostic assessments about some stranger's life by comments made from ink blots, which are not just ink blots mind you, but creatively contrived ink cluster duplicates that every single one of them look demonic!

I remember being so painfully uncomfortable with him staring at me, coupled with knowing my mother might be in hearing range, unwilling to let the sound of her clothes ruffle, that I turned my head toward the window and pretended to hone in on something, slightly squinting my eyes out toward the green in the tops of the pine trees, and I kind of tilted my head on its axis as if I were slightly intrigued by something, acting, and also saying in a way, "catch me if you can!" "What do you see?" he rushed in "when you look out there?" completely over-stimulating the already intolerable moment and violating my personal space, but probably sensing I was antagonizing him. I may have said in a reluctant monotone something ambiguous like, "I no-no, tranquility …n… beauty." He wouldn't expect me to report to him, "it's ape men, always ape men, hundreds of them, laughing at me!"

THE PART ABOUT THE SERPENT

But what I wanted was out.

When he walked me down, there was a short transaction between he and my mother, who was still wrapped up tightly in her coat, where I overheard her ask him his thoughts and he said, "Well it appears that Joe does have some good and evil conflicts" and then there were no more words… It was as if my mother's pride prevented her from inquiring further, as if she conveyed an understanding and kind of latched on to what he said, because when I searched to see her reaction, her head was lowered and her eyes set out toward the dismal future; as if she now knew what she was dealing with and was taking inventory…not quite certain if she was equipped to handle raising a child with G&E, and not quite certain it was her responsibility - while on a deeper level, checking her tracks.

It was as if my mother were getting all dressed up, taking me places where she could try to sell me…

…

Dr. Williams tested my asthma by drawing a grid on my back and then exposing my skin to different substances that were suspect to trigger allergic reactions. I tested positive for so many unusual things that I can't remember them all. There was turkey, potatoes, herring, halibut, cotton, cat dander, and he mentioned ash trees but I thought he said, "ash trays" giving me a thrill because I thought that meant my mom might have to quit smoking! He then put me on a long-term regimen of homeopathy injections and an endless supply of Isopryl inhalers; including huge glass bottles of Elixophilin that tasted exactly the way it sounds, Elix-awful with an out of tune violin. It was like drinking Pine Sol-flavored schnapps, with the added ingredient of some old lady's perfume from the 50's to purport some kind of medical authority. It was like, "How did I let someone trick me into drinking this!?"...

I would get so sick at home that I got to know respirators and humidifiers intimately by hugging them. Any child who remembers being medically treated by machines this way knows what I'm talking about. They are of no value to anyone else, but you are left alone with them in the quiet for hours, mostly in the dim lighting of the night, listening to their paternal suggestions as you grow a respect for them... I suppose it is the same principal as why we love our books. Truthfully, my mom's instant coffee made a difference too. During that time, doctors warned against the use of caffeine for asthmatics, however, I told my grandpa Kacin who was a pharmacist, and he said emphatically, "...then drink it!"

So, while I was sickly, anything that came near me effected me in manifold proportion: taking two puffs of my inhaler made me light-headed, where even sounds became less threatening and I would see tiny, white, effervescent floaters; Elixopholin burned my stomach

THE PART ABOUT THE SERPENT

and gave me a false-sense of wellness as might watered-down wine, and then coffee would stimulate my breathing and give me the false energy that food was supposed to give.

Being left alone was all I wanted.

I was basically incapacitated, and sometimes I remember being too weak to get the cap off the Elixopholyn, and I think we rightly switched to non-child-proof caps. But whether I took medicine or not, I was so deeply withdrawn; it was like being buried in a haze, and if an assailant rushed me to attack me with a knife, I would not be able to stop him and I might not be able to feel it. Like someone shouting at you in a nightclub, where the music is so loud that all you see is someone shouting at you but you can't hear the words - strangely authenticated by feeling their spit on your neck and seeing the bulging veins in their forehead...

Nothing killed me worse than going up north to my grandma Bezesky's. We are talking bent-over-hands–on-the-knees wheezing, and good and lingering sick for a long time afterward with a humiliating cough that spelled N-E-G-L-E-C-T. Ironically, however, I would do anything to get my mother to take me there, even working to clean the house if she said she was behind on things and said she couldn't manage the trip. It was that there was not a place in my neighborhood where you could escape the eyes of the neighbors and everyone was a threat to me. But when I would go up to Houghton Lake, allowed to roam the woods behind the high school, realizing no matter how loud I screamed no one would be able to hear me, I loved that! I told myself that I could make it out there if I had to, alone in the woods...

So after my allergy tests were done, it was pretty much left to my discretion as far as determining what my triggers were, and I attributed my worsening at my grandma's to one: the huge ash tree in the yard. Two: the fact that my grandmother never could turn away a stray cat. And three: the place was filthy with the perpetual soul-penetrating odor of my grandpa's urine rusting out old coffee cans inside the house.

I remember evening-time once when everyone was lighting up inside and having a good time while I was left sitting across the road on the back of my mother's Granada. I was wearing a surgical mask on my face, listening to them as the sun was coldly setting. I still recall how the powerful smell of that house threatened me even at that distance. As if it had a mind of its own and it chased me out; I was well aware I was still too close. It was kind of a precursor glimpse in preparation of deeper isolation, because everyone else had the luxury of someone to talk to, and if they didn't, they'd just make sure they did. But my dialogues seemed to be with the elements and assessing the shocking snapshots of real life, touching that reservoir deep inside - where although everything registered - words were becoming inferior as long as no one else needed to understand... And so someone attempting to strike conversation with

THE PART ABOUT THE SERPENT

me was probably painful and awkward for them and me, to begin with...

My grandma lived on Sunshine Alley, and fittingly, the morning sun always blasted that place.

That urine smell was next door at my Aunt Jenny's too, and no amount of cleaning agents could ever diminish it, it only of glorified it. Kind of the way a hospital glorifies death. It was like, going over to visit Aunt Jenny as politely as possible, but automatically compelled to pan the room for traces of the body! She had rare antiques and a never-ending supply of lemon drops to offer you, which were really the same lemon drops that where in that same particular candy dish last Easter vacation that were all stuck together in one big cluster. But they were still good.

She had wall scenes of two little ceramic girls, dancing, that could have represented contemporary angels; and an old oriental man smoking a pipe next to a woman - we kids used to attribute to being Aunt Jenny and Uncle Roy. On the wall behind the couch, tucked away from their view, but in sight of company, was an air-brushed painting of a bearded Jesus looking heavenward and praying. Plus she had lots of cold Catholic artifacts. Consequently, the lady was scared out of her wits because she always saw demons...

They always had horrible ice storms up there, everything structurally was oddballish; and even the water lines were built with military, aircraft fuel lines

THE PART ABOUT THE SERPENT

left over from the war, and every individual family member took a shot on working on them, as if working shifts, when visiting. Having work done very much stressed my aunt Jenny's nerves and once my brother told me while my grandpa was over - the power suddenly went out and Aunt Jenny exclaimed, "Oh thank you Jesus!" to which my grandpa angrily replied, "Now whadiya' thankin' *him* for!?"

At my grandma's there was an old, bowing bookcase near the door and the bottom shelf was lined with *Awake!* magazines and color-assorted Bible Tract Society books that resembled the color scheme of a cheap box of crayons. I used to help myself to them, where no one else did, indifferently studying the imagination-invoking artwork denoting an almost sort of science fiction. But this was science fiction that I was encouraged to imagine myself in as a reality, and their books heavily stressed the word, "new" and a "new world", more so than any other Bible content I'd ever been exposed to. And to be honest, the word "new" or "improved" always meant that the original had failed, and therefore I was inclined to avoid that as a sales pitch.

At home, my mom solemnly told me, and I think it was after Danny Brown asked me what our religion was, "If anyone ever asks you what our family's religion is, tell them we're Protestant."

I used to take the questions I had from what I read at my grandma's and simulate them to the beaver pond

THE PART ABOUT THE SERPENT

and the nature scenes I would fantasize about behind the high school; "a place for owls" ... "porcupines" ... "a pool of reeds" ... Those correlations and visions started becoming my personal, privatized lessons.

At times when I was my mother's sole confidant, she would let me in on bits and pieces of what it was like growing up down in Farmington. I know that my grandpa kept an exceptional garden and always kept his hoes and garden tools extra sharp, and you could tell my grandmother had seen her share of hard days canning vegetables because she could run her hands under scalding hot water that would send a normal person to the hospital! They lived in a tent, a family of six, while my grandpa traveled the country to work masonry jobs, like the construction of the Colorado Damn, returning intermittently to build their house, one room at a time. He had to use oak lumber because it was war time and nothing else was available. They got their water from a pump, and basically I can tell you they were dirt poor.

My grandfather owned a bar at one time and it still fascinates me that I often heard how he used to water down the ketchup - trying to equate in my mind what kind of tremendous loss of revenue might constitute an act of deception so minuscule in an industry intended to make profit off liquor - he might make a gain off some poor bastard's tablespoon of ketchup!... Nevertheless, he made no real financial gain whatsoever being that all of his money went to drink. I was under the impression, just as everyone else was, that my grandpa's side of the family were known to have made their fortunes from an old junk-yard down in Farmington, and some of them obviously did quite well for themselves. Neither could I connect the profit of old car parts, when cars weren't even big yet - nor around long enough to constitute being serviced with outlived parts - with their lifestyle, and then tie that in to match the retributive condition they were in.

They traveled and owned bars and joint-owned strip clubs, and it wasn't until I was an adult that all the pieces started fitting together when my mother finally admitted to me that they were all bootleggers. On top of that, they were heavy gamblers. Because, visiting them was like visiting a military hospital but no one ever asked any questions, where as if an outsider took a philosophical or an anthropological look at our family, he would be shocked to discover that everyone was dying.

There was barbaric violence that my grandfather took out on his family at home that was so freakish and abominable only a couple of us have ever dared to speak of it, and that, facilitated by bizarre crises in our own lives three generations later. It seemed to have spread out throughout the family and there was an Aunt Chris - acquitted for drowning one of her children, and according to one familial account, she was known for holding her babies heads under water because they made "googly faces". Another aunt, who was always said to be crazy, had her kids taken away from her for

THE PART ABOUT THE SERPENT

beating them, and I know it had to be serious for the law to have intervened, especially back then.

Although my grandmother was very poor, she valued more than anything her Jehovah Witness study books. My mother told me the milk-man came one day and they had not paid their milk bill and no longer had money to buy milk and were going to have to discontinue. My grandma sent my mother out to mediate the issue with the milkman, but after hearing my mother he said, "Well then where are you kids going to get your milk from?" and set the rack of fresh milk down and left...

My mother said she was embarrassed to have people over, however, she spoke of a doctor who lived nearby that she was always so impressed with, who's home was beautifully decorated inside. And I heard that my mother's bedroom was uniquely decorated and furnished, from other family members who remembered it.

You could see clearly in the photographs of my grandpa, a long, dark indentation running up diagonally across his forehead that apparently came from a rare moment of self-defense from my grandma, striking him with a rod-iron fire poker. Once, there was a standoff where my grandma was going to leave with the kids but my grandpa detained one of them. She was probably unable to leave with the one child still in the house and as the detained child was crying for her, my grandpa asked, "do you want yer' mom back?" and then he hit the child, causing my grandma to surrender.

There was an intervention planned at one time where the men from my grandmother's side paid a visit to my grandpa to beat him up. Now, you have to understand that my mother would only throw a very small revelation at me at a time - like a confession - done only on rare occasions, and though I could tell she was restrained from doing so, she almost couldn't help herself, either. Then, when she spit something out, her mouth would kind of trap shut and she would freeze, like she caught herself saying something forbidden. Therefore I would be left to process it alone for years to come. So, over time, comparing her testimony with other accounts, I could tell that my mom was giving me a biased view of the picture, and I had to learn which ways it was leaning, and why.

My mother tried to admonish my interest about the physical intervention taken against my grandpa because I called her to ask her the names of the men while I was doing some writing. She'd only known me to passively listen up until then, and I was 30 years old at that time. The full story was apparently that the men showed up to do my grandpa in but my grandpa overpowered them all, humiliating them.

Another time, my mother told me, slowly swinging her head side to side in amazement; her eyes fixed to some shame in the corner of the room - that she saw her dad's arm swing and grab my grandma's hair so fast with one

THE PART ABOUT THE SERPENT

fist that her feet came off the ground so that she was perpendicular with the floor.

Mostly it seemed that my mother was prevented from telling me things that seemed as though they might have went to the supernatural level, and then she would protect her father. Before they went to bed, apparently, they would have to line the stairs with glass jars to alarm them when he was coming… The kids were taught to walk through the house and give the Nazi salute shouting, "Hiel Hitler!" Years later a cousin informed me that my mother had confided to her that my grandfather had been raping the girls...

My grandma's Bible books - my grandpa burned.

Apparently, my grandpa separated from my grandma and moved to Houghton Lake where his sister lived, but my grandma eventually followed him there to care for him. There in the office of the Stroup's Resort, on Sunshine Alley, in my grandma's bedroom, she had nightmares so terrible that we could all hear her mumbling, moaning, pleading, and acting out, every night. "Never was there a night that grandma didn't have a nightmare" my cousin Kim admits.

My grandma's bedroom had one window that swung open across her high bed but it was always covered with blankets, as were often the rest of the windows throughout the house. Like she was aware of the unusual amount of sunshine blasting the place, but as a form of martyrdom, she denied it. It was as if she did

THE PART ABOUT THE SERPENT

not respond to sunshine. The bedroom was so dark that you had to enter it blinded by the dark and then reach above an offending dresser to twist the switch of the wall-light that was always unsecured, and then you would see piles of clothes; old, cheap suitcases, and the closet was sloped to the ceiling with newspapers. The floor was centennial tile adhered with asbestos and if you dared lay your palm to the floor and brought it up again, it would be covered with dust, grit, cobwebs, and cat hair. It was punishing; kind of quarantined and condemning, and when you entered it by the twin burlap curtain and then sensed the curtain behind you - privatizing the sounds within the room - it gave an oppressive, claustrophobic feel as if you were in threat of having your face shoved into it, and the air so dense that if you spoke an audible word, it might sound back at you the way your own name does when you catch yourself saying it.

My grandma had black hair and jet-black eyes - keeping mostly to herself with her back to us in the kitchen, working, or fixed behind her *Sun* and *Star* tabloids. She was quite witty, and excellent with rhymes and riddles, or games where you had to come up with fun words on spontaneity. "Did you take a bath today?" she would say. And you might say, "…no, but I took a shower" and she'd say, "…good, because yesterday you smelled like a pig." She used to take us kids for car rides and ask us if we wanted to see her do doughnuts in the church parking lot. Then she would drive into the center of an empty church parking lot, cut the wheel, and lean her head out the window and go around and around super slow while we all laughed in hysteria. But sometimes, at least when *I* was alone with her, her sarcasm would alert me to visually hold on a frame, like a dare, and then an invisible membrane would open on my eye, indicating I was vulnerable and I could see that the jet-blackness in her eyes was nourished by a mischievous spirit. "You think I'm shhhtupid don't you?" And the scariest part about it was that she was aware of it and she wanted me to see it! It delighted her somehow.

My mother was forced to struggle against being the least favorite of her kids, which drove my mother to vindicate herself against their injustices, ultimately becoming the whistle-blower of the family. And so naturally I was the second-generation-least-favorite and I took a lot of passive-aggressive treatment from other family members as a means for them to punish my mother. I respected (and not because I heard the saying) everyone until I had a reason not to, individually, so, although I kept catching the brunt of my family's aggression toward my mother, in my heart there was nothing between me and who ever it was who happened to be despising me, personally, and therefore I would continue to put myself in harms way by naively approaching them. Another interpersonal twist growing up where I had no idea what was going on...

THE PART ABOUT THE SERPENT

"Jo-Jo the Dog-Faced Boy!" my uncle Roy used to call me, spoken very slowly, metering his energy where sometimes all you could see was his long, prominent chin moving with a slight smile. So you could guess what he was saying and catch up with it even if you couldn't quite hear him at first. He moved so sloth-like and I don't think I ever remember him standing. He dominated a vinyl recliner set further up in the room with his back to my aunt, like on an airplane. It is hard to understand, but it was almost as if, if you ever completed the thought, questioning what it must be like for my aunt Jenny and uncle Roy to go to bed at night… it was probably worse than staying awake - hardly able to walk and talk and seeing demons all the time...

Their days lacked any wholesomeness that might induce a good night's sleep, where it seemed they perpetually lived in their chairs - having been stricken with the inability to sleep for the past 50 years, but had become accustomed to it. It would be no less appalling to visit them to discover their arms and legs amputated, but not mentioning what happened, while telling you small jokes and humorisms to palliate the dread of it and to divert any vein of gravity that might slope attention back down toward it, but for always! As if they were paddles in a pinball machine, causally and effortlessly kicking the ball back into play, when you can hardly tolerate to feign another moment of it! In fact, the only place I remember my Aunt Jenny and Uncle Roy ever going was to the Knights of Columbus lodge.

THE PART ABOUT THE SERPENT

The jet-blackness I saw in my grandma Bezesky's eyes was stealth compared to the times I would see it in my grandma Kacin's, who was a white-Russian named Anne. She was a small-framed woman, slim design, with a space between her teeth and she was an artist who seemed to remain too calm at all times. I don't think anyone ever made the connection, but I believe I got more of my grandma Kacin's physical attributes than from anyone else in the family, where I used to absolutely loath myself as some kind of ethnic-looking oddball until I saw the resemblance myself. And then realizing how beautiful my grandma was, after the sobbing and sniffles stopped, was like, "See? it's not so bad!"…

I think what hid that connection was the fact that my grandma chose to wear professional wigs, because my mother said she complained of her hair being too thin. My hair, as a matter of fact, is so thin that you want to keep it away from sparks, and the price that any of my close friends or lovers have had to pay is they get to eat some.

Funny, on the wall above my grandpa and grandma Kacin's television were two golden impressions of the two angle-looking dancers I saw at my aunt Jenny's…

And although my grandma was not versed in saying bad things about people, as Gothically Catholic as they were, I knew she never approved her son marrying a divorced woman with a kid.

THE PART ABOUT THE SERPENT

My grandma Kacin was also a diabetic - one of the first ever to go on insulin and definitely the longest living insulin user. "Hit and miss," she'd say. And there were times when visiting my grandparents where my grandma would be slipping into diabetic shock, for lack of a better term. And while my grandpa had a non-verbal way of pre-occupying everyone with how important what was on television was, my grandma would sit across from me on the couch and begin to glare at me with those jet-black eyes (although her eyes were blue).

She would begin taunting me with subtle curses, followed up by intensifying the deviousness in her eyes. She would start to giggle, but not a fun giggle, an evil giggle, and then she'd spit out another one at me. And then my grandpa would say sternly, "Anne? Get some orange juice!" But you could tell that she was enjoying herself as I sat there in horror, unable to blink. Then she'd grumble little words at me and then one would be a strike, and then my grandpa would get up and fix her a glass of orange juice and bring it to her and place it between her hands. But she kept her eyes fixed on me and when she got too carried away my grandpa would increase the sternness, "Anne drink your orange juice!" And still staring at me, she would drink some only to appease him with no intention of really stopping. Then it would be, "Anne! Drink the orange juice!"

She was cursing me.

THE PART ABOUT THE SERPENT

When my family was still together, they made a trip to Florida, but left me with my grandpa and grandma Kacin because I was too small to go. I remember one particular incident during that time, as if nothing else happened that could be remembered: I believe my grandma was angry with having to change my diapers, and as an off-color joke, I stuffed a big bulky, toy tug boat down the back of my diapers and told her I pooped my pants. Although she never said one word, I learned something that day: don't ever piss grandma Kacin off!

According to my mother, my Grandma Kacin used to manipulate people with her illness, because she told my mother, "I can get real sick when I want to!"

I find it peculiar to discover how there was Catholicism and pharmacology on my father's side of the family, and how my Jehovah Witness-grandmother on my mother's side wound up taking the roll of servant on the property of my aunt Jenny and uncle Roy who were practicing Freemasonry; which I learned to be a Luciferian cult under the cloak of Catholicism (hence the subtlety of the Jesus portrait hidden around the corner but in plain view of visitors), and how it is my mother came to be working many years for a pharmacy 120 miles away, owned by a Shriner, AKA Freemason…

My cousin Kim told me several times, she found a swastika buried in my grandma's yard. And I attribute the persistence in her repeating it to a lack of better words, because I am certain Kim understood by the depth and location et cetera., taking in the familial clues - that she was emphasizing its being deliberately buried there. Soon there was an occult family who purchased the only house next to my aunt Jenny's. The man was a militia weapons retailer and the woman publicly purported herself to being a "white" witch; complete with the long, faded brittle hair that looked ruined, who worked for Dr. Pezco's office - the general practitioner in the area of you wanted to see a doctor.

On one of our trips up to Houghton Lake, as little kids get to be the full spectators in a car, I saw a black cat running across an intersection we were approaching. The light was green (if there was a light) and amidst the chaos and looks of horror from every other vehicle, I saw an oncoming box truck barreling down the fast lane with what appeared to be a man delighting in some cat's predicament, and rolled the cat over about the moment we were passing. I visually latched out the back widow to a cat laying in the highway in a spasm; every non-black body part hollered out. I even noticed his penis was erect.

THE PART ABOUT THE SERPENT

Losing Touch

AS A VOLUNTEER for The Lion's Club, I remember going to Oxford to assist handicapped kids in physical therapy. I remember it changed me, that these wheelchair-bound kids could have so much fun hitting a balloon with their elbow, or being assisted to walk through ladder steps (which I believe too strict a path for a *coordinated* person), and I was at a light jog the entire shift, sweaty and even staying late to do all I could do.

I was also given the privilege of leading warm-ups and calisthenics on my soccer team, which, to the team's dismay, meant running laps, though they never bitched. And I think that was because they knew it was essential for them, as this particular team had been grossly undisciplined, while none of the adults were assertive enough to get them out of it. So it didn't take assertiveness on my part - no one ever didn't listen - it took someone to lead them, who practiced what he preached and continually got MIP by disciplining himself, and I believe the coaches were simply telling the team to model after me, in that regard.

I refused to entertain the possibility that any of my grade school teachers may have had immoral lifestyles until forced as an adult to research the abuse within the godless, public education system. The rumor came from adults long after I was out of grade school, but it kind of scared me into assessing what these people were all about, given my adverse experiences from day one.

Now there was Tammy Fisher and Brain Bailey in my homeroom class. They were the two star students. Brain's dad owned The Music Shop; and Tammy was the front row, sweater wearing, textbook-toting brunette who probably brought her own travel-sized box of tissues to school with her. Tammy was another girl who kept to herself, like Regina, but Tammy was too guarded to be an introvert, and this WAS a romantic noticing!

For the life of me, I can never forget sitting behind Brain on a day we were to have a chapter essay written when the teacher randomly called on him to share his, and probably because she had an important point to demonstrate to the class. He then lifted up a blank piece of paper between his hands, still resting his elbows on his desk, and proceeded to read aloud his entire thesis without missing a beat so convincingly that it seemed even to drive home the point the teacher was trying to convey! And her point wasn't that Brain was a little con-artist!

Nevertheless, Brian and Tammy, everyday, rather than going outside during recess to work up a sweat on the most wicked playground in the land - asked permission to go to the library instead. So, I, everyday, forfeited all my passionate, precious outdoor-time to go to the library too, but not to have anything to do with books and schoolwork, but only that Tammy might notice me...

I deliberately wore a scarf just like Tammy's, red and blue knit, and where I got it - I would be surprised if I had not stolen it. Someone teased us (me) about it one day and all I saw was Tammy throwing barbs around with her eyes. She was the embodiment of the color brown I described in the name Ruth: book-smart, a brunette with perfect hair, good posture, loyal to her cause; and the name, Tammy, which is burgundy – is a close cousin of brown - and has that antagonizing girlish sound in the Y, like Shelly and Wendy.

All year long, I don't know what I was doing in the sterile environment of that artificially lit library when outside, they called me Speedburner and loved me to play wide receiver. And why it was I was so attracted to Tammy; she had a little bit of weight on her, attributing that to healthy, and if she ever showed emotion, I don't know what it was...

THE PART ABOUT THE SERPENT

David and I were both at the roller rink. I remember the music: Love is Like a Rock, I'm Gonna Keep on Loving You, Centerfold…and Tammy was there. I think she may have been grouped with Angie Dicks and Linda Patterson, I don't remember for sure. But I asked David to go ask Tammy if she would skate with me. David was more than willing but he kind of looked at me the way all the neighborhood kids looked at me when I was drunk, "Tammy Fisher?!" Anyway, the answer was no. I somehow kept my composure until I made it home and walked passed my mother to lock myself in the bathroom where I proceeded to have an emotional breakdown. I remember my mother consoling me from the other side of the door. I had to be rebuilt.

"*Fuck* the *library!*"

…

Now there was Dawn Furman, not a romantic noticing, but Dawn was probably from a poor home, and when I should have been loyal to her - standing beside her, as I was in the same boat, even if only done non-verbally - I was morally digressing at a fast pace. Dawn was the oppressed type, probably lived only with her mother (I do not know), and she yielded to poor treatment, even that of myself.

THE PART ABOUT THE SERPENT

While on my paper route, not far from my house, a high school girl, who, I believe may have spent large chunks of time between parents, used to leave her Nike sneakers outside on the porch, and to vindicate some of my own poverty, I took them. I started hanging more around a kid named Mike Livingston and less around Brain O'Brien. Eventually, every part on my bike was hot, and Brain used to love how my bikes were so streamlined. Then I remember trading Brian my Gibson SG guitar for a pair of his used Nike tennis shoes…

Mike and I were both blondes, were both on soccer teams, and both had large paper routes, same as Brian…Often the customers on my particular route were loose about their drug use and all too inviting, and if their invites didn't get me, their influences did. But Mike introduced me to an older couple, Bill and Elaine Adams, who had fostered children in the past, including Brian O'Brien's new stepfather who on one occasion came home from the bar with a knife wound, bragging of what the other guy looked like…

Bill was a decorated, retired police officer who had been in a horrible auto accident necessitating the Jaws of Life. On Sunday mornings he would drive Me and Mike on our paper routes, and then take us water skiing while his wife painted ceramics in the basement.

I remember the awkwardness of taking unwrapped Christmas presents and food to underprivileged families with kids in the area through the Lion's Club, with Bill, who was a member: The parents were still asleep, probably knocked out from depression, while a houseful of kids with no shirts on took from us paper grocery bags full of naked Barbie Dolls and other donations of unwanted items sticking out of them... And I remember the awkwardness of Bill straddling me and Mike - the way my Mother used to straddle me – but with our pants off upstairs at the Adams' home while he played with our genitals in demonstration of what we should never let anyone do to us...

Bill had also made a strange comment to my Mother one evening at our house. Apparently my Mother mentioned I needed to take a bath one night and Bill commented on how pleasurable it must be for her to dry me off with a towel; something she never did, would never take pleasure in doing, was bizarre to say, but Bill had become accustomed to that out on the water.

Then it seemed all I remember is a blackout death-wish for the next 30 years...

...

My Mother not only remembered, but instantly tied in the inappropriateness of Bill's comment 30 years later when I disclosed to her as an adult what he was doing to me and Mike when we were kids.

Around this time, during summer vacation, Brian and I were riding through town out to his house and while crossing M-24 to get to the party store, I came upon Dawn Furman who was walking unusually upbeat when I spit on her a huge, wet sticky spit that spread as it caught wind-resistance before landing on her. Brian was ahead of me and never knew of it. He wasn't cruel like I was.

Another day, after making a deal with Mike that I would lead him partway home – the bridge – the big kids in my neighborhood grabbed hold of my forearms and dragged me into a wooden fort behind their parent's property where they locked me in and dropped fireworks on me. I didn't break until I made it home and then my mother took me to the doctor's. Dr. Williams said to her, "You're suing, I hope?!" There resulted a small lawsuit against the parents of the bigger kids for Kidnapping and Entrapment and soon we were loading our things on a moving truck for Houghton Lake.

...

For years to come, I would recall looking back toward the street my house was on (seemingly with crumbs falling out of my mouth) and seeing the silhouette of Dinky - the runt of the litter - now a giant wildcat with a massive chest and a beard; who chose to live a life of hardships outside, rather than to subject himself another day to a bunch of abusive freaks like myself, inside - in so-called luxury, and it appeared Mrs. O'Brien had taken to feeding him out of their boathouse...

THE PART ABOUT THE SERPENT

Down Time

AFTER MY MOTHER AND I MOVED to Houghton Lake, we hit a level of poverty that lingered and haunted us awhile. We rented a small, red three-bedroom house on a concrete slab that didn't match our royal-blue Granada with the white vinyl top so much anymore, and took to upgrading our circumstances by hard, impossible work. My mother was good about watching the papers so we bought a portable washing machine that would wash and spin our clothes, and then we would dry them on a dowel-rod clothes rack. In hard water, you could pick up your stiff garment off the rack in the same form it dried - before breaking it open to slide a limb into it.

The house in Lake Orion - we rented, but it was sometime before I learned that the tenants were not paying rent, and had brought dogs into the house, which we prohibited. My mother was still receiving child support from my dad, and even though it used to concern me that she always prided herself how *she* bought the house in Lake Orion, which was secondary to the other house *she* bought in her previous marriage, as if she bought them single-handedly - I don't think I ever spoke up or demanded to know where any of that child support went. I knew the answer, "room and board!"

Furthermore, I was to report to my mother the actual amount my father was drinking during visitations which went to court against him, causing him to lose his custody rights of me which were only instated to appease his parents in the first place. I could tell, because every elaborate toy my father ever bought me had to be opened in the presence of my grandma and grandpa, and then they were broken and in the garbage in a week. And not that I didn't love my father, but my heart knew they were no true gifts. It would be less awkward for a father in that situation, and less painful for a child, to simply write the child a void check with the words "I love you" written on it and mail it to his parents.

And the court didn't hear about the stories like my father cracking beers before breakfast, or falling backward with his pants down through the glass shower...

Nevertheless, as one of the formal courtesies my mom used give, we bought my dad some gifts at Christmas -

me being the medium - filtering the choice of gifts through my immature hands just enough to signify authenticity, though I was totally too irresponsible to execute such a procedure (i.e. being thoughtful, saving the money, being somewhere to buy the gifts, wrapping the gifts, tagging them with addresses, making allowance for estimated time of arrival while also considering the holidays, and waiting in line at the post office to step up and have them shipped). We mailed them to his Clawson address but this time they came back with someone else's, penciled cursive on them that appeared to be written by a well-disciplined female, "Not at this address."

I had more freedom in Houghton Lake and after noticing my coming from down-state intimidated people, I began flaunting it and wound up doing dirty things like throwing rocks at occupied houses in broad daylight, smoking, and cussing up a storm to impress my friends. From a BMX stunt gone awry in Lake Orion, I had a temporary crown on one of my front teeth, which often didn't hold, and makes me look like a street fighter from Detroit. My mother received an anonymous letter during that time which condemned her for bringing white trash into the neighborhood. The letter may have been endorsed by more than one neighbor, and I know that my mother tried diligently to find out who it was, to dispute it. It seems as time went on, my mother must have bore the guilt of that accusation alone, never inquiring if I may have had anything to do with it, but I am certain it was because of what the neighbors witnessed in me.

THE PART ABOUT THE SERPENT

A car stopped just past our house one night while we were in bed, and perhaps because Pixie, my dog, growled, we noticed two young guys trying to siphon gas from the car. I grabbed a tennis racket and ran out the door, kind of after they were alerted to us, and they were in their car and speeding away by the time I hit the end of the driveway. I remember knowing I was at no risk so I turned up the toughness and ran down the road after them, knowing they could see just enough of me in the glare of the moonlight shining off the road behind them.

Things start getting a little fuzzy for me; there was still trouble going on at home, and I was at the age where I wanted to see girls and be with friends, and go to dances.

And I also remember needing a role model, but which came via MTV.

In the middle of the night I would creep toward my mother's bedroom where the door was always open, paying close attention to the sound of her breathing while she slept to determine the likelihood I could steal a couple cigarettes out of the open package on the nightstand just inside the door, next to her head. I would lay down on the floor and shift myself in augments without rubbing against the carpet, and then pause and wait...taking enough time to let my mother fall back into a deep sleep, knowing that even unconsciously, noises are still registering to her. I would go through the whole routine of lifting my arm so as to not make any ruffling sounds, sliding the contents very carefully - making sure not to cause a honk from the vibration of the cigarette being dragged crosswise the paper edging, all while paying attention to my own breathing. Enduring all the patience and muscle-resistance to do all that was a practice for me that took what seemed like half the night.

One night, I wanted to go to the Rock House to a dance they put on on the weekends. I would have taken my bike, anything. I believe I may have been grounded or something because my mom WOULD NOT let me go, and it swelled into a passionate fight. It went so far that it regressed to my mother physically beating me even though I was thirteen or fourteen, and she was sitting on top of me on the couch, beating me with her hair brush. This particular time, however, I grabbed hold of both her wrists and then squeezed hard. She dropped the brush and folded in agony, sobbing in complete loss. And soon I was seeing a professional...

I remember my Uncle Dick was the only male my mother looked up to now (although being her baby brother) because he resembled so much her father. So when this counselor asked me what I wanted to become, I told her, "A mason contractor", just like my uncle. She wrote in her notes that my mother and I had a symbiotic relationship, which meant that it was apparent to her that we were both dependent upon one another, but in a sick way.

THE PART ABOUT THE SERPENT

I used to jog the streets at night, favorably during snow storms, even running backward, and rather than ride the bus to school, I would ride my bike to my grandma's while it was still dark out, where I could drink real coffee like an adult while determining the importance of my actually going to school or not; whereas if I rode the bus with all the bunch of fawning immaturity, unwittingly laughing their way off to the tailored demise of their industrialized education, dressed in their favorite Scooby Do and Batman winter-things, my mindset would follow and my resistance would be gone in just the half an hour of the sound of it...

The woods, the sunrises, the red dawns over the giant pines gave me strength.

My grandmother also knew first-hand the troubled relationships in our family and offered an almost unconditional place of respite. Consequently, my brother lived with my grandma for years and years, occupying my grandpa's old room; as did my cousin Kim, who occupied the couch or the chair.

We always made fun of my grandma's place and her kitchen habits - cutting up liver with her rusty old liver-scissors to feed to the cats, who would lean their ears to the floor to crank down on the liver, enjoying it so much they would forget to breathe – making snarling sounds and growling at one another like little liver demons. My brother never stopped marveling that he once discovered a mouse's face on the carpet of the kitchen floor.

THE PART ABOUT THE SERPENT

My grandma's favorite cat was a pretentious Siamese, rightly named Princess, and when you were in right alignment to see the blue-orange and gray of her eyes beyond her thick cataracts, all you could see was greed. And she had a peculiar voice, as many Siamese do, which was a raspy old annoyance with a little grueling touch of dying agony broken into syllables, and we swore the cat was audibly requesting liver. We then went around imitating the cat's pronunciation of liver. The cat didn't know - protected as she was by my grandmother - that if she carried that attitude and made those sounds outside that dysfunctional environment, something would just kill it.

One night, feeling mischievous, while everyone was asleep, I sabotaged stuff around the house and planted a chunk of liver down in the coat pocket of my brother's blue-denim winter coat, hoping he might find it out in public somewhere, standing at a cash register with a line of people behind him... It wasn't until years later that my brother told me, "One of Grandma's damn cats put a piece of liver down in my coat pocket!"

I was enrolled in Middle school which was a step down from the junior high where I came from, and initially I was right up front and fresh faced, even volunteering for safety patrol. The principle, Mr. French, however, was not so keen on my choice of friends to enlist on the patrol and eventually I held my loyalty to my friends above the safety of his students.

THE PART ABOUT THE SERPENT

I could never forget some of the rules and procedures that were passed out on the first day of school at Houghton Lake, such as, "No chewing tobacco", and school was closed for opening day of deer season. I also remember them offering Elk on the menu in the cafeteria on one occasion, which I suppose couldn't be any worse than the turtle soup we were served in Lake Orion that George the janitor caught!

Things were almost unbearable for me emotionally, and knowing I drew too much attention made me so uptight that I began to limp when I walked. On one hand, it told of a conscious forfeiting; putting on an air of defectiveness that might prevent a full-blown confrontation between me and the older and bigger kids who were threatened by me, and on the other, it spoke of a hardness to warn anybody else below them not to mess with me. It was a semi-volitionally self-imposed imperfection - else I would break!

I remember limping down the hall in front of everyone at a fast clip one day, with just a few members of our class in the hall behind me, on the way to another room. It must have looked peculiar to see a fast limp because a guy named Larry shouted down the hall, "Kacin! Why do you limp?" I looked back and I could see everyone's head tilted inquisitively, and I slowed back to give Larry the person-to-person spew about having Osclosis in my knee from playing soccer as a kid. Osclosis I did once have, but not anymore, and Larry pegged me however obtrusive he was about it.

THE PART ABOUT THE SERPENT

So, I knew I drew attention so - that I drew attention by deliberately not trying to draw attention, and then I walked some hallucinogenic line between trying not to draw attention and wondering if I was deliberately trying to draw attention by not trying to draw it, because I'd be following the cues of people around me - whether they were understanding me correctly or not. If misunderstood – I'd go into a tailspin of inner-conflict, sending me into deeper desperation, knowing it could be a long, long time before I could ever be exonerated; the defeating voice of all the bad things my mother ever said about me pouring into that hypersensitive vacuum like acrid sand...

My mom recalled for years what Mr. French said to her, and I think it was, "I have never seen a student more sullen and withdrawn than Joe."

Nevertheless, I still had to fight the big kids, and other times I would employ the attention I seemed to have been cursed with to make statements. One day, I dared, dared to wear a tied bandanna around my left leg, just above the knee. Something I think Chatchi did in Happy Days but was probably more Van Halen 1984. Even though I rode the bus that day, anyone noticing before my statement made its debut had already been swept aside in a blackout of determination. Not until recently could I acknowledge that a fad had started because of that, and kids even from other socioeconomic levels began wearing some very nice, very fashionable bandannas (of higher quality that I could ever afford) and not just around their legs, but as collars and belts too, from that one very inconsequential statement.

I remember Mr. Haley's study hall during last hour where he would often let me go to his art room, having never been his curriculum student, and unfortunately, though he was so good to trust me, I would smoke in one of the interior rooms of the art room. Moreover, on the days I didn't go – there was a young, overweight, lazy looking kid and his friend who taunted me the entire hour I sat in Mr. Haley's study hall. Pausing to mention here that my mother reported all of my behavior to professionals and I was probably very close to probation, in addition to whatever disciplinary threats might have come from school; "living", as they say, "with a hammer over your head." So I tolerated this kid.

"Whatz' a matter huh? You speaka no English?" … "No understando Engleso?" "Can't hear?" … "Hard of hearing?" … "You stupid? You dumb?" "Huh?"…

One day, with respect to Mr. Haley, after the bell rang, I waited until we were in the hall just as it began to fill up, then I picked this guy up by the collar, slammed him into the lockers and glared at him. In three seconds Mr. Lewis – a 280-300 pounder – picked me up and slammed me into the lockers all the way across the hall, and said to me, "How do *you* like it?!" There where kids behind him giving me signs, including Eric Williams, who mouthed with his fist up, "Hit him!" I just diverted eyes from what was happening and took it.

THE PART ABOUT THE SERPENT

I never went back to talk to Mr. Lewis to tell him what had been going on; I knew it was too far from him, but that kid was my friend from that day on. He would always say things at me (from the opposite side of the hall) when going by with his friends, but he knew as well as I that I had bigger things going on and could hardly do more than barely acknowledge him.

A guy named Bill had befriended me at the time, and I turned Bill on to how I would eat orange peels to get high off the dies, and on Open Gym night at the high school one night I was drinking schnapps and shooting baskets with my pant down. Bill approached me alone one day. "Joe, I have to tell you, how you told me you eat orange peels to get high from the dies and act all crazy...getting drunk and playing basketball with your pants down...for the sake of my reputation, I am going to have to stop hanging around you." Anyone else, and I would have rebelled against that, and maybe I did in time to come in unspoken ways. But the way Bill approached me, alone, solemnly... Although it hurt, Bill was only protecting himself, he wasn't trying to injure me, and I am still impressed he was such a man about it.

My mother and I moved into another red house at 665 Nellsville, this one much larger, sided with faded aluminum, white trim, and black shutters. It had a large wood stove in addition to an oil burner, and a two-stall garage attached in which the doors remained permanently open; housing wood and unimportant things we wanted to keep dry. It was set back in a field,

THE PART ABOUT THE SERPENT

high on a hill and had a trail running down behind it full of character with dips, turns, raspberry bushes and beehives; crossing a two track, then Nelsville again after Nelsville turned into dirt.

The field around the house was all high weeds and there were a couple non-producing apple trees in the yard. My mom worked me to take the weeds down by hand with the type of grass whip you swing back and forth – that probably came from Lake Orion, or from a garage sale, and hadn't had its blade sharpened in years. All I remember was it was blistering murder that never ended.

The house next door was a vacation home and when the people came up they brought a terrier with them, but all we knew about the dog was that his tag said rabies, so we called him Rabies. Across the front of the house, the view looking from the house was of a good mile stretch of field interrupted by a huge sand pit, and to the right was the expressway with one lot between us and it, housing an old tar shack; the kind where you'd expect to find old, faded *Hustler* magazines and a rusty can full of roofing nails.

One of my friends in Houghton Lake, after getting to high school, was Don. He was short and thick, his brown hair registering as long, but only in the back (a mullet) and his face was so long and full of character that it resembled something you'd expect to see on Mount Rushmore. Don's parents appeared to be at the grandparents' age (which I now attribute to their heavy smoking) and owned a small resort on the north shore. They were from the south and I was always strangely impressed how they furnished Don with many different, high quality vehicles to drive – as if he needed them to drive to the party store for cigarettes, and he drove them harshly at their expense.

The most memorable of those vehicles was a red Volkswagen bug, and if I remember correctly, it didn't have heat. My first ride in Don's bug - crashing through snow banks and driving a gravel pit like we were in a derby, proved to me that they were little German tanks! When the bug was down, Don would drive an automatic diesel sedan with duel batteries and I remember him shifting it into reverse when speeding down the road on icy snow! And if he wasn't in that, he drove a Kawasaki Enduro.

Don was a strange friend. Even though he had bigger fish to catch in life, and came from more money, he was humble enough that he fit right in with my friends, even dating my girlfriend's best friend. He was power driven above authority, he thought nothing of it, and it was obvious that his family's mindset despised law to shame. My mother never seemed to outwardly reject Don as she usually did all my other friends, perhaps, I believe, because she sensed his disposition to an older generation and Don didn't hide; Don was Don. But sometimes he was embarrassingly immature (which kept us on equal footing), and although Don never really ever lashed out at me, never sensed him ever wishing me harm - which was very, very unlike most anyone I have ever befriended - Don had a malignant anger that often revealed a state of fearlessness, almost as if he were in a trance. And although Don may not have appeared to be expressing anger, you could tell that he was hell-bent, toying with danger, and that he'd been doing it so long he was desensitized to the thrill of it, including your own! That made Don absolutely scary, and parting ways inevitable.

A typical day with Don would be sitting with him in wood shop, snickering after laying two joints of Cincimillion on the instructor's desk, who me and my cousin Doug called Woodbuddy; then sending a girl or two home because he fashioned a wood catapult with a bolt on it, smashing his fist down on it - sending the bolt 18 feet straight up into the florescent lights, showering down chemical-laced glass in everyone's hair, but not intending to do so much damage!...

Or, once Don was at home, super stoned, and there was a bird out on the power line… It was the huge, thick, black kind of power line that draped low over the driveways running the length of the highway. Don took a shotgun to the bird and took the line down with it, knocking out power down the entire north shore of Houghton Lake and then went back inside and laid down to take a nap. Apparently, he didn't wake up until his parents came home who were being accosted by law enforcement with every type of fire truck and emergency-crew vehicle out in his driveway.

THE PART ABOUT THE SERPENT

One day, Don showed up at my house on his Enduro, driving up over the downed fence from the expressway having just outran the cops. One night, during winter, there was so much snow that school closing had already been determined for the following day. Don came and got me and we fired up two of his snowmobiles and ran them down the highway, right into what would be referred to as town, raising hell. I remember a pick up truck with a light on it, chasing us this way and that way, confused by the chaos and duality of it, but he was hot to catch *one* of us.

I remember coming to the end of a street by the bowling alley and turning around, getting stuck in the ditch with too much snow in front of me. He was right there behind me while I had to get off the sled, walk out in front of it, and lift the skis up and walk them to the side and then get back on it and hit the throttle, praying it wouldn't flood out! Somehow, the confusion must have saved me from that, and I don't think I saw Don again until the next day, who said he'd went straight out onto the ice.

One day, me, Don, my girlfriend, and my girlfriend's best friend, skipped school by climbing into his bug. And as we were leaving the school grounds, Don quickly put a motorcycle helmet on his head, as one of the first buses were pulling in while we were pulling out, so he couldn't be identified, as if no one would notice the only red bug in town leaving school! We made it out as far as the other side of the expressway from my mom's house and killed the battery. There was an old lady we tried to get help from who refused us - wise of her - being that we should have been in school, and we must have push-started it and made it out to my mom's.

The next day, possibly due to me having been known for trouble in the home at the crises level, I was threatened with the charge of statutory rape, even though no such thing ever occurred. In an act of appeasement toward my girlfriend's mom and dad, my mother and I made a visit to my girlfriend's parents', and imbecilic as it may sound, subsequently, my girlfriend's mom told her how cute I looked sitting there on their couch while being reprimanded, after we left...

I remember having friends over at my mom's and we were hyperventilating; something me and my friends had been doing for years, where we would bend over and suck air in and out as fast as we could and then raise our bodies upright and choke ourselves, either with our hands or something else, with the object of passing out, or passing half-way out - entertaining everyone in a brief demonstration of non-sensible communication that sometimes seemed to draw up a burst of emotion. This time I fell through one of my mom's glass end-tables and woke up to my friends staring at me like a bunch of ghosts. I told my mom I tried smacking the dog off the couch and it jumped onto it!

THE PART ABOUT THE SERPENT

My friends and I loved pot and I took to making pipes and water bongs out of household items, though I was stingy with my pot. I started carving small, one-toke wooden pipes and I would draw moonscapes on them in heavy ink, depicting the night sky I used to worship while walking home late at night - usually miles and miles in the dead of winter, grandiosely stoned. I recall a guy names Art from school requested that I make one for him, but without the drawing. I was eating my mother's Darvon and Darvocets now; a good buzz being four at a time, and I took so many of them that I used to dismantle her Darvon capsules and re-fill them with sugar. It was a tedious operation; I also had to keep the sugar taste off the outside of the capsules. The powder was bitter-awful, and in the end of one side of each capsule was a separate stimulant the drug company added to keep you awake while pain-relieved. I used to mix the powder in my coffee and the tell-tale sign of my usage was that my pupils, including my eyelashes and all the surrounding components to my eyes, would turn dark black. It was also how I could tell when my mother, not getting enough of the effect from the sugar-filled Darvon, increasing the dosage, would happen upon a cluster of those I hadn't tampered with.

Sometimes I would lay in bed in the afternoon in a meditative state and the side-effects from the Darvon would cause vibrant sounds to shake me right up into wakefulness, but I always rationalized them into being harmless. Once, I remember trying to cross the highway on my motorcycle to get to my grandma's. And while I waited there on the curb for the four lanes of traffic to

THE PART ABOUT THE SERPENT

clear up, I was so high and my coordination so discombobulated that I didn't know if I could keep from hitting the throttle and just shooting out into traffic or not... or, if I could tell when I actually should hit the gas... or, maybe I might just hit the gas by trying not to hit it!...

I carried a pair of fold-up, designer sunglasses in a zip-up pouch to school, which where "in" back then (somewhere), and I used to carry pills in it. Mr. Jury, a counselor from the high school who had a form of naivety that could only be blamed on his genuineness, approached a group of us outside smoking in the woods one morning before first hour. He gave us all a slight interrogation and he happened to grab my glass's case that rattled with pills in it. He unzipped it and saw 10-15 little yellow pills with a V cut in them and said, "Joe what are all these little yellow pills in here?" And I said most indignantly, "It's for my asthma!" And he zipped the case up and handed it back to me as quickly as he took it from me.

I preferred speed, and we all ate 357 Magnums, which I believe is just caffeine, and then we would get white crosses which had a little more sensation to them. They would "dry you out" and cause the hairs on your head twitch. I took to snorting magnums so that I kept a crushed stock in a folded piece of paper down in the breast pocket of my fake, black-leather jacket with a pen sticking out of it, having removed the guts of the pen so I could snort at will. There were a few times I would feel so ill from it, and semi-fearless from the unreal energy, that I would have the office call my mom to come and pick me up.

I remember Darvon gave me enough false confidence and love-feeling that I casually told my girlfriend I loved her before school one morning, which, normally something like that had to be written in hieroglyphics and then mailed as a piece of chain mail across the continent before it reached her, because I was really too immature to express anything like that in person.

Don had headed down south for a while and he left in my possession a large Indian pipe we used to smoke dope out of. While he was gone I took to scraping the bowl out which brought up so much black resin that I was not only smoking it myself for a good long while, but I was sharing it with everyone else. Then I took to drilling the end out to get all of it. When Don saw it, he said, "Dude! that was my grandfather's grandfather's pipe!" Apparently I'd broken some sacred Indian tradition.

...

My friend Alden dated Wendy. Wendy was a plump, little brunette who always wore denim blue jeans and a denim jacket, so she was all denim, all the time. Her mother was, or had become a substance abuse counselor, and I remember there was trouble in the home. There was a period where she and Alden had broken up and she happened to call me and let me in on how her mother never let her go anywhere, and basically, I was right where she was with my mom. My mom and I were still fighting where she would chase me through the house on Nelsville and I would try to get behind a closed door. It would be an all night *t*rauma. She would press her weight into the door while I wedged my foot at the bottom, like my brother once taught me, who took martial arts and knew things like that. She would wrap her fingers around the top and side of the wood-slatted door like an animal, breathing like she would in Lake Orion - like she just ran down a train - bending the top of the door into the room, chugging, "Oh God damn you!" "Oh God damn you!" Oh God damn you!"

There were times when I knew she was not going to let up - that in order to make her stop and to call it a night, knowing it would not do any lasting damage and sensing she might over dramatize it - I would stiffly jab the door once onto her fingers. Then she would slowly slide her bathrobe-covered back - down the other side of the door, curling up at the bottom, sobbing at what a monster I had become…

And at that point I waited there with no choice but to remorsefully absorb every pound of the guilt of it.

Although, Wendy's call didn't seem to me to be unusually personal, it was, however, unwonted that she called me at all, and within a matter of days Wendy fatally shot herself.

THE PART ABOUT THE SERPENT

About that time, on a day unexpected, my mother walked right up to me with her head down and growled, "If you think you are not going to do what it is I tell you around here, and disobey me, then I will get a 2x4 and you *will* obey me!"

One day, my mom would not let up and struck me repeatedly with a three-foot, chrome vacuum attachment. This time, I took the weapon away from her and stopped her with one very deliberate blow to the front part of her quadrecep. That night she was on the phone for hours with her old boss, Christine. Her thigh swelled up black and blue; she must have rolled her pant leg up because it was exposed the rest of the night, and I knew by these calls that my mother was feigning the victim while intensifying my guilt by publicizing it.

Another occasion, a spirited verbal fight broke out between me and my mom. I remember countering her with a defiant "I-DON'T-CARE!" and my mom crouched and shrugged with her head tipped back, and yelled out in pain - exactly as she would if someone wearing boots had stepped on her bare toes. Although I could not see it at the time, I had been taking the blame for so much of my mother's misery for so long, that she felt confident enough in that deception that I might not know the difference between physical and emotional pain when I saw it; because the rule not to resist my mother was law above everything, including making sense. My mother knew she could cripple me with guilt that I hurt her. And why I feel it necessary to disclose

these details is that I've learned this personal type of attack is not unique to my mother. And so has the devil…
My mother's dependence on prescription medications had made her bones weak and her skin necrotic-like, and she would break a rib simply riding in a golf cart, while years later she would tell me I had done it to her in a fight…

I was put on probation and I remember sitting in my probation officer's office with my mother one day so she could scold me in front of my mother. Apparently, my mother had complained to this woman that I would let a fire go out in the wood-stove of the house on her, so she said to me, "You wouldn't do that to your friends! … You wouldn't let your friends go cold in your mother's house!" But it was inappropriate, and my mother had been grasping at things to accuse me of now that she was actually sitting in the county probation office after indirectly leading me there.

The probation officer hadn't taken into account that I myself would not let the house go cold while I was in there if I could help it, not to mention we were often without firewood and took to burning rolled up, tied up – newspapers that we soaked and dried, and that my mother wasn't my friend. Nevertheless, I was court ordered to live with my mother until I was eighteen...

I got caught with a water bong at school one day, a probation violation, and another day – I got caught pulling the fire alarm before school one morning and I took the blame as if I did it intentionally, which was not really true; I simply tested the device for tension, not intending to pull it off the wall!

I was also taken to a shelter home for bad kids hosted by a family in Roscommon. I remember them asking me at the shelter home, after they had learned my temperament, "Why are you *here*?" and I said - knowing the nature of their question – "Well…I fight with my mom." My answer allowed validation to the legal explanation of why I might be there, it also showed my taking my portion of the blame, while not entirely, hence, I fight "with" my mom, and that was the closest I could come to casting aspersions upon my mother at that time. If they had asked me that question with a free-healthy mind and spirit, and not someone who lived in fear of their mother, I would have told them, "I'm here for trying to defend myself."

Was I a good kid? no. Was I bad kid? yes.

There was also an unhealthy obese couple across the street from county probation I was taken to for counseling. My mother was there in the room during the session and I remember being so furiously insulted with them trying a form of play therapy with me – by throwing pillows at me – that I pretended to play along in order not to insult them!...

I had purchased an Electra Telecaster, a very rare guitar unbeknownst to me. It was brown with a high gloss finish, semi-hollow with an f hole; and it had a blond, tapered neck that made it the easiest guitar ever to play. My strap was rainbow-colored and I found a way to power it out of my boom box. Were in poor country however, where you couldn't even buy guitar strings if you had the money, and my cousin Doug and I were hitting a spiritual level that resonated with Led Zeppelin, though there was very little of it around.

While everyone in high school wanted nothing more than to buy a stupid car, I told Doug that all I wanted was a Les Paul electric guitar and a Marshall stack. And eventually that became a reality, even insisting on a Sure 58 microphone with a 25' cord.

I remember one particular day Doug and I stopped by someone's trailer and the two young men living there asked upon greeting us outside "You guys wouldn't happen to have any LED ZEPPELIN would you?" Doug and I both kind of leaped forward in response without looking at one another, party to appreciate, and party to console. It felt to us as if the question had been staged and their inquiry and need held all the base elements of a drug deal, including the, "No, I wish I did though." Doug and I had for some time been glorifying this type of irony to the superstitious level.

And the more we did, the more it came.

Me and Doug, his girlfriend, Kelly; and Eric Williams were out in Eric's little red car in the woods one night during winter while Eric showed us how to spray starting fluid into a bread bag and then hold it to our

THE PART ABOUT THE SERPENT

face to breathe in the fumes from the ether to get high. It seemed that he and Doug had already done it, or Doug was not unfamiliar with it, or more appropriately, the sophistication of drug use itself caused Doug to abandon any fear of it. It is highly volatile and makes you choke until you endure enough of it that your nervous system starts to respond to it as something pleasurable. Like when scientists drop rats in glasses of liquid to demonstrate how they can breathe under oxygenated water. But not without a consistent form of consent.

I remember each of us taking turns and the suspicious looks and non-verbal communication between us was, "Oh my God!" I remember huffing, then visually being in a very small, black and red carpeted room. I wound up so elated by the end of my trip that I remember leaping with my hands into the air with a shout of ecstasy! but I hit the interior of the roof of the car... then I looked to see if anyone noticed, or cared; if I ought to be humiliated or not, or if the crazed look in my eyes and the spit on my chin gave it away...

When we started the car and turned the headlights on to go home, all the leafless branches and twigs from the bushes and trees were pronged in an evil, threatening way that I'd never noticed before; like pitchforks.

And it didn't go away.

Doug and I started doing ether together often, and when faced with people, I often couldn't speak. There were things we were seeing and being told; we were gaining a knowledge from some form of intelligence that no one else was aware of, but we were too far gone to communicate it...

I started doing ether alone as a study, say, just as if I were going to the library (I was actually taking notes and encouraged Doug to do the same), and I started queuing in to what were behind things; what people were really up to, what they really meant. Consequently, I started spending all my time alone, bringing back to the motel room more books from the library than I could carry, where it seemed my hands had a preconceived notion of what to grab: Carl Jung, Alistair Crowley, Yoga, Poetry...

I had a vivid dream at that time where I saw three men walking down the crowded hallway of my high school. The man in the middle was the superior to the other two, even taller, and his clothing kind of draped in a sublime gold color that was far removed against the simplicity of the football jerseys, shameless 80's prints, and sleeveless t-shirts that all reeked of Old English and Brute cologne. He walked without lifting his feet much off the floor as if he were shuffling. It was apparent that he was carrying so much head-knowledge that concentration on things like walking lost priority; like a handicap, or more of a curse. It was as if he needed guides who carried stacks of books and statistical data-graph charts to confirm his every notion and minister to him, while so preoccupied with the martial perplexities of things that no one around him posed him any real concern. Although these three men were indistinguishable to all the other students, I knew the man in the center was Satan and when I tried to reveal it by shouting it out to alert the other students - he telekinetically took away my voice and elevated me to the ceiling, pinning me there. Then there was no doubt...

At times, when I would hear certain things coincide - similar with what is referred to as "jogging a notion" or "rigging a bell" I would get a spermatic sensation - a tightening into my inner left thigh that would threaten to disable me; tugging between the valley-like area of the front of my hip and my testicles. The more profound the coincidence (whether I *re*-cognized anything or not), the more intense the not-quite pain, but almost agonizing sensation... I never understood it, but when it came, I was supposed to try. It was an indication of some lurid message and I was probably not less than literally spellbound.

I remember seeing things - fantastic futuristic scenes, or maybe past. One in particular was of a meek and contented young woman hanging her laundry out to dry on a clothesline while listening to a short-wave radio on the only radio station available to anyone. The sky was cleaner, like out of the 70's, but for some reason, I was always persuaded to attribute it to a time deep in the future:

The singular radio station and the use of a clothesline indicated to me the past; I remember being shown how crystal AM radio's work in grade school, knowing how quickly broadcasting spread across the dial since that time, as if 10 stations were all trying to fit into the same frequency at once. On the other hand, the eyes of our future in the 80's were in anticipation of almost unavoidable nuclear devastation (someday) and the clothesline and the short wave radio were also indicative of a remnant of what may have survived a nuclear fallout; the radio now under government control…

Another: the cover of John Lennon's Imagine album came to full-life color to me while huffing in my grandmother's motel room one day. It was like one of those drawings where the artist drew the entire picture with one continuous stroke of his instrument, only it was as if it was being drawn out before me … John's face, then his glasses, his forehead, and then the colors began to bleed out as they filled in the contours of his hair - like a stunt pilot draws smoke messages in the sky. Although I never owned that album or ever studied that image, it appeared to me that Imagine contained the highest form of human deity and kindness the world had ever known. "Imagine was hope for the world!"…

On one occasion, while Doug was huffing in my motel room, I saw all the cigarette-smoking and poverty-stricken lines on his face deepen and elongate all the way down his cheeks, joining the lines in his jaw, and from there - connecting to the protruding tendons of his neck, as he stood there; eyes squinted shut, lost in a soft hilarity that didn't stop when it should have… As if the

THE PART ABOUT THE SERPENT

laughter were vindictive of all his poverty and reproach...

I remember hearing moans and groans coming from the leafless, nearby woods when doing ether near Doug's mom's apartment, just before it got dark. I remember standing there looking at Doug while he was sitting on his mother's couch. "This ain't good. This ain't good." he said.

I recall being at my brother's friend, John's. He and Doug and I would do ether during broad daylight hours, listening to his home stereo - powered through two, tall home speakers. I remember going way too far. I remember seeing shapes floating out of the speakers in accordance with the sounds. They were each definitive, having their own cookie-cutter shape and translucent color. Moving slowly, they kind of grew as they came into the room toward me, growing more subtle - almost evaporating as they threatened to reach me.

That same day at John's, I noticed myself sitting in an armchair: my arms must have been bare, but I remember all the hair on my body stood out like weapons; like I was a big pin cushion – each follicle was three inches long (and would have had to have been supporting me where I sat)… In another vision, I was looking down into a small paneled room from where the ceiling should be - kind of like a human looking down into to Barbie-doll house. Below my chin, where I looked down, there was a ship's wheel flat against the wall, as if it were a window, turning surreal-

THE PART ABOUT THE SERPENT

like. Then I saw an older man with very little hair, stick his head through the hole of the wheel, his head turning counter-direction the wheel. He looked right at me, and I asked him, "Is this real?" and he said, "Yes, this *is* real."...

In lucid moments of hindsight (some recollections of my youth I believe were either too bizarre or too horrendous to acknowledge, and I lost huge chunks of memory) I had to go over some things, like remembering the moment I questioned in my heart whether the shapes I was seeing coming out of the speakers at John's that day might have been a deliberate hallucination (something the devil was perpetuating), as it seemed they were there for me to see - the shapes suddenly shed any trace of mischievousness, floating benign out into the room as if they had changed their very trajectory in that instant... Like how people suddenly divert their gaze upward and away when pretending not to notice you...

...

I remember consensual warnings imparted to my conscience while doing ether. Everything around me was storm-dark and violent while I accelerated downward like a plane in a nosedive. Intermittently, what seemed like a door - would open with what seemed like a loud, stouthearted call coming from beyond the threshold; the proverbial beam of sunlight

THE PART ABOUT THE SERPENT

coming down out of heaven, but terrible. Its message, though rejected - I understood so intimately that it could not be completely ignored:

Warning: "Your soul is at risk!"

Me: "I know!"

Warning: "Your soul is at risk!"

Me: "I know!"

Warning: "Your soul is at risk!"

Me: "I know!"

Warning: "Your soul is at risk!"

Me: "I know!"

Warning: "Your soul is at risk!"

Me: "I know!"

Warning: "Your soul is…!"

Me: "I KNOW, I KNOW, I KNOW, I KNOW, I KNOW!!!"

THE PART ABOUT THE SERPENT

All the way down - you consent. You fall like lightening.

At the end of the fall, when I'd hit bottom, where I'd tear the bag away from my face and gasp for oxygen as if I'd decided I really did want to live at the last minute after all, I would hear a riot of spirit beings laughing hysterically and ringing bells. Bells of all kinds: church bells, jingle bells, silver bells, sleigh bells, timers, buzzers, and gongs... Literal pandemonium. All I could do was listen, stunned.

The whole thing was akin, however uncouth, to the slippery ease of self-gratification, followed by an inevitable let-down and a damning. Like a cheater's glory - of which there really is none - and as quickly as one grasps at the object of his affections he's charged with the penalty of proceeding to apprehend an allusion for which he was well aware did not exist all the while he pursued it. It's the kind of thing they should have been teaching in the public education system: cheaters lose, robbers go to jail, and sinners go to hell.

And to be frank, each time I did either, knowing I was at the doing-damage point, I hastened it because I fucking hated myself.

...

THE PART ABOUT THE SERPENT

Back on Nelsville, hidden in the depths of an excavated landmass that ran in front of our house, I was doing ether in the tall grass on a sunny afternoon under a clear sky. My jaw dropped as I looked up to see a colossal pinwheel turning in the sky. It had pointed flags atop the end of each spoke, and was so massive; turning so steadily and impeccably, that it was nauseating to witness, threatening to throw me off balance. It was a dark entity, holding no allegiance with the physical world around it. Whether the sun shone on its face, or at its back, no rule of shine or shadow followed; it was exempt from the elements. Dark it was, in the sense that it was an organized power obviously defiant of natural law, and shocking it was, that I was to be its sole witness.

Another occasion, though I may have been tripping in the house, I was lifted high above those fields… The wind blew the tall, green grasses below and I saw my mother and my brother - there with my little dog, Pixie, running about - holding out a parachute as a signal to me, in which all the pie-shaped sections of the parachute held the color scheme of the rainbow, calling out:

"Joe!" "Come home!" "Come home, Joe!"

The rock song Don't Fear the Reaper by Blue Oyster Cult especially fueled my abandon to doing ether, as well as my memories of a foreign cult flick aired out of Detroit on the *Ghoul Show*, called *Psychomania*.

THE PART ABOUT THE SERPENT

We had a party line and unbeknownst to me our neighbors took to eavesdropping on the deep conversations I was having with my friends late at night, because they called the police to inform them that I was planning on running away from home, which further necessitated that into becoming a reality.

All I had was my cheap acoustic guitar and the clothes on my back. I tried to orphan myself to my cousin Michelle, Doug's Sister, and her boyfriend Ken, who lived in a trailer nearer to town on the other side of the expressway. They let me see their eyes looking at one another enough to make me feel too uncomfortable for the idea. There were a few gravel pits linked together in that area and Ken took me out to the edge of the woods were I could make a lean-to. Ken mentored me in that he had been a runaway himself. What we found was an overturned stump overlooking the fields, and Ken cautioned me that we should stick to only two ways to get in, so that no one could see the grass beaten down.

The woods came to a sort of point at the location so that when you were up there behind the stump, it was kind of like being behind the bow of a ship. I cleaned all the leaves so that there was just black dirt (stupid of me) and I made a nice nest under the stump. One of the gravel pits near by was filled with junk and I would haul whatever I could use back to my camp. I still have

THE PART ABOUT THE SERPENT

vivid memories of roaming the fields and sunning on a rock in the morning with my guitar, while the dew was still cold on the ground. But it wasn't cold; I was sunning on a rock and there wasn't anyone out there threatening to me…

One evening, just before sundown, while I had a fire going behind the stump, a backhoe came bobbing across the fields. In fear, I tried to smother the fire, which only sent a stream of smoke out through the trees, but thankfully no one came back.

Things were hard then: The police were looking for me, I lost my girlfriend, and my friend Dale told me that my brother would start crying any time anyone would ask him about me.

I was riding in Eric William's car one day and I remember Kelly's mom sent me out some cold pizza wrapped up in tin foil with a message - that she herself ran away from home when she was a teenager. I still couldn't acknowledge that the food in the foil was for me. I mean, Eric and Doug probably haven't eaten all day either, right?…

Another occasion, Eric was driving me through some side streets. Suddenly I saw my mom's car pulling up to his and I knew it was a set up. I bailed Eric's car, leaving the door wide open and ran. I went miles, miles down the north shore behind the houses toward John's house. It was cold with the wind blowing off the largest inland lake in Michigan, and my energy level was

THE PART ABOUT THE SERPENT

dangerously challenged before I was anywhere near John's. Subsequently, I don't even think I went there.

I had to get to the house one day. I remember I could crawl the drain tube under the expressway about a half-mile down and then take the woods up toward my house. I remember the tube blasted sand in your eyes because it was so long and windy in there. I remember being so hungry while watching my mom's house that I brought up the most lush field grass and began eating it. It is impossible to chew, but there are probably nutrients in the juices. I made it to the old, tar shack and then climbed up on it and laid down on my stomach, where I watched for my mom to leave; then as I would when I was locked out, I could jump up to catch the eave over the front door and go hand to hand over to the bathroom window and slip down into the house. I remember it was sunny and warm on the tar paper this particular morning, and I fell asleep... When I lifted my head, I saw my mom's car was gone, and went to the house.

I still don't know how it happened but my mother had baited me into the house and then tried to reason with me. I kept my distance and let her know by my level of excitement that I was not going to be apprehended. While this was happening, I heard the tires of a car creeping up to the house. Being that my running away was a protest, I was in authority of the situation, so I went to my bedroom widow to see, and certainly, there was a squad car. I shouted more protests as I ran through the house and I went out the back door so hard and fast that nothing was left behind me but an open door and pollen dancing in the sunlight.

I was nearing the tube through the woods when the officer pulled his car close. I was still in the thick and he said meanly, with his arm resting on the door "Come here *boy*!" And I shouted back, "I ain't no *boy*!" And already exhausted, I remember having to face my lack of energy to pick my legs up high enough to get them over some fallen trees and high branches to get away from him before going over the barbed wire to enter the expressway, then again on the other side, after traffic.

One evening, I was at my cousin Kim's apartment in Grayling, thin, sun-darkened and ravished – toting my guitar as if to say to my cousin - I was in full control of everything that was happening to me. I was there only minutes, it seemed, before Ken, who had driven all the way from Houghton Lake just to come get me, arrived to take me back to my mother's…

It was dark outside while the lights were on in the house. I called out to my mom as I walked toward her bedroom until I heard her respond from a drug-induced stupor. I could tell by the time of night it was, and the particular choice of lighting on in the house – that my mom's mental faculties were together before she crashed. I stood far enough away from her bedroom door - that resonates to the times I would shout up the stairs to my mom in Lake Orion. As soon as I heard an empathetic response, sensing she was willing for me to come home but unable to talk to me, I went to my

THE PART ABOUT THE SERPENT

bedroom with a certain security on two fronts: that my mother would wake up in the morning relieved I was there - but also that my being there would decrease my mother's need to knock herself out - the very embodiment of what they term symbiosis...

THE PART ABOUT THE SERPENT

Born into the hands of the Devil

MY MOTHER KNEW IN HER HEART that my aunt Pat was going to suck the life out of her - as if that were her very intention for moving to Houghton Lake shortly after we did, as my mother complained of my aunt always helping herself to my mother's belongings when they were kids, and as an adult would call my mother for rescue late at night having slit her writs. My aunt's oldest son, Jack, basically lived in jouvie-homes and prisons throughout his life, and her youngest son, Doug, and I were court-ordered to stay away from one another (though that never stopped us), while my aunt would buy us both liquor.

There was a time when the three of us, me, my mother, and my aunt were out at Reedsburg Dam. While I was off swimming to my heart's content, my mother and my aunt sat on a blanket over a strategic patch of the grass; near the river but not too close to be overwhelmed by the rush of the falls, harnessing the protection afforded by two tall poplars while still out in open view, as if conscious they were once attractive young girls who had had their share of run-ins with all manner of perverted bastards, sipping beer. My mom pulled me aside, "She's taking pills out of my purse. I am going to the bathroom, watch her!"

I remember the dark outhouse was far enough away that you could only see my mother's bright clothes slip into the door, but you couldn't see her looking back with the door slightly ajar. My aunt leaned way forward, keeping the position of her legs in the same place so she could sit right back up again to resume the same posture after she closed my mother's purse.

My mother made a plan that she was going to show the new house on Nelsville to my aunt (we hadn't yet occupied it but we had the keys) on the way home while I was to wait in the back seat of the car with solemn instructions to go into my aunt's purse and get my mother's pills back. I still try and imagine what it must have felt like for my aunt to have gone home in anticipation of getting stoned out on the spoil of pills she stole, only to discover she'd been discovered…

Another time, I waited at my aunt's while she and my mom went out to the bar. When they got home - as I traded the passenger seat with my aunt - my aunt looked into the car and said, "Ruth, I had a nice time tonight but next time don't be such a bitch" and then closed me in the door… Miles and then miles my mother kept silent as we drove home… It had to be after one in the morning and there was frost blanketing the ground. I had been prepared for doom even before my mother put the car in gear. "Slap!" my mother slapped me with an audible narration, as if she were joking, but I had every reason to be scared out of my mind. "Slap!"(Then I pretended to laugh). "Slappy! Slappidy slap slap SLAP SLAP SLAP!"…my mother simultaneously let go of the wheel while bringing the car to a stop in the middle of the double yellow – bringing me in close with one arm while the slaps rapidly escalated, as if my mother was playing music, until the slaps transposed to blows. It seemed the anticipation of what my mother might do to me that night actually antagonized not only my fears into being fulfilled, but even exceeded them as if to mock me! "Oh my God, I can't believe this is happening…!"

We loaded a 24-foot U-Haul and headed for Florida. Although I lived in Florida on two occasions, about two years each time, I think it only noteworthy to share here a couple instances as my intention is not to share every detail of my life in this book, but those of pertinence and personal import. One was, after buying my first car where I hadn't much to do outside of work but drive around getting high. My mother, now working for the Collier County Sheriff's Office, had been in communication with my brother back in Michigan, and I was still court-ordered to live with my mother until I was 18 (which was something my mother held over my head, but was probably jurisdictional). I was 17. One day, a day off work, while my mom was at work, I was feeling sorry for myself and accentuated it by watching

THE PART ABOUT THE SERPENT

Pink Floyd *The Wall* and trying to find pills in the house with some notion I should die, but was really only sad. Some nice looking young man about my age knocked on the door and told me he just ran out of gas and asked me if I could help him out. He pointed back to his car, it was not even a block away, pulled conveniently over to the side.

On the way to the gas station, he asked me what kind of stuff I was into. I told him he probably didn't want to know. He told me that on Saturday, he and his friends were getting together for a football game. He told me their were some girls, and who else would be there, and that I could come with them. I never did; the out-of-gas scenario looked to me like a set-up by my mom and perhaps one of her Sheriff friends at work. Whatever it was, it was too neat to be real - the timing and all. But I asked myself many a time over the years what course my life would have taken if I would have opted for the healthy choice of socializing with people my age - at a healthy football game and taken him up on it. Because he was simply sent from someone.

My mother talked my brother into flying down and soon he and I were partying together on a nightly basis. We took my mom's big bedroom and she took my little one. One night, we all went to Marco Island. My mom stayed and drank with our aunt Isabel, our uncle David, and our uncle George, Julie's (the oldest girl in my mom's family) widower, while me and Steve drove around and drank, using the hot tub at one of the resorts via permission from my aunt, sometime around midnight. I vividly remember watching the effervescent bubbles in the tub, splashing and teasing under my brother's big Polish nose as his head bobbed closer and closer to the water as he was passing out... Then watching his head giving birth to vomit into the tub as I backed my way out of the tub so fast I was dry!

In the wee hours we went back to pick my mom up, who herself was bombed.

It was raining a monsoon Florida-rain. My mother was relentlessly trying to pick a fight with my brother who was in the back seat, but he was too passed-out to defend himself. She kept picking at him, saying things to hurt him, which was reminiscent of the time I saw her whipping him with a coat hanger. I screeched the brakes to a halt, "Get out!" My mother looked at me in astonishment. "Get the fuck out!" She got out. Me and Steve drove to the house, got our things, emptied the dresser full of beer cans into the lot next door, said goodbye to my dog, and we headed for Michigan.

It rained all night as we drove, visibility was getting worse, the windows were fogging up with no heater in the car, and the alternator failed. The next day we put another alternator on my brother's credit card and headed on through more rain, and then more rain, and then snow, and then a blowout, and on and on...

There was a stench crescendoing in the car. At first we joked about it - that perhaps we brought the dog and didn't know it and she died under the seat. And then we were trying to get each other to be honest: "Dude, if it's you, just do something about it, ok!?" certain that one or the other crapped his pants or something. I did all the driving because I did not trust my brother's coordination with my car, and we were smashed through every county; every county that wasn't dry, that is.

Looking back, I recognize the particular type of drunk my brother was on too; a coma-drunk - to blanket out the nightmare associated with dealing with my mom... the same drunk I was on...

The storm followed us the entire 1,100 miles back to northern Michigan. As soon as my brother opened the door to greet his girlfriend - it was obvious it was over; my mother had already telephoned. She told her we ransacked her house, among other things. As my brother always said, "She talks a good show." When I got to Houghton Lake and dialed a payphone to call my old girlfriend, it was obvious that that was over too...

In the grand picture of things, I believe to this day, no matter had I made some long-forgotten commitment to God or not, somewhere in my youth; no matter how unfairly I may have been treated by my mother, I received due retribution for cursing her like that.

As it is written:

> "Do not curse your mother or father."

THE PART ABOUT THE SERPENT

And,

"Do not despise your mother or father."

Now I was back in the motel room huffing ether.

Soon I would be working in a number of restaurants. There, I would rush the entire shift - scrubbing down appliances, wiping down walls, hoping no one would notice the damage from the ether. I would be employee of the month, I'd be the star employee; for if I did above and beyond what was required of me in my workload, maybe that would offset my inability to function socially...

There were times I would walk upon a group of my co-workers who suddenly went quiet... All I was allowed to hear was, "...it's sad."

...

I lived in a horror of isolation. The disciplines from my music and my physical exercise afforded me some immunity from guilt and what would otherwise be a wasted existence. I would jog deep in the woods after dark in the wintertime, forcing my voice to sing things it couldn't, deliberately sloshing through puddles beneath the broken ice, strengthening my endurance. The image of the sun setting through the bare trees was like death to me. The sun *setting* was the future rather than the sun rising. "Today was unbearably cold and lonely and tomorrow will be unbearably cold and lonely…"

In the midst of that place, where actual tears would breach any misunderstanding, reaching across the chasm that now separated me from the rest of the world; to be understood and to dwell safely in the company of others, to laugh at what they laugh at, to aspire to what they aspire to, and then to sit down next to them to watch TV – was more a death sentence to me than the one I already faced…

What a shame it is to find yourself more alone among the company you wished you had when you were alone wishing you were among their company. Perhaps they just hadn't considered that I may have had a greater quest going on inside...

My brother at that time said that the Van Morison song, Domino, reminded him of me, because it said something to the effect of kids needing heavy rest; because he told me, "....you need some heavy rest." I have heard of victims in extreme cases of Dissociative Identity Disorder as not knowing when to be tired as they shift from one identity to the next. Although I do not have DID, I can identify with not knowing when to be tired because trauma won't allow it. In an extreme DID's situation, you have to imagine - one individual identity might have run the victim to exhaustion before passing the piton to the next, without leaving any details... But in my case, it's been static. I always thought I'd make a

THE PART ABOUT THE SERPENT

good bounty hunter because of that, and not the run of the mill type, but a guy who had the patience to locate and take down the creeps who were responsible for the Texas chainsaw murders (knowing today those stories were fictitious), because I can endure impossible things and I know how creeps think.

…

(I had let my mother talk me into coming back down to Florida to buy another car. I stayed with her a while, and now I am back in Michigan…)

I was desperate. All I could recount of the relationship between my mother and I while I was down in Florida again was sucker punches and handcuffs...

One day, as I was pulling something out of the freezer, I noticed my mother passively wander into the kitchen from her bedroom. I remember her eyelids were lowered as she began nonchalantly fondling the decorative items on the stove…the tea pot…the spoon holder…touch the control to the burner…inching her way my way until I saw her Frankenstein face and a sucker punch coming for my head. I saw it in time that I deflected it with a roll, instinctively returning it with an open hand to the side of her head, just as swiftly as she delivered it. She let the air out of her mouth in a tight cry the moment I caught sight of her swing coming because she knew she hadn't been quick enough. And although not condoning my actions, it was as if her swing, which began sneakily and delivered with intent to harm – but missing the target in that the whole thing was out of control - landed right back on her own head just as if it were the continuation of her own motion; only humiliating in that the return, after being filtered through resistance necessitated by her false-accusations and guilt trips, was done mercifully and in open self-defense. And in no way was I not enshrouded in so much guilt to understand that at the time, but there really was no possible way she could blame me for it, yet.

Thus was the pattern of the relationship between my mother and I: she hated my guts and wanted revenge, and she hated my guts and wanted revenge…

There was something so dominiative about the work expected of me from my mother while I was down in Florida: I was washing her car by hand and watering all her outdoor plants on my days off; helping her with her home projects and handling any spontaneous maintenance issues, while her lawn seemed to epitomize a kind of penitent sentence… Any pursuits of my own outside the import of her home and her needs, she loathed. Keep in mind I was 19 years old at the time and a full-time employee with a major utilities company. My objective was (after the work was done) to get as far away from her, for as long as I possibly could, and get as high and smashed as I could possibly get. I took it to music, and played my acoustic guitar -

singing and writing songs down by the nature preserves and back-road canals. I was always trying to covey a "hey, some people like me!" message to my mother, and one evening after swimming out to a tide pool on Tiger Beach with my gear over my head, I took a photograph of some symbolic sand-art I made consisting of sea-shells and mango-tree parts that said "If we could just join hands" which came from a Led Zeppelin song.

But sometimes my staying as far away from my mother as possible while intoxicated wasn't entirely possible.

If you were drunk, my mother could not leave you be. My mother hated slapstick comedy, especially *The Three Stooges*, but my brother told me my grandma told him that she couldn't get my mother to stop watching it when she was younger! And I recall a photograph of my mom when she was young; wearing denim jeans, rolled up widely at the bottom like they did in the 50's, sitting quite informal in a lounge chair, blocking the view of the camera from her face with a copy of a paperback entitled *Smarti Pie*. Taking this, with my mother's dry sense humor, even cruelty, and the way she did foolish things when she herself was drunk - followed by a day in bed to recover – I can't help but to wonder if it was not her own accusing finger, as they say people hate in others what they hate about themselves, that would interrogate me and harass me and even call the police when I was drunk?...

THE PART ABOUT THE SERPENT

It was almost as if my mother instigated me to drink to the end that she could blow in hysteria once her suspicion had been confirmed that I had indeed drank as she suspected I would! And I would have to say, that type of entrapment was not uncharacteristic of my mother, and if it were true - how vile and very sad at the same time - but liberating in that that level of confusion, which blinded me with emotional pain for half a lifetime, can now be deduced with words...

It was so ironic to me that my mother bought me, or gave me, a six pack of Michelob upon my arriving in Florida, but then would come to be calling the police if she knew I'd been drinking, that I told my brother about it. And unbeknownst to me, my brother caught the irony of what I told him, but the irony only; and it wasn't until many, many years later during an upsurge of self-justification from my mother – that she accused me of telling Steve I told him she bought me beer and then called the police on me, as if it were an isolated incident I'd conjured up against her. She had no other explanation in her head and I wasn't in a place where I could defend it at the time.

Another thing that came up during the time of that particular upsurge was passive mention of my mother contacting The Tenitis Foundation, or a tenitis organization, while I was describing the severity of my own tenitis (that I have to pretend the buzzing in my ears is Katydids, making mental allusion to summer and better times), because she said I hit her in the ear so hard with a cupped hand while I was drunk down in

THE PART ABOUT THE SERPENT

Florida, that the ringing in her ears had never gone away. The key words, "you"… "me" … "while you were drunk" floored me so bad - I would never contest such a thing. And only after recognizing the well-worn subtleties and tying that accusation to the sucker-punch-incident in the kitchen, did I realize my mother's reaction to the drama of my complaint was done in defense of a sense of bad-motherism, and the reason why I couldn't tie the incident together was because I wasn't drunk during the sucker-punch-incident! I would not have had the mental faculties to recall the details, nor would I care to be making myself something to eat. It was early afternoon and had I been drunk my mother would not have approached me stealthily - she would have been yelling from across the room. Furthermore, the reason I was able to anticipate the sucker punch was because the tensions had carried over from the previous day, hence the tight cry that came out of my mother's mouth…

Across the street from my mother's was a yellow building hosting a dance-beat radio station where the employees would smoke outside, and once I recall an actual dance going on in the parking lot. One night, I laid down exhausted on the cool concrete of my mother's driveway after storming out and yelling back at her the last word. Then to my surprise came a carefully initiated applause from across the street while I lay there. And what I mean by "carefully initiated" is that I could tell that they were not simply applauding the rebellion of some drunk bastard yelling at the top of

THE PART ABOUT THE SERPENT

his lungs, nor was it entirely sarcastic, they were careful because they didn't want any of it either.

Down the road at an apartment complex were a couple of high-ons I used to smoke dope with. Sensitive as I was, coupled with extreme guilt, I would be either kneeling by the door or standing; never could I just sprawl out like other people. And one day at their place I woke up having fallen backward onto a large, black garbage bag full of garbage by the door. I actually passed out and fell backwards, not knowing what happened, but they didn't even notice until I tried to apologize for falling on their bag. They themselves were no less high because they thought I was joking.

One night, I was speeding down the road on shell rock (roads built from dredged shells) and my rear end began to swing. I went nose first into a canal and then tried to re-start my car which sucked water into the intake. I walked out to the main road where there were police car lights flashing from some other incident and I walked up to an officer and told him what happened. He told me to go home and sleep it off and then deal with it in the morning. When I returned, all my belongings were stolen from the vehicle, including my classical guitar. I made the police report and called a tow truck and the police told me that a guy in a little yellow car had reported my vehicle. Consequently, that morning I came upon a little yellow car with a woman driving it at the party store and noticing my guitar in the back seat - I reached in an took it despite the fact she denied knowing anything about it and tried to keep me from doing it.

The saltwater killed the computer on the car and it was months before I got it running.

Out walking the neighborhood with my mother one evening, I noticed a very attractive girl my age visiting her grandma who seemed just as attracted to me. Any time I would walk by her house I would whistle and she would be out in the street in a heartbeat. Once I showed up drunk and I must have turned her off because she went back inside. I came back after dark, smashed. I went up to her window to try to get her attention without the other occupants of the house knowing about it. I saw her enter the room and as she was walking closer to the window, I rapped on it. She stopped, turned white, backed up, and screamed a blood curdling scream! I ran through so many yards and so many sharp bushes in my shorts that my legs were bloodied up, and by the time I got back to my mother's someone had already been in contact with her about it because they knew it was me! And for the record: I wasn't watching her, and peeping Tom's don't knock on the window.

I remembered my fishing pole broke during this time, and so did my need for healthy recreation. I lamented to people in years to come, "The devil broke my fishing pole!"...

After a fight between my mother and I – an evening when my mother had called the police again – the police having knowledge that I was intoxicated, pulled my car over and took me to jail for drunk driving.

My mother worked with the bondsman to hide the fact that the title of my car could be used as collateral for bail for fear I would bond out and head back north. How I bonded out, I don't remember. There was also a party-store nearby my mother's during that time who received a phone call from a woman accusing them of selling beer to her 19 year old son. They never sold me alcohol; I would usually ask someone else to buy it for me, but the cool Turkish guys in the little gas station right next to her house always did.

I couldn't be driven to and from jobs in my work truck at work for very long without a driver's license, and when I loaned my car to a co-worker with the only condition he pick me up and drop me off for work, he informed me that he was repeatedly getting pulled over from the police, who were assuming I was driving…

I sold my car and bought a moped. I rearranged my face with it one night falling in the gravel on the street. I moved in with a group of rednecks that had stayed together since they were living homeless in the woods. I was thin, drunk, and destitute, but I tried to clean their house for room and board. The bathtub drain was full of male hair and the tub was the worse I'd ever seen. In the kitchen, I knocked down a mountain of dishes from the counter, and when I emptied a metal garbage can full of beer cans that sat next to the sink, the bottom was swarming with maggots.

THE PART ABOUT THE SERPENT

I was into cocaine enough that any time I got a hold of some I would always be desperate for more. Once I remember setting out late at night to see if I could score at any of the 24-hour convenience stores by the Cuban neighborhoods where you would often see them hanging out. Now, where normally they – not able to speak English - are always at the mercy of the white people, here's some desperate white guy looking for blow, and I remember them laughing among themselves. I had $20! That should get me hooked up, right?!... I remember giving it to a black guy who told me to drop him off down the road at a house where there were no lights on… He kept saying, "I won't rip you off! … I won't rip you off, man!" But after 10 minutes turned into 20, and then 20 minutes into 30… He had simply rounded a house and walked out their back yard, and I never saw him again.

I wound up selling my moped (for beer money, nonetheless) and when I had the place to myself I would jam, still dreaming of working a stage someday. Next morning I'd be riding my mother's ten-speed, I bought her as a gift, through the cold damp four AM air to a day-labor program to dig trenches in the 90 degree sun for another few dollars.

One night, while they had people over and a card game going with country music playing, they unplugged me while I was playing guitar. Another night, the big guy of the house, outweighing me by 115 pounds, blasted me in the eye. Shortly after it happened I called my cousin

THE PART ABOUT THE SERPENT

Doug up north and told him what was going on (I was initially going to ride with these people back to Michigan), and fearing that this guy was going to pull his firearm on me, Doug hung up and called the police while I fled. There is a picture of me - my mother took the following morning of that incident - laying face-down on the indoor/outdoor carpeting of her patio in a wet-spot of my own urine.

I remember a Halloween party at my stoner friend's apartment-neighbor's and as the night started growing old with people fading from the party and crashing here and there, standing there looking like a blonde crack addict with a black and blue eye, I overheard the host of the party asking my two high-on friends if they knew me. And I remember hearing them tell her, "No, no, we don't know him."...

My mother couldn't deal with me anymore; I was damaging her reputation at the Sheriff's Office, so she sent me on a bus back to Michigan.

THE PART ABOUT THE SERPENT

Sacrilege

The day my grandpa Bezesky was put in a nursing home:

Nurse: "Now Red, are there any religious preferences you have that you'd like us to be aware of?"

Red: "It's none of your goddamn business!"

Nurse: "Well Red, if there's anything that you'd like to know about *me,* you can just ask me and I'll tell you."

Red: "One look, and I can already tell!"

Nurse: "Well, what Red?"

Red: "You're stupid fat and ugly!"

THE PART ABOUT THE SERPENT

I left - at church one night, where the doors were always unlocked, expecting that the pastor, whoever he be, might be obliged to reply in the same covert manner – a secret note. This church was creepy, but I would force myself through the dark, inch-by-inch, stopping to study each blunt figure, listening for the repercussions of my trespass. It had that eerie air in it, like in my grandma's bedroom, and I half-anticipated a large man to step into a stream of moonlight and ask, "May I help you?" If anyone could see me through the windows from the outside they'd see two tandem silhouettes tip-toeing along - a big one and a little one; Mutt and Jeff.

Blue-white snow gave standing ovation to the mercury light outside the low kitchen windows where I would boil a pot of water on the industrial sized gas stove in a tea pot with a real, whistling spout; and make myself Folger's instant coffee, and sit on a stool. Here I was as secure as my eyes could detect any danger, and think like an adult again… It marshaled the atmosphere of anywhere my mother would dare to venture, or take me, or think to find me. In spirit, I felt appropriately sheltered here, for it was God's house, and as long as I had legitimate concerns – those were mine alone. My mother could never stand in the way of that; she could only see from the direction I'd abandoned, the back side of me, leaving with my head cocked to the right in that inquisitive manner as I stepped further on and upward… But the truth is, I didn't belong there on Sunday…and I didn't belong there now... Regardless, it kept me from roaming the streets in the cold dark, where I often would get chased by cars and whatever

THE PART ABOUT THE SERPENT

drunk derelict. And on the other hand, it kept me out roaming the streets in the cold dark...

One week to the day of leaving my note, I came back to find the reply, but there was none. I do no know exactly how the note addressed the Pastor, who's name was on the office door, I simply asked if God was a spirit.

I don't remember how much time lapsed, but before long I invited Doug there. We did the same thing - tiptoeing around in the dark. As he and I were wrong together, I sat him down in a wheelchair, then dashed him through the building with enough force that he could only cry for me to stop, helpless to get out.

We crept up superstitiously around the alter as if we were watching one another's back while we examined everything. There was so much import given each artifact; it was like a haunted museum in the dark, and whether we saw a statue of the virgin mother Mary standing there, or a bronzed bat-winged Lucifer towering beside us that night, all the same! When Doug moved to where the holy water was between us, I splashed it on him with a hiss!

...

As Doug and I were walking through an old resort just after dark one summer, we stopped to spy in on an old man through an open screen window. It was a one-room efficiency, and looking down through the screen, there sat a not-so-able-bodied man, sunk in an armchair with the glare of the television on his block-like glasses. He was the embodiment of the resort-town type: a hapless chap that had lucked upon a room where he could give his liver a break while awaiting his next welfare check. I spoke into the room like a vamp, "The devil will possess you!" "Damn it!" he said, without moving an inch... It was so weird that we inflected our laugh as we ducked down to run away. Doug's laugh burst out in a snort but he grabbed hold of it until we got far enough away... It was as if this guy'd been through it before, or maybe he'd really had a problem with hearing strange things like that and/or was too piss-poor and hopeless to do anything about it!

Doug and I were feeding on my brother's Judas Priest album. We could only stare off in wonder as we heard Rob Halford roar into the mic during a live show, belting out notes that were abnormal for a human being. One day after school, Doug and I were heading to our grandma's through the back yards of the neighbors. These were houses that sat high up on a hill, which overlooked a marsh that accessed the lake. Now, Doug was bigger boned and more crude in the male sense than I was. He sucked in, stuck his chest out toward the lake, and roared!!!!!!! As soon as all his air had extinguished there was a little old man standing behind him with a yard rake in his hands, who said, "whaddya sick or somethin'?" Doug, shocked – instinctively pambied up his hands together like a prairie gopher, and we scampered off!

THE PART ABOUT THE SERPENT

Doug and I obtained a couple motorcycles. His was a silver and burgundy Suzuki road bike without a headlight; and mine was a red and black, Elsinore dirt bike with no kick-start, a defective clutch, or light of any kind. We rode the things, the mental cases we were, all wee hours of the morning, sometimes super-smashed. Everyone in town knew those bikes and once a neighbor rushed into the street to flag me down, where I used to drop down the hill from the motel room to jump-start it, to tell me that I can't just ride an illegal dirt bike through the neighborhood like that.

One night, we were toying around on the bikes behind the Community building where there was a good deal of marmalade streetlight. It must have been pretty loud to the neighbors who were trying to sleep, and it was within eyesight of the motel room. Behind the building was a grass birm and then poplar trees making a fence at the woods. There was a foot trail back there but impossible to find - moving along on a bike in the dark, as the street lights were out in front of the building. There was one entrance off the road to the Community Center, which then let on to the highway, and then the other direction was basically foot traffic for the tennis courts and the middle school. As there was only light swaying back from the sides of the building, we approached the school-end and a state police car's nose pulled into it. When we headed back to the other side to try and make our way out, the police car met us again…

We were nervous, trying to keep our speed up enough to keep the bikes balanced while also trying not to run into each other. As soon as we made way to the other side again, we saw the passenger-cop jump out of the door of the car (which they were going to try and use as a road block) and we knew the cop on foot would be ill equipped to stop us should he try and get to the other side before we did, so we turned around and nailed it! We went right at him, as if he were the flagman for a race! Doug went to the left like a speed demon out to the highway, and I went like a country-Joe-horseback rider toward the school, right under the lights, in a slow second gear, praying that my clutch would engage!

I saw Doug at an intersection in the woods that night, flashing his blinker so he could make his way, but we didn't meet up again until it was early morning and foggy out; behind his mom's apartment, exhausted.

One night, Doug and I were going up to get a bag from his drug dealers, who were EMS driver's nonetheless. We had a routine with that. I was on the back of his bike this time, still no headlight, and the State Police came after us. Doug hit it!... Now I have to tell you it might be fun and everything to outrun the police on your *own* motorcycle, but it is not in the least bit fun being on the back of someone else's motorcycle while they're outrunning the cops!

Doug took to the winding side streets; he was actually quite good at this, but I patted him and pleaded with him and patted him and pleaded with him – every time he would slow the bike down a little bit to take a turn, "Let me off! Let me off, man! Let me off!" But he was

THE PART ABOUT THE SERPENT

hell bent, and the lights from the patrol car fishtailed from one side of our felonious shadow to the other as they were in hot pursuit!

We made it to the top of the hill and Doug went for a trail. As soon as we hit the dirt to go up onto the trail, the chain slipped of the rear sprocket. I ran up the trail with my helmet still on. Doug bent down to try and slip his chain back on. I hit a wire fence and flipped right over it, just several feet into the trail, it was hopeless... And then I listened as the officers took Doug down like a pack of wild dogs.

It started to sprinkle cold rain and it got quiet as the more aggressive officer stayed busy with all the tow-truck arrangements et cetera, and I think they took Doug away in another car.

I went with helmet in hand and presented myself to the "good cop." He at first tried to raise a commotion but I said, "I wasn't driving." Then he thought inwardly and said, "well, put the helmet down, we don't want…" But I assured him I wouldn't resist.

One night, on Doug's bike, I was going back to my work were I had about 300 beer cans stashed in a giant, clear plastic bag. That was going to be our party money for the night. Doug waited down the road about a half-mile at the party store. I stopped just outside the dumpster, killed the bike, and before I could lift my leg off from it, the State Police pulled along side me in exact proportion to the way I pulled in - mocking me in that they were the big fish. I kicked Doug's kick start so fast that I didn't even know it was running before I kicked it again and the throttle started taking me. I wasn't used to a fast heavy bike and I burned across the greens of the establishment while the officers darted out civilly on the pavement.

I flew across the highway regardless traffic and then down a long, dark side street; remembering the trail at the end I once took while running away from my mother's set up with Eric Williams. No headlight, going way too fast, I approached the end where there was a marmalade street light with a bunch of black garbage bags and a split rail fence coming up under me. I let on the rear brake with my right foot, and not used to street tires either – I started to fishtale on the sand of the road, Bam!!! One wheel was still turning while I lay upside down against a tree. The officers casually walked up to me... "Don't even try to run or I'll just shoot ya!" I could already tell I wasn't in as much trouble as I could have been. Doug told me he *knew* it was me when he heard the squad car.

Another night, Doug and I were partying at the motel room with our girlfriends, and intermittently we'd go for short motorcycle rides. I even took Kelly on my bike that night, because she said she wanted to ride with me. The inside of the motel room looked like this: there were so many empty beer cans on the floor that we had to wade through them; and a lamp with its shade, still plugged in and on - was laying upside down in it all. We were just getting comfortable from coming back

THE PART ABOUT THE SERPENT

from a ride and sat down when a knock came at the door.

"Who is it?"

"State Police!" (Certainly it was a joke from one of my friends)

"Go the fuck away!"

Four seconds of silence followed before I went straight out the door and closed it behind me.

"Joe, we know you've got underage girls inside and we know you guys are drinking…Can you do us a favor and just stay of the bikes tonight?"

Back before I really squatted in the motel room, when I was still in school, I often slept temporarily in the middle motel room. The middle motel room was always kind of made up in that it was the last profit-generating motel room on the property, and wasn't full of junk. This room had a made bed in it, and couch that fit perfectly into an alcove facing it, but no heat. After Doug and I were there once, knowing how my grandma snooped though everything, I left an ominous collaboration of signs and letters for her to find, in full view on the night stand. On a piece of paper I wrote OX NAM PAX or something like that – unwittingly discerning something wicked in that Latin propagation of characters, and it may have been centered into a pentagram (I don't remember). Then I took 13 pennies,

THE PART ABOUT THE SERPENT

and placed them in a terribly symmetrical circle around it – revealing whatever side of the penny seemed most magical. Although the paper was white, and everybody sees pennies every day, my writing was always death-heavy and stressed, especially when it came to symbols – and giving the acute attention to the precise arrangement I left everything, the spiritual message was, dark!

It is strange to me today to try and understand where that abandon came from - that neither Doug nor my other cousins ever seemed to engage themselves with - not with books, or with symbols, or with music, et cetera. They never dared put their own hands to those things, but they did very much watch those who did...

I stole an eight-ball on devil's night one night with my friends. One of my friend's alleged that his elderly neighbors ran over his dog. While he and Doug waited around the corner of their house, I went up and pounded on the door. Both the man and the woman came to the door while I held the eight-ball up to their faces, "You killed my dog and yer gonna' pay, you Alistair fiend!!!" They're jaws were dropped, and my friends jaws were dropped, and then we ran away. We egged cars that night from between two cottages, so we couldn't really couldn't see what was coming. One of them was a patrol car – probably dispatched to come find us, and we waded through the cold October water of the lake that night to get away from him.

THE PART ABOUT THE SERPENT

During my time in the end motel room, I wrote poetry as a form of vandalism. It always began neatly metered and rhetorical like everyone else's, but then I'd blast it with something profane that only mocked the very art. Like a painting class where all the students are assigned to give their best shot at canvassing the Mona Lisa, when one of the students presents his piece to the class having painted a mustache on him/her and then steps back and throws a bucket though it!... I did my best at studying biofeedback, as I learned Jimmy Page did, and I used to swing behind the Community Center on the swings in pendulum style until I would get a sick feeling in my stomach, as a time-keeping exercise.

...

I wrote a song on my twelve-string back then that makes people cry to this day when I dare to play it for them. The second word of the first verse remains a word that I made up (though I don't think anyone ever notices) because sometimes writing song lyrics, for me, is more about what it's saying through the sound…

"Be dealder, lay your precious sheaves down
On this swollen pain
You'll be better soon
You'll be better soon

THE PART ABOUT THE SERPENT

And be fearful
You'll be giving your life back
Believe this reign
and you'll be-come someone soon
and all your friends will welcome you
So what you like to do
I swear, you'll be better soon
I swear, you'll be better soon...."

I remember telling Doug's girlfriend that I'd been trying to make contact from the spiritual world – that I was looking for a sign – and then I showed her what it was. I had drawn on a small piece of paper the head of an alien-looking demon, waving.

I attributed power to demons by drawing them; actually, anything I went so far as to draw – I kind of worshiped.

My brother's friend once got a hold of one of my ink drawings who had also happened to be someone who had given me quite a few Led Zeppelin bootlegs. It was the depiction of a rock star guitarist – fairly normally proportioned in one side of his aspect which then mirrored into a very profound Alice-Cooper meets Jimmy Page-type character in death-heavy ink that actually looked as if the paper were reflective itself. My brother's friend looked at… "I can't even understand this! It looks demonic!" "That's what this guy does" my brother told him, slightly touching the picture with the back of his fingers in a suggestion he

THE PART ABOUT THE SERPENT

was referring to the guitarist, but which subtly cloaked the fact he was referring to me...

I always had natural leadership abilities and sometimes I could keep my friends out of trouble as long as they were partying with me. I thought of myself as Lord of the Animals though I never uttered those words; it was too arrogant, but me and my friends, I assure you, were animals! Sometimes performing music or entertaining people while I was on drugs, when faced with apprehension - when I needed to improvise - I would sort of black out and lose the ability to critic myself – taking a leap of faith into the unknown where I was certain I all but blew it each and every time. It was like, looking back at myself during that time - I see three standing mirrors, side by side. The first two mirrors from the left show my reflection equally. While the third mirror, that was supposed to reflect me, was empty, even clouded... And the third mirror was symbolic of where I would let go. Then I would hear rave reports about what I'd done, even from other circles.

One day, I was the oldest among a small throng of partiers and we went out to Canoe Camp where sandy banks sit high above the Muskegon river. While everyone was at the top, I slithered down the sand on my belly - still in my clothes – all the way down to the water and then began lapping at it. I heard the story told to me days later by people from another town who said the witnesses were fascinated, as if it were supernatural.

THE PART ABOUT THE SERPENT

Once I remember a row of mail boxes going up over the top of my car calling my attention back to the road...

Once I remember seeing an Amish man waving his fist at me in my rear view mirror...

Once I deliberately blew a stop sign at a four lane highway with a car full of people...

And once when I was in Florida, I sought perhaps to burn down a church...

THE PART ABOUT THE SERPENT

The End Motel Room

MY BROTHER OCCUPIED the End Motel Room at one time but he never really moved into it; he never really hung his artwork on the walls like he did in my grandpa's old room, and by the time I started spending time in it - it was semi-commercially straight again, even though the water had been off for years. It still belonged to my Aunt Jenny who lived in the big house, and my grandma was still responsible for taking care of it.

Actually, before my mother moved up from Lake Orion, out of frustration with me, she sent me on a Greyhound up to Houghton Lake, though all I knew at the time was that it was so my grandma could enroll me in school. I remembered, here, the office of the school first asked you if you had a phone before asking you what your number was. But I was in the End Motel Room.

THE PART ABOUT THE SERPENT

The safety I experienced in the End Motel Room caused me to think independently; to nourish big dreams again. At one indefinite point, I stole one of my grandma's crayon-green *New World Translations* of the Holy Bible off that old bowing bookshelf and made a solemn vow to myself that I would read every word of that book from cover to cover for the sake of the impoverished state of my family (whatever exactly that meant). I *knew* that whatever had happened to my family - whatever it was they so terribly missed - whatever retribution they had incurred; the answers were in that book! Consequently, I disciplined myself and made time every day to sit down and read; sounding out each one of the names through the genealogies the best I could. I took long, exploration walks around the beaver pond behind the school…my grandma started having to answer big questions…

I dreamed of having my own library, full of unreachable shelves, stonework with ferns on it, comfy chairs on the end caps, and hanging lights...

After my mother moved up, the End Motel Room became storage for some of our furniture until we moved out to Nelsville. However, I could still go to the middle motel room in the interim, as the motel rooms rather became respite anytime there was trouble between my mother and I.

Now, after my cousin Doug and his mom moved up to Houghton Lake, before Doug had enrolled in school and before I was court-ordered to stay away from him, I

THE PART ABOUT THE SERPENT

was basically not going home - but going to school from the middle motel room. I kept it nice and plugged in an old, electric-coil heater at night that probably weakened the power of the entire premises. And one day I decided not to go to school. Apparently, a truine officer came immediately to my grandma's, and my heart sank as I came upon the sight of my stuff piled in a heap outside the motel room. Doug and I felt doomed. We went into my grandma's when she was gone and sat down on the edge of my brother's bed, hiding. A moment later, Doug's sister Michelle walks into the house and out of the house yelling, "Doug?... "Joe?" while we held our breath in full daylight on the other side of the burlap curtain, until she was gone.

I told the school that I didn't have any clean clothes to wear, which was not totally untrue, but not entirely true either. Subsequently, they called my mom into school and we all sat down at a long table. My mom was wearing her blue, suede-like coat, with the fake, white fur on it and I was in my black, nylon jacket that was supposed to pass as black leather – that I paid my mom back for for buying me. When the blame started falling on my mom, she grabbed my coat near the collar and twisted the fabric and said, "Who bought you *this*?" "I paid you back!" I said, in such honest defense that she let go and sat back. No one could say a word. It was unfair to my mom, though at times I considered it a defeat on her part; now the school was shining a light into our home-life and I got the chance to slightly exonerate myself from constantly bearing the blame.

THE PART ABOUT THE SERPENT

Now there were summers, and now I was working. I gave my grandma $20 a week for my using the End Motel Room even though she would probably have preferred that I didn't stay there. There was a heater in this room, a Warm Morning Unit still hooked up to the old lines that ran from the propane tank outside my grandma's house. There was never any water but I would use the toilet anyway, and urinate outside after dark. I bought distilled water in gallon jugs and always a jar of instant coffee in the smallest jar possible – because my philosophy was that I didn't know where I was going to be tomorrow – or even if there was going to be a tomorrow. During daylight hours I would urinate in the empty plastic jugs.

It was summer. It must have noon and it was like 98 degrees out, plus humidity. I was passed out face down on the asbestos tile, like I fell there from off a tall building and was still pressed into the same position upon impact. I remember my body - thin and wrecked as it was, drawing the coolness from the concrete slab like a reptile draws heat from a rock. I was so sick and dehydrated. I was certain to throw up before I even tried to lift my head up from the floor. I worked at it, looking down at the floor while letting my hair slightly shelter my eyes from the memories of what might have happened... Then I got myself up on one hand enough to reach one of the water jugs. I shifted my weight as I brought the jug close so I could use my other hand to support the back of the jug as I began to chug. And as you may have guessed it, I grabbed the wrong jug!

THE PART ABOUT THE SERPENT

The place was probably at the tuberculosis-level. With the onset of 30 years of a raging intestinal imbalance, I blasted diarrhea in the toilet and then I would use the curtains, or a sock, or anything I could find to wipe myself with. Sometimes it would be swarming with black flies and a couple times I tried to emolliate the stench by pouring Old Spice directly into the bowl which caused a yellowish-green and dark-red orange chemical reaction and a lifetime vehemence of anything resembling air freshener, potpourri, aroma therapy, scented candles, I hate you!

What was going on on the outside was just as vile as what was going on on my insides: I wore no socks, I wore no underwear, and the clothes I *did* wear weren't clean. I would lift my shirt from my stomach to blow my nose in it while I continued to wear it. I even remember blowing my nose in a black, plastic garbage bag on one occasion out of spite. I crashed on the floor with no pillows, and I don't remember any blankets in there, if there were, they became toilet paper; and I had a mouth and the attitude that makes all that look pretty.

My brother told me one of our old co-workers asked him at one point, "Your brother used to be a gentleman; what happened!?"...

Strange as it may seem - and perhaps to offset the savagery - I still brought in armloads of books: *Etiquette of the English Language* (which I never read but it made me look smart because it was as big as a pillow), *Magician of the Hermetic Order of the Golden*

THE PART ABOUT THE SERPENT

Dawn, The Seat of the Soul, Confucius…crap like that. I always had a guitar or two, plus I drew pictures and wrote poetry. Not to mention, I did drugs.

My grandmother's property was sad and run down, like it was condemned. It thrived with stray cats, and abandoned dogs who had all been beaten by previous owners, and they were all misfits: one missing an eye; one oddly deformed; and at times, a cat would drag himself home with his front paws because the neighbor shot it and paralyzed its back. And I myself was drawn to that property with no less sense of entitlement....

THE PART ABOUT THE SERPENT

After Dark

DURING MY BUS RIDE back to Michigan I had bonded with runaways and victims of domestic violence who had fled their homes in the middle of the night, sharing the booze they had stashed in their shampoo bottles, and passing joints at the bus depots along the way. The toilet in the bathroom of our particular bus was so full that it was overflowing and then running down the rubber-grooved track in the middle isle all night, and you had to walk on the edge of the seats to make it back to the bathroom if you dared to go. Then a woman boarded with a baby who's diapers had not been changed and it was obvious she was helpless to do anything about it.

When I arrived in Houghton Lake there was no one there to pick me up (no surprise, but same feeling I had at a bus depot late at night when departing Michigan; my family's not so subtle ways of passing their aggression on to my mother)... I called my cousin Michelle from a pay phone, who sighed a bit as if she'd have to drop everything to come and get me, but kindly inflected the sigh to the fact that no one else in the family who knew I was coming, came to get me. Then she wrapped up whatever she was doing and drove over.

I met Doug and Jack at my grandma's and I began rooming with Doug in my grandma's old house, the motel office. My aunt Pat was living with my grandma again. I was abrasive toward Doug, and one night, he brought his pimple-faced friends home from work with him one night and I cursed at them from my chair. I just came from a nightmare; being involved with the law, cocaine binges and black eyes, and I worked heavy utilities while down in Florida. Doug soon left and roomed with his girlfriend. I could tell no one wanted me there, although my grandma remained the same - leaving containers of soup outside my door; supplying me with potatoes, and a dozen eggs on occasion, and sometimes she would buy me a can of mentholated tobacco. It was as if my grandmother, held subjectively, some responsibility for the plight of her grandchildren. Michelle, on the other hand, defending her mother's complaints, suggested to me that I ought to find somewhere else to live, but in a drunken confidence I blasted her for trying to kick me out of "grandma's" house.

Jack came over one night screaming at me. He kicked me in the balls and threatened to smash the remainder

THE PART ABOUT THE SERPENT

of my bottle for the night. I had put notice in at the restaurant across the street, now owned by a woman I will call Dee, whom I worked with before, that I was available, but they didn't need me yet. I went to work with Jack for a small manufactured housing company, assembling modular homes on site with a three man crew. The work paid by the job: $140 per home which supposedly took two to three days. Our first home took a week and I still received $140. One morning, I showed up hungover and my boss caught wind of my breath. "Gotta' be a drunk…gotta' be a drunk!" he said.

Jack started laying in to me one morning while driving around in his car before work. He too was defending his mother's complaints about me living at my grandmas and he pressured me about paying rent. Now, the only reason there was propane in the office was because I was paying for it; my aunt and I agreed to $20 per week - the same amount I gave to my grandma voluntarily when I was in the End Motel Room. Jack, on the other hand, would never so much as give a dime to my grandma, would never work around the house or do repairs, and repeatedly kept my grandma's phone service in threat of shut off due to $140 phone bills. Not to mention how my grandma would cook a meager meal for those present, and Jack, coming in out of nowhere, would plate up as if food was just there.

So, I asked Jack, "How much rent do *you* pay *Jack*?" and then it was like the cardboard box he was standing on broke beneath him. But now I knew I had to fight - that he was going to redirect his accusations, probably within the next moment, and it could be long uncertain battle. The same as Michelle, the same as my aunt - anyone who ever stayed with my grandma and then tried to accuse *me* of being a mooch were far bigger a mooch themselves.

The deep-seated guilt I bore for so long, and fear of defending myself seemed to give license to any old derelict to try and exercise their authority over me. They trusted so confidently in my passivity - testing and encroaching upon it over time - that they forgot I actually might have known in my heart why I was in the predicament I was in; as if making sense or even being a full-blown hypocrite wouldn't matter.

My 21st birthday was approaching and I could finally buy. My grandma and grandpa Kacin sent me a card, and trusting there would be a check for $25-50 inside, I ripped it open in front of Doug and another friend, dumping the check out without opening the card…

About that time the man from the witch's house came to the door to ask me to take down a badminton net I had erected in the back yard (because technically it was on his property). Within a few days, I remember looking out the back window from the kitchen, where the ground is about chest high, and I saw some kind of Indian dancing going on around a fire pit. It looked like a flippin' rodeo, but I saw mostly only people's legs. When I went to the window I saw they were all wearing real animal heads. They were having occult ceremonies in the exact place were I'd had my badminton net. But I

THE PART ABOUT THE SERPENT

was so preoccupied with my own personal miseries that I paid no attention...

I was drinking cheap whiskey and Stroh's beer, and I hated them both, but they were the easiest in availability from the drug store. Then I would play guitar till dawn every night, making a few recordings, and I jammed with a couple professional musicians on one occasion, even though they probably didn't want me back, knowing I had to be intoxicated to play.

I was back at the library, and doing extreme yoga. I disciplined myself to sit in the lotus position for the duration I ate every meal (which is painful business), and I started writing curses in poetry-form.

My past was haunting me down... "Why co-workers who had been faithful to their employers for years would suddenly quit after I was hired on to work with them... How I heard one of the guys at the utilities company I worked for had called me a dog-back... That I never took that scholarship like Bucky Stimpson or stayed in school like Brain O'Brien... The blame incurred upon me from defending myself against my mother's attacks... Feeling I betrayed my dad... Sensing my grandparents despised me... Spitting on Dawn Furman... Dinky..."

Every night seemed a test of desperation and something usually got broke.

THE PART ABOUT THE SERPENT

I compiled a written oath, using the same devotee-terminology I learned in Alistair Crowley's writings: "service", "reverence", "duty", "honor", et cetera., and in lieu of abilities, recognition, and vindication of all wrongs committed against me (in other words), I sold my soul to the devil.

Sensing my grandma's old bedroom was the spiritual center of the house (of the entire property for that matter), where she encountered nightmare after nightmare after nightmare – I performed a candle-lit séance on the floor beneath the place where her bed once was, and I let the devil in. Strangely, I didn't notice anything…

In days ensuing, Dee sent her son over to get me to come for work. I started the night he came, and after work I made it to the beer store with an advance. Now I started socializing more, and friends and co-workers seemed to be lifting me up and away from my grandma's, and the defeating influence my family used to constrain me.

I knew my aunt Pat was going to try and enforce some kind of authority over my staying at my grandmas, as she conveniently defaulted from the years of being a freeloader at my grandma's to the roll of caretaker, because she wanted to have a meeting with me. I wanted nothing but to avoid it, and one night she caught me outside the office with my friends who were going to help me move my stuff. She tried to speak something stout-hearted about all the chances she had given me

THE PART ABOUT THE SERPENT

and that I wouldn't even come over to talk to her. I never said a word back to her. My friends, without a word themselves, almost rushed and started moving my things out and across the parking lot to the shack outside the restaurant, where I was going to room with my buddy, Bobby.

Now, me and Bobby were about the heart; writing songs, loving girls, living life. One of our more well-behaved colleagues witnessed my ability to play lead guitar by ear and mentioned that if a talent scout heard me, he'd pick me right up. Another girl asked me, "Can you do that with any song?" Even Bobby made a solemn drunken vow to me one night that he would give up his life savings to promote my music.

Our circle of friends was large and not without serious problems. Bobby and I were both having affairs with married women. There was a sting operation watching the restaurant, and one of Dee's sons was turning state's evidence against my cousin, Jack, who was still running up the phone bills, living rent-free across the street at my grandma's. There was a point in time, before I left for Florida as an adult - the notion crossing my mind and making an inroad - that I would be doing society a service if I rid the earth of Jack. I'd simply do my time in prison while I catch up on my drawing...

Dee's daughter Christine (who I call a very powerful person) took a particular interest in me, not in the romantic sense, but more in an empathetic sense. She was dating my friend Alex, and at times I would crash

THE PART ABOUT THE SERPENT

on their floor, wasted. Christine was more of the Fort Lauderdale-Spring-Break Go-Gos kind of girl; she didn't hide much. Christine was also deep, she was smart, and she was going to school for psychiatry. She overhead me scream in my sleep often enough that she began trying to treat me for it. She said it sounded horrible, like is was some kind of regression or something. She told me to set my alarm three times throughout the night so I could get up and write down what was happening. But I wanted to avoid it, it was too dark.

Christine furthermore had connections with a professional spirit medium and I would carefully distance myself from any invitation in her direction. The reason why? I *knew* that if some spirit medium saw me, they would instantly see how black I was with the demonic. And it was darkness I couldn't bare to deal with myself.

On one occasion, Christine had disclosed confidential medical information to me she obtained while visiting Dr. Pezco's office (who apparently left the information unguarded and in plain sight of passing patrons) about the father of my girlfriend from high school. Another occasion, one of my girlfriends approached me and told me that Christine told her that I used to stutter and beat up my mom. And I knew the only way Christine could have heard anything like that was from our eavesdropping-party-line-neighbors on Nellsville during the hours my mother would dramatize stories of my behavior to her old boss on the phone, as a guilt-provoking device against me. "...Did you?" she asked. "No." "I didn't think you would do something like that."

Christine also threw a surprise birthday party for me one night. There were so many people and friends there; she must of worked a long time at it. How they kept me sober until I arrived, I don't know, and I remember mentioning to the two friends who took me, that some of the cars parked on the sides of the road on the way to Christine's looked familiar... This was before her brother took state's evidence against Jack, who was also there, and handed me a big fat doobie as a gift.

The sting operation knew about the party and invited themselves undercover, posing as a teenage couple. Christine, unbearably smart as she was, figured out that they were undercover cops and stopped the party to question them in front of everyone. "What are your names?"... "Who invited you?"... "Are you undercover cops?"...Then I am going to have ask you to leave, no one invited you." The astonishing thing was how Christine could handle such situations without losing her cool.

Bobby was moving in with his girlfriend and he left me his old cat - a south American bobtail that weighed 20 lbs. who kneaded the waterbed by your head when you slept. When friends of mine who worked late at the restaurant needed some sleep – I often let them crash at

THE PART ABOUT THE SERPENT

the Shack, but they would wake up at 4:00 AM with their head soaked!

Christine had a friend, Samantha, who I'd actually had my eye on since high school. She was the hottest girl ever, she was elusive, and she was wild. I knew, because of a visual memory I had, seeing her back in school, that she was angry. I worked for her parents at said restaurant for years and only caught one glimpse of Samantha - sunburned, just up from Florida, and only in the restaurant long enough to cuss her family out. But now she started coming around Christine's, and the restaurant. Apparently, Christine invited her over on the night of New Year's Eve while I was already there, but apologized because there was some drunk that hangs out there, evidently referring to me. I remember sitting at the same table with Samantha, drawn in to her good looks. I asked her if I could kiss her and she said coldly, "It won't mean anything!" But I leaned in and did, even though it was like kissing a corpse that was ready to bite.

Nevertheless, that night at the stroke of midnight when the ball dropped in Times Square on the television, Samantha and I were jumping up and down on Christine's furniture with abandon while Christine played the mature one.

In the days ensuing, I didn't want to blow it, so I pretended nothing happened. Samantha started coming to the restaurant every chance she could and would say things at me every time I went by, but I wouldn't hear what she said; I wouldn't listen. I was playing hard to get, in a way; keeping in mind what she said the night I kissed her, and also not giving myself the credit in her presence of being anything desirable to her. That seemed to be antagonizing her and soon she started inviting herself over to the Shack. The more she talked, the more she talked – the more I felt the need to console her. The initial kiss (or the second kiss), she had to come and get, she had to work for it and appropriate the moment. And I could tell she knew I was working for it too.

Then the day that I noticed Samantha's curling iron on my bathroom sink was an ethereal confirmation to me that orbits collide; and all that playing hard to get, though seemingly like walking on a tight-rope, had drawn together as reality.

It's just a game.

Because Samantha was an extrovert (and a very outspoken one at that), her clamor - all those hours she talked and talked to me – she was testing me. It didn't matter what she said; she was sounding me out. It's like a broken-wing-syndrome: the more she speaks, the more I hear her hurt – the more, me, being a contemplator, has to come and rescue her. And once I do, she is pacified, and for like the first time ever. Then everything changes. But when she needs me, she clamors; she wants attention, it means she hurts; even if she's complimenting someone or just talking about how puffy the clouds are...

THE PART ABOUT THE SERPENT

People thought Samantha and I were the epitome of the 60's because we wore flagrant clothes, everything we did was symbolized, and after auditioning for a rock band that came to the restaurant looking for me one day, the drum kit wound up in the corner of the Shack and that's were we proceeded to jam.

I often felt inferior to Samantha, especially like waking up in the morning next to her, trying to stifle an emphysema-like cough from an unhealthy lifestyle and home-rolled cigarettes that followed me from my grandma's. She was so much more cosmopolitan than I was, and she'd had more experience with other lovers...

One night, I remember waking myself up in bed laughing. But it was a degenerate, ghoulish laugh - something alien to me and too embarrassing for me to ever imitate. It disturbed me so bad I couldn't acknowledge it until years later. And if Samantha would have heard it, she'd have been gone.

The laugh, I believe, had something to do with why it was I feared mediums and what was happening in my dreams; while at the same time, akin to the profundity of relief I'd experienced when smoking pot, where I'd not known how painfully oppressed my spirit was until suddenly - every constricted room in my mind and every cruel dictator lording over my thoughts gave way to wide-open entertaining spaces...

THE PART ABOUT THE SERPENT

Samantha and I ran together, I had a weight bench in the kitchen (because the drum kit took priority in the living area), and we went to the library and analyzed things through empathy and conjecture. But Samantha's once-benign need for attention started betraying a deathly serious jealousy that contended for the object of our studies. It was the broken-wing syndrome, only scary. It was how she was hurt as a little girl, here, and there... How she had a little dog, a precious dog, but it was run over by a steam-roller!... How her painting endeavors held psychic clues into the repressed memories of her bizarre upbringing... And for whatever reason, the images and depictions she conveyed to me still stand out more vividly in my mind than any realities I personally experience. Her rants were movie-like and captivating; authenticated by tantrums and tears.

I'd played Samantha a cassette tape that came with me from Florida where I was rooming with a drummer in a Cuban trailer-park were our trailer used to catch fire every time it rained, and was filled with cockroaches. The tape was of the drummer's band who played gigs professionally (something I had never done) and plagiarized by telling her I was the guitarist, despite the fact it was fast-paced Motley Crew stuff, and obviously not my style.

I was pretty sure I had an ulcer and needed permission from her mom and dad to take time off work for a doctor's appointment. Samantha's father said to me,

"Samantha finally got to you, didn't she?" Then he said, "Don't tell Sam I said that!"

While Samantha was on her childhood theme, she dug up as many pictures as she could find of herself. On one occasion, while I was waiting outside in the passenger seat of her car, she came out and invited me into her parents' house to show me something while they were gone. I followed her in and she showed me around the living room, at the pictures. She showed me how all the pictures in the living room (and elsewhere in the house) were full of her brothers and sisters, with not one of herself. Then, having a clever look that defied the insult, she lead me into a bedroom and we got down on our knees where she lifted up the blankets from the side of a bed, revealing a professionally photographed, portrait picture of herself she had framed, and sent to them from Florida, laying broken and heavily dusted under her parents' bed in the dark...

Samantha had purchased a high quality camera on her Discover card (so it would be insured) and began taking hundreds of abstract photos. Photos, many of people's most awkward moments; their worse moments. For instance, she might take evidential photographs of a window I broke out and the events surrounding the scene, with the intention she might use the evidence against me at a later date...

She painted the interior of the Shack, and while she was at it, her mother warned me what to expect: painted door knobs, light fixtures, everything!... Although

THE PART ABOUT THE SERPENT

Samantha didn't get the door knobs, she did go over a guitar chord hanging on the wall, and she did cover the kitchen windows, and then etched symbols on them with her bare fingers. Her mother came over while the painting was being done and Samantha had brushed something abstract onto the wall behind the front door. When her mom looked at it, Samantha said, "It scares you doesn't it Mumzie!?" in a taunting voice. Her mother vanished.

Apparently Samantha liked to paint; one of her childhood photos shows her using a wide brush to slap paint onto a brick wall. But now she arranged a visit with the widow of her old art teacher from grade-school. She came back from her house with a handful of poster-sized paintings, obviously done by more experienced painters (at least more experienced than grade-school students), she found in the art teacher's basement, claiming they were hers.

She showed the paintings to me and my friends, explaining them, until one day I said calmly, "I think those paintings look to be a little pre-mature for a grade-schooler." Then things got hairy.

The next day when I showed up for work (where Samantha had signed on as a waitress) my friend Lyle came up to me to warn me, "Dude, if you knew what Samantha was saying about you, I don't think you'd be going out with her any more!" I got the same kind of greeting from everyone in there, but Samantha never even looked at me. Her mother consoled me, "Oh Joe, when are you going to find a *nice* girl?"!...

In retrospect, what I see visually of that day is the back side of a demonic little girl, running from one person to the next, setting fires... Moreover, I hadn't taken into consideration back then that my plagiarizing that cassette tape may have had anything to do with it. This still was the most stable and normal relationship I'd had as an adult, and looking back, if I hadn't been so drunk, I probably should have been afraid for my life.

Nevertheless, Samantha was the biggest fan of my music. She could tell me when it sucked without telling me *I* sucked, and then she could tell me when it would send shivers up her spine when I was getting it right. She became sort of my spokeswoman, and would get in peoples' faces who crossed me or took me for granted,

"Do you know who this guy is!? Do you have any idea what this guy does in his spare time!?"

She planned to be a model, she even quit sunbathing and refused to wear makeup (something even the glamour models won't discipline themselves to do) and she solemnly told me she would never pose naked for some stupid magazine, but she would do it for an album cover of mine, if I wanted it. Every girl alive envied Samantha's hair...

THE PART ABOUT THE SERPENT

She and I moved out of town and I couldn't stay sober. Often when we would fight, she would simply drive home to her parent's house, and it was obvious that that had been the pattern with all her relationships. Then there was the reverse - when she would fight with her parents and needed a place to crash. We were living in a motel room now, almost destitute, and in dire of need of vital things like toilet paper and rent. Having just gotten paid or something, I asked Samantha if she could let me run into the store for some cigarettes. She said, "Joe, please don't buy beer!" She pleaded with me again before I exited the car, "Joe, please don't buy beer." I walked out of the store with a twelve pack and opened the rear door and threw it on the seat. "Oh, I am impressed!" she said.

There were nights that I would prowl because the tension was too high in the same room with Samantha. My guitar was always fighting the TV. My music friends called me the homeless guitarist because I would play my twelve-string under a nearby overpass at night. And then at times Samantha left I would have to be with other people. One night, I found myself at a college-age basement party, where I was half-welcome/half out the door, probably due to the fact I was older and drunk and not able to prove myself to be any asset to anybody. But I remember a young man that had been sitting down on a couch across the room from me - approached me to hand me a picture had been drawing of me. It was a portrait of my head and my left eye was blanked out with cobwebs in it…

THE PART ABOUT THE SERPENT

I would call Samantha at her parents' house in the middle of the night to tell her that I met a girl and that I was thinking about inviting her back to our place, even though it wasn't the truth. Then Samantha would be back (even in the face of nearly crashing her car) by daybreak to comfort me as I blacked out.

Samantha's older brother fatally shot himself and her family came to get her. On their way north, their vehicle apparently flipped but there were no serious injuries. I called my brother and told him what happened, "He was about a creepy fuckin' son of a bitch!" my brother told me… "What are they doing to my girlfriend?!" I said. "I…..don't know," he said. Samantha had tried protecting her brother by telling me that his gun fell to the floor and it accidentally went off, shooting him in the head.

Things got worse; I almost could not tell.

…

We moved into a new apartment while Sam's intelligence became too much for me to understand. She spoke in code, like the way Charley Manson spills out self-centered metaphors expecting people to know what the hell he's talking about, only I could understand Charley Manson. Then she quit showering but would still go to work like that.

THE PART ABOUT THE SERPENT

She allowed me to believe that what was happening to her was foreign while I faintly sensed my sexual advances had something to do with it, because regrettably, I remembered there was a time that I came on too fast and she started to cry, but I didn't know what I did… Nevertheless, I was on the phone with endocrinologists, anybody, and we wound up going to a counselor who told her she just needed to get back to church. (At least that's what Samantha told me).

I called Christine in Florida were she was now living, and told her what was going on. "Oh Joe, Samantha is sick…"

The air in our apartment seemed to hang, filled with a fuzzy hue of horizontal colors of pale yellows, reds, grays, and blues; like what you would see on a television screen in the 70's after station sign-off…

Then I woke up next to the bed, where Samantha had been lying. There were empty beer cans making a half-circle around me indicating I must have sat there talking to her and had blacked out. She was gone to her parent's again, but that fuzzy hue still hung in the air…

Then her mother called me, "Joe, what kind of drugs is Samantha on!" I told her, "We drink beer, and she likes her pot, but that's…" "OK," she said, "I'll call you again." She never did, but her family came and took her stuff while I was across town trying to get a job.

THE PART ABOUT THE SERPENT

I could not go a day sober…I admitted to myself in a letter to Samantha's mother (that I never finished) that I was attempting to build a monster out of Samantha. I coached her – when she started going soft I told her that I missed her intelligible rages at people (but not at her parents, because I loved them). She said, "I can't…I can't do that anymore." I believe it was the same night I wrote that letter, realizing also the kind of brother my brother was – someone who would not hesitate to give me one of his kidneys - while I realized I was not that type of brother, and would have to think about it if the situation was reversed, that I tried to kill myself.

I knew from cases such as a homeless drunk down in Florida who slept with his neck on a railroad tie, that you can cut off your circulation and die that way. I mounted a barbell between two half-walls of the apartment with a noose hanging just off the floor. I got as drunk as I could possibly get and did the hyperventilating thing me and my friends used to do when we were kids so I'd pass out, and then die out. It didn't work, though one of my eyes herniated with blood for weeks to come.

I called Lyle to come and get me. He had to beat on the apartment to wake me up. We were both spooked by the whole thing, I'd told him everything that had been going on with Samantha, and the eerie air of the apartment still hung there; although I can't speak for Lyle - I may have been the only one who saw it. After dark - after we packed my music equipment into his car to head north. As soon as we started driving, everything crashed in the back seat! Lyle hit the breaks, and everything was fine…we couldn't figure it out…Lyle started driving again and then, Bam! Bam! Bam! Bam! "Get out!" both doors swung open and we bailed! We were scared out of our minds! We then discovered we had been running over the power chord to my Marshall stack with the rear wheel! We laughed so hard we thought we were going to get arrested for laughing so hard, and we had to try and keep our composure and move on.

THE PART ABOUT THE SERPENT

Hard Stuff

THERE WERE TIMES I woke up not knowing where I was. Sometimes I woke up on a concrete slab in jail. Sometimes I woke up having wet my pants, and other times I woke up having soiled myself. Sometimes I woke up with my face rearranged. Sometimes I woke up to homosexuals touching me. Sometimes I woke up on disgusting people's floors. Sometimes I woke up by law enforcement or people rapping on the window of my vehicle. Sometimes I woke up beat-red on the beach with the next day's visitors bustling about. Sometimes I woke up to turn on the lights and would see a swarm of cockroaches spread from a huddle in the middle of the floor to pervade under the baseboards. Sometimes I woke up with my throat raw from screaming in my sleep. Sometimes I woke up being held down in bed and molested by things I couldn't see. Sometimes I woke up by something trying to get down my throat. Sometimes I woke up to nurses shouting at me, "Good morning Joe, do you feel like hurting yourself today?" And sometimes I didn't want to get up.

I was 25 now, and me and Lyle had heard about some drunk in Traverse City who staggered the down the double-yellow lines downing mouthwash while trapped in people's headlights. We set out to find him around the fourth of July in 1996 – we wanted to get him *really* wasted - but a storm came on us so heavy it was blowing birds out of the trees and slamming them onto the ground.

The storm was lifting our car at the shocks while we were parked. We made it three-quarters of the way but turned back. After the storm cleared, we paid admission to a put-put golf course. It was dark out, and there were so many people ahead of us in play that we couldn't proceed. We started volleying balls using our clubs like hockey sticks... We started spiking balls... We started spiking balls at moving cars... Then I didn't know what happened... Lyle pulled my hands away from my face, "*We* gotta' get to the hospital!"

I had to be wheeled in. "We're going to give you some Demerol...it's going to make you throw up!" Then it was an ambulance ride from West Branch to Saginaw, St. Mary's. They couldn't let me sleep; they couldn't give my any blankets. All night long, they prodded and probed. I remember hollering with the cat-scan technician through the two-way microphone while in the tube. I took one of Lyle's through-swings into my left eye, busting my eye-socket out.

THE PART ABOUT THE SERPENT

The next morning, I woke up to a Dr. Stephen Morris hostility throwing water in my face. "I don't have time for this!...and we'll probably never even see a dime from you! You'd rather go buy yourself a case of beer!" I had to be taken by ambulance again to an Ophthalmologist, Dr. Jardenico. Dr. Jardenico was very self-restrained, Oriental, probably practiced eastern spirituality; I remember him trying to joke with me, and how strange the silence and peace was in his facility. When he started talking in parables I knew I would never see out of my eye again. I remember I glared at Stephen Morris, while he diverted the welcome-back smile he wore to appease his colleagues as they were pushing my gurney back into my room, but I deserved what he said.

The phone rang and rang and rang next to my bed but I was too far-gone to answer it. I remember going to the bathroom with one, long single stitch hanging down my face, and I wouldn't look in the mirror. I called Lyle at the restaurant where I knew the number by heart, "Lyle you have to come and get me." Lyle arrived with my brother and they were jollying. I had to go to the front desk for paperwork and the woman there pleaded with me, "Your going to have to get some kind of financial help to pay for these medical bills...your going to have to apply for financial assistance right away!" But I was still too far gone to grasp the import of what she was saying. My discharge papers were blood-soaked, as was the shirt I wore in, and I wore my gown out the door. I took it upon myself to cut my Vicadin in half, then altogether, in just a couple days.

THE PART ABOUT THE SERPENT

Just prior to this, my brother had let me stay at his place, "No booze, Joe, I mean it, no booze!" Bobby and my old drinking buddies stopped by to drag me out but they couldn't understand how traumatized I was. All they could see was that my left eye was swollen shut, everybody's had that! "No!" I told them, "go away!"

I remember opening the phone book several times, crying, then closing it. I remember all I could do was cry and sleep. My first day back at work, I remember having to feel my way home through a wood-path in the dark because I couldn't see at night. I would sneak out into the nearby woods with my twelve-string and a twelve-pack, writing songs and suicide notes by the fire-light. Among those songs is one I kept; and this one too, still makes people cry when I play it for them:

> "Her flower necklace needed rain…
> and it gets it if she cries…
> She found the hand of fait is gen'rous…
> But that's only if she lies…
> And so goodbye, my love…
> And so goodbye, my love….

The song was about Samantha and a large, purple daisy necklace she used to wear around her neck. Samantha had gone home and done some bizarre things on her parents' property. According to her older sister, she took a shovel after putting gloves on and was looking for dead babies. She taunted her parents, saying, "Are you afraid of what I might find back there!?" They called the police and she was taken to the hospital. Samantha screamed for 16 hours after they put her on the psychiatric unit. She became a ward of the state, was sent to the state psychiatric institution, and they even sought to sterilize her. Her sister also told me how inappropriately Samantha had taken pictures at her brother's funeral, even pictures of the casket...

My brother talked me into walking to the grocery store with him one night but I waited outside for him because I didn't feel good. I was crouched down, wearing a homemade eye-patch I fashioned from an old pair of black denim jeans when the police drove a direct path across the parking lot, probably 300 yards, and got out and questioned me - almost as if it had been arranged ahead of time. Apparently, there was a warrant out for my arrest; a one-year delay-of-sentence for an attempted breaking and entering. Payment for my fines never made it to the court on time as I relied on my income tax refund to cover it which never came in the mail, likely, if I remember correctly, because I was too disoriented to get my own address right. But I believe the payment had been made. Nonetheless, a warrant was a warrant, but they were kind enough to wait for my brother (and his case of beer) and they even gave him a ride back home so he could get my medicine, at his request.

A very long, dark quiet ride it was out to Roscommon from Houghton Lake that night... I remember the "good cop" said, and quite sincerely, upon hearing my recent experiences, "It'll get better..."

THE PART ABOUT THE SERPENT

The officer who booked me asked me from a list of questions, "Have you ever had a suicidal thought?" I said something to the effect, "Well, yeah, haven't you!? He said emphatically, shaking his head from one side to the other with his eyes squinted shut, "I have never...I have never had any thoughts of suicide or thoughts of doing harm to myself!" But I was certain he was lying.

I slept the entire week I was there. Unbeknownst to me, I had a surety bond: 10% of 1,000 - and could have gotten out with a hundred bucks at any time. I remember the bond's-man (who reminded me to take care of my eye, because he himself had lost one) was being smart with the officers, making sure they had extra copies of my release papers, et cetera, and today I wonder if my cousin Jack's reputation with the police hadn't had something to do with my being kept there a week without being informed of the surety bond. At any rate, I really didn't want out, I just wanted to sleep...

My music equipment was in the middle motel room because it had a decent lock. Every night, I put my experiences to music. I sang Samantha's song through my Dean Markley vocal amp, and miked my twelve-string through my Marshall stack. About the time I got that song right, I admitted myself to the psychiatric unit; the same place Samantha had originally been escorted. I slept on the unit for so long upon arrival that they said I scared them.

THE PART ABOUT THE SERPENT

After getting familiar with people on the unit, one of the patients (who I call The Sad Girl) protested to Dr. Adams during a group one day, that she couldn't talk to the staff, but she could talk to me. And peculiar to me was that shortly after, Dr. Adams and the staff voiced concerns that we, the patients, were conspiring against them!

My brother thought I was being foolish. My mother was on her way - moving back from Florida to Michigan where her family was, because, I believe her doctors who had been treating her for Myasthenia Gravis suggested it, given the prognosis. I urged my family not to tell my mother where I was, but within days she was at the front door of the psychiatric unit with her boss from the Collier County Sheriff's Office who was helping her move up. Now I was living with my mother on the shore of Lake Ann… The idea didn't just spring, but she made the offer and I thought about it. The Sleeping Bear National Lakeshore would be respite for me, I've camped there… The lakes and the dunes and the sunsets and the woods… I appraised the sustainability of a location by the health of its jewelry stores and the jewels advertised in the local papers, and Traverse City had been on the map for a long time; it was cosmopolitan enough that I wouldn't stick out… I would move up there to heal…

I watched many sun-sets there, or perhaps it was just one, very intense sun-set that suggested to me, like the "good-cop" said, things would get better. But it was as far away as the sun itself from my cold patio chair…

THE PART ABOUT THE SERPENT

...

Now I was working dark to dark swinging hammer for my family. I used to wake up for work still laced up in my work-boots from the previous workday. No one understood... My mother took me to Grant Parsons P.C. for my eye injury and he was asking $375,000 from the golf course. He sent me down to Spectrum Rehabilitation Centers in Saginaw; he told me it cost something like $900.00 just to get in the door of the place. Grant did not know that I may have had brain damage prior to my open-head injury because I'd been hiding it. Nevertheless, the actual testing itself was so grueling and humiliating – I went on a walk-about for the next four years, not caring if I lived or not, nor ever did I inquire to the prognosis of the tests.

The employees of the golf course admitted in depositions they themselves spiked balls for fun. The golf course had apparently purchased false-insurance, they filed bankruptcy, someone lied, and my old friend Lyle was defaulted the $375,000 because he didn't show up for court. Lyle thought it was personal, but it wasn't; I had told him that. All Lyle had to do was show up for court and say he was there, and 90% of the judgment would have fallen on the golf course, bankrupt or otherwise. No one saw a dime. My medical bills estimated $30,000 plus a lifetime of having only one good eye and double vision between the two.

THE PART ABOUT THE SERPENT

Although I was told that suing Lyle was in my legal right, I could have just as easily hit Lyle with my club as he did me, and I wasn't going to do that to him.

My mother was taking control again – lining me up with counselors and doctors. We were not getting along and I am now grasping part of the reason she was so vehemently opposed to me drinking anything - was that alcohol afforded me instant defiance to her manipulative devices. On one occasion, my mother arranged for me not only to come to work late, but to have an emergency meeting between me, Joe Garrety (a counselor she set me up with), and she and her counselor, Becky Vincent - both from then Great Lakes Community Mental Health/now Northern Lakes Community Mental Health. Keep in mind I am a 26-27 year-old full time construction worker. They were astonished to discover that I was not willing to have such a meeting and the only thing they could do was let me go. The same thing happened in Florida: my mother arranged for me to enter a David Lawrence treatment program for which I had to pay cash for, but when they discovered my mother was the one who had the problem with me drinking, and not me, they simply refunded my money. Only these counselors were not so keen, they were not your picture of health, I'd been wary of them breaching confidentiality to my mother, but apparently they presumed I didn't need any.
I set up a storage unit for jamming, complete with drum kit, propane heater, and new recording equipment. During that time, I torqued my voice into something so hard - I've never been able to un-train. The Storage

THE PART ABOUT THE SERPENT

Unit was usually black-out territory. I also kept a piano at my mother's an old girlfriend had donated to me, and I took to refurbishing it; but which remained in pieces, in boxes, upon boxes, upon boxes for almost two years until I couldn't face it anymore and had to burn it. My mother would call me, "Joe, you have to do something about this piano."

Anytime I stayed at my mother's, I slept endlessly... A little girl my mother was babysitting asked her, "Why does Joe sleep all the time?" and when it was revealed to me what she said, I deemed myself "eternally sad."

I actually was afforded more life in my mother's basement apartment than when being in close quarters with her. I was teaching myself Sanskrit and doing extreme, self-denial yoga again. And as an exercise, I walked about the basement doing my daily living with my eyes closed to better appreciate what it means to see.

I learned that it takes a blind person years of training just to learn how to walk around a block. And I heard a blind person say, "My world is not like your world..." Once, I automatically caught my balance doing yoga with my peripheral vision, then instantly remembered reading that peripheral vision is one of the ways we keep balanced. I learned to track a tennis ball round a Frisbee which would leave my eyes with that massaged feel you get after doing moderate exercise. I would share with the staff at Cedar Run Eye Center that I exercised my eyes, and though one technician condescendingly told me that our eyes get enough exercise throughout the day without having to exercise them, the ophthalmologist could not dispute it's benefits, and recalled having a patient who does Yoga herself who is her nineties and is in excellent shape. Plus, I don't think the technician considered seriously living with a permanent eye injury, nor would I dare take on tasks like parallel parking if I didn't exercise them. Not to mention, staring at a computer monitor all day as many people are now accustomed to in the work force (and otherwise) should not be considered exercise for your eyes, but a health hazard.

I still studied bio-feedback, which I think is the same concept - how a dog rolls on a dead fish to gain autonomy, and I chased Krishna through *Bhagavad-Gita* because that was exactly how *I* saw God. The names of the masters of my music tapes were things like A#1, Jesus, and Zeus, and I had poster collages filled with eastern proverbs. I wore three, high-quality Moroccan bracelets on my left wrist, and I had a couple middle-eastern shirts I wore that got compliments, and laughs.

I booked a room in a downtown hotel that was one grade higher than a homeless shelter, and would traverse from there to the storage unit, plus I bought power equipment to run out of my Cherokee so me and my drummer could jam out in the woods. I told myself that if I ever got pulled over intoxicated again, I would bail and run. Plus, (as often as I wouldn't finish it) I kept a bottle of bourbon next to my seat in the event I would get pulled over and then swig from the bottle - which would be recorded on the dash-cam of the patrol car where a breath-test would not be able to determine whether I had anything to drink prior to that. But I did, and when I did, I surrendered, because I was absolutely tired of living that way. It was January 2000. The officers were kind enough to park my vehicle off the road and lock it, and they even went back for my wallet.

I was facing a one-year, third offense. The bookies in the Grand Traverse County Jail put me on suicide watch because I was sarcastic with them. I had asked them if jail activity worsened during full moons but they only ridiculed me. But that is exactly where the term "lunatic" comes from; "lunar." When I saw the magistrate, my hair was a long staticky mess. I happened to have approximately the amount of bond set in my wallet the next morning though I tried to get it through other sources which would give me more time to hang on to what I had. And as soon as I got out, I cut my hair.

I knew that if I ever quit drinking I was going to suffer. I'd been reading *People of the Lie* by M. Scott Peck – fascinated with what was in it, I had a copy of *Power for Living*; and I still had my crayon-green, *New World Translation of the Holy Bible* - which was now the oldest material possession I owned, or stole. Early on a foggy morning, I drove out to my mother's with a camp-bag packed with a pencil and that *Power for Living* book. I parked at her house while she was still asleep and hiked around through state land to the other side of the lake. There, I sat down close to the tranquil water and I made a formal commitment to surrender to God.

I was advised by my attorney to enroll in an outpatient treatment program at Munson Medical Center which would make a good impression on the judge, and part of their treatment was to get family involved; my mother. During one visit between Sandy, a counselor, and my mother and I, my mother began explaining my head injury to her. I remember tilting my head and resting the bridge of my nose between my thumb and index finger, with my elbow resting on the arm of my chair. I was kind of taking the back seat with that gesture when Sandy quickly shoved a box of Kleenex at me with her yes wide opened, certain I was starting to cry. She took control of the situation with a pronouncement, "Joe is suffering from a frontal-lobe injury…he needs to be admitted to the Center One psychiatric unit!" What a surprise, but cool, I was all for it. Maybe I could sleep! My sentencing was coming up and maybe the judge would know I was in the hospital and would be more lenient…

I remember Neil Fellows from Community Mental Health was one of the doctors who screened me for intake at the hospital. I remember he wrote in his notes that I appeared to be of average or below average intelligence. He asked me when it was I had my last seizure, but I have never had seizures…

THE PART ABOUT THE SERPENT

Now, the kicker in admission to a psychiatric unit is whether or not you have a suicide plan, and anytime anyone would ask me that question I would tell them, "yeah, I've had one for about five years", which was true. But whether or not I was in any place to act on that, was a different story.

Every morning the nurses woke me up shouting, "Good morning Joe, do you feel like hurting yourself today?!" which I thought was a method to embarrass us into saying that we didn't, which somehow psychologically prevented people from actually doing it. However, I later found that their medical notes indicated I was hard of hearing…

My court date was approaching about the time of my release-date from the hospital. So one day I decided not to get out of bed. They sent Lyn Conlon down, the psychiatrist, and she dryly threatened to take the blankets off my bed if I wasn't out of bed when she came back, but I was. They called it a "crash" and kept me on the unit longer, even contacting the court - exactly what I had hoped for. Peculiar to me too, was that Lyn ordered a B-vitamin for me, and when I asked her why, she told me it was to clean the toxins from the alcohol out of my system, because I had been sober for three months… Not to mention they treated me for benzodiazapine abuse, certain that because I was prescribed Ativan by other doctors and had a drinking history, I had to be abusing them (hence the one they discovered in my pocket that was to be taken on schedule following my intensive outpatient meeting the night I arrived). But I was a speed-guy if I were going to abuse pills, and Ativan put you on the floor.

The arresting officer greeted me at sentencing; he'd never seen me cleat cut. I was given 14 days in jail. One of the things the judge, Judge Michael Haley, said to me - I could not internalize for along time afterward, that sent me on my heels - was that everyday a drunk comes into his court room; everyday is a new case, "but" he said, "I have never seen a case as bad as this."

While I was in jail a call came over the intercom, "Alcoholics for Christ?!" and I was the only man in my 16-man cell to heed it. I sat down at a large table, chaired by Philip Asplund, a registered social worker who was volunteering for the jail ministry, and a few other green looking inmates. He had ties to a prayer warrior, Lois Hawley, and asked us for written prayer requests. I left the jail before he returned, but Philip took it upon himself to look up my last name in the phone book and contacted my mother, where I was staying again. He told me that he had a personal prayer package for me and to come to a meeting they were having at the Bethlehem Lutheran Church, downtown.

I'd been getting stronger, and my mother and I were not getting along because of it. I was even subtly threatening to leave her by disappearing for extended periods during the day, though my Cherokee had a lock-down arm on the front wheel. I stayed occupied with a new, one-year study Bible that had an air-brushed

THE PART ABOUT THE SERPENT

portrait of Jeshua (Jesus) on the cover, and I bought myself a fishing pole...

My mother drove me to Philip's meeting and then returned to pick me up when it was to be over. I kept her waiting, talking to Philip outside. Philip was very interested in talking with me, and she began picking at me as we started home. As we drove through town, she started flaring up. I politely asked her to pull the car over to let me out, but she refused. I tried to step out at a red light but she stepped on the gas and ran through the red light, threatening to do it again if I tried to jump. I told her I would draw attention to the vehicle and I shouted for help to a group of people at a gas station we passed, who all stopped what they were doing and watched us pass. Then I pretended to relax, and when she came to the next red light, I grabbed my leather brief bag and bailed. She was at that moment between not knowing if she should try and step on the gas again or stop – because she saw either method was going cause physical damage. I got out in full control, shut the door in one sweep and walked calmly in the opposite direction.

I then heard the sound of the car I feared in my soul since I was a little boy – flee the area; picking up speed as it gained camouflage amidst the sounds of the other vehicles. My mother was not dumb...

I went back to the hotel, who still had me on file, and I insisted that they block any calls. I was wearing a white dress shirt with a black leather jacket, toting a black

THE PART ABOUT THE SERPENT

leather brief bag. The room they gave me smelled like urine but I didn't care; the prayers were what I wanted to get a hold of. I went through them as my sense of awareness heightened. Lois, who represented Alcoholics for Christ and New Covenant Ministries claimed in her package that she did not give advice, however, one of the suggestions she had for dealing with the devil was to speak out loud in a commanding voice to Satan as you draw a Jesus line, saying, "Satan, you can't cross this line!..."

I went out to the lobby to chat with an old acquaintance – to tell her what just happened to me, and she easily recognized my mother as criminally psychotic. Suddenly all the brutality started making sense, only I was scared. She told me about her husband, Greg. "They make toys of people," she said. The man across the room from us, sitting in an armchair – pointed toward the television - but too far away to actually engage in it – began giggling. All I could see was the glare off his glasses, like the hapless chap's in Houghton Lake who happened upon a room to give his liver a break, but his giggling was at my fear. My friend glared at him and he stopped. As she started talking again, he would giggle creepily again. Aware now it was spiritual, I imagined a grand neon band around my perimeter, complete with crosses cut out of it, turning round me... As in meditation - always the image begins to break down, and as soon as it would, the creepy-guy would start to laugh. So I tested it: I acknowledged that when I abandoned my "do not cross line" nothing happened. In turn, when I would pick up my "do not cross line" in full force, nothing happened. But as soon as my "do not cross line" began to crumble, where parts of it would disappear here and reappear there - desperately trying to hang on to it – he would start laughing, as if I were entertaining him.

I was so nerved out by it that I spoke up, "Let me guess, acid?" "No, Vietnam shit!" he said. Then I asked my friend if we could continue the conversation up in her room.

My friend informed me the Vietnam thing was a lie. If this guy disrespected me so much to lie to my like that, I knew he was, or something in him was, laughing at me.

"Greg was raping our daughter…things were bad…I even saw the devil…he had maggots, maggots flowing from his mouth, and the stench!…Greg witnessed a murder at a convenience store on the Ohio/ Michigan border…the killer knew Greg saw him and Greg fled… the killer chased Greg on back roads, north, into the night at speeds of 100 miles an hour…the killer crashed into a corn field, broke all four axles of the car, and burned…Greg was so screwed up when he got home, I called the police…they took him to the hospital where he was on a gurney awaiting a psychiatric evaluation….someone drew the curtain back between Greg and the patient in the bed next to him, and it was the killer, who noticed Greg, and told him, 'you thought you got away from me didn't you!' The officer assigned to the situation was scared and warned the guy, 'If you

THE PART ABOUT THE SERPENT

lay one finger on me you will die!' He was chewing through his face restraint...

"Greg was never the same after that...they wouldn't let me testify in court (regarding her daughter); they wouldn't let us make eye contact..."

I asked her where Greg was now, and she told me he was walking the streets of a certain northern Michigan town, as a bum.

I took notes of everything she said. She told me, "You have to make an evacuation plan." I went downstairs and called the Women's Resource Center; she said they deal with battered men as well as women, including psychological issues. I would not give them my name, I couldn't risk it. When I walked by to the pay phone, the front desk informed me that they did in-fact have someone who had been trying to call me, and I could tell by the urgency in their tone that the caller was persistent.

I knew that anytime I yielded to the devil he would take the upper hand. And times when I was stronger, he would yield. For instance, times when I was very passive and beat down - when driving the winding, double-yellow highway out to my mother's, I noticed the oncoming cars would encroach over the double-yellow at me. The greater I yielded, the greater they came; however diminished my strength was. And on occasions where I was stronger - and could even coach

myself to test it - no car in a million years would
encroach that double yellow as I approached them!...

I was up at five or six the next morning at the hotel;
prayed up, on my toes, and prepared. I remember
walking across town to the Women's Resource Center
in a righteous strut. I'm a white nigger from Detroit.
Concerning the times when I'd yielded to on-comers,
this was not one of those days. Even if a car came
barreling down the sidewalk at me it would either have
to stop, or something would have to stop it!

I met with Gilda Allen at the Traverse City Women's
Resource Center. I noticed the offices were behind
wire-meshed glass, but I was puzzled that the
conference room Gilda took me into to talk with me had
no visible camera or recording equipment as did
modern attorney's offices. She needed a contact number
and the only thing I told her I could give her was my
pager number, but which the batteries were dead. She
happened to have a pack of batteries for me and used
the opportunity that I might know how to set her pager
as well...

I told Ms. Allen that I thought my mother was trying to
make me sick; and I did not mean that she was
poisoning my food, but she was playing the mental
health system as a surrogate accomplice, and long as
she could convince them of the possibility I was sick –
the greater her chances of them convincing me I was
sick, and over the course of time it became easier to
wear the disgrace than to resist it. This was in collusion

with my mother's constant reminders of every bad thing I had ever done to her.

Feeling bad is feeling un-well. When you remind someone of something they may have done to you that they can never take back or change, you are, in effect, making them feel un-well, which is the equivalent of making someone feel sick (unless the reminder is executed with the intention of bringing sorrow that leads to repentance i.e. change).

"For godly sorrow worketh repentance to salvation not to be repented of: but the sorrow of the world worketh death." (2 Corinthians 7:10)

All my credibility went out the window when Ms. Allen found out that I had a therapist, and insisted we call him, never considering that I probably never would have had a therapist if were not for the woman I was there asking for protection from... Like a fool, I went along with it.

I remember having hours to kill before I could catch a bus back out to my mother's. I crouched down outside behind the garbage-bin, smoking, certain that my mother was going to find me there. I wrote Gilda a desperate note: "Gilda, call my therapist and tell him not, not to call my mother's house!" and gave it to the receptionist.

I walked a couple blocks down to the hospital to wait for my bus, my pager rang. It was Philip. "Philip, how did you get this number!?" "From your mother... Joseph, you must be exhausted!"...

Eight hours later, I arrived at my mother's. I was so suspicious of her. Prior to these evacuation warm-ups, I remember audibly reading a Catholic rite of exorcism I had hand-copied from the book *Michelle Remembers,* in my bedroom, which was right next to my mother's bedroom, where I heard my mother moan as I read it... I remember how my uncle Dick, a Jehovah Witness, always marveled how the smoke from a fire always followed my mother, saying it was a sign she was a witch...

The house was full of stagnant cigarette smoke; my mother had been sitting in the dark silence, calculating. I was scared for my life. If she knew what my thoughts had been the past 24 hours...if she knew I'd been talking to people about getting help to get away from her...if she knew what I'd been recognizing from *People of the Lie*... if she knew I knew her strength was abnormal and that she was under the influence of demonic power - as my friend said they would not even let her and Greg make eye contact – and how Greg's assailant bent on killing him when he discovered he was a murderer, I was scared out of my wits...

She went outside to do some chores and I got on the phone. I phoned Grant Parsons and they said he was away but they'd track him down. While waiting for his call, I called Gilda Allen, certain my mother was going to hurt me or herself, who told me condescendingly,

THE PART ABOUT THE SERPENT

"You just need to call your therapist" and I shouted into the phone, "Forget it!" Grant Parsons called me right back but he only gave me the number to the local crises line...

I barricaded myself in my room with a gallon of milk, a hunting knife strapped to my belt, and my Bible. My friend Kevin (whose mother was a paralegal) and I often humored about stretching the law when it came to vocabulary. I knew exactly what constituted a threat, and the difference between a threat and a warning, just like the officer who was standing guard of Greg's assailant when he told him, "If you lay one finger on me you will die!" That was not a threat, but a warning. I went out with my Bible in my hand to approach my mother. I was standing across the living room while she was crouched down in her chair with a horizon of smoke hovering motionless in the air. I said to her (the first words spoken between us since I jumped from her accelerating vehicle) "I don't hate you mom, but I hate what you represent." "And what do *you* represent, Joe!?" she said in an eye-for-an-eye fashion. And I held out my Bible and said, "this!" I then told her, "If you lay one finger on me I will gut you like a rotten tuna!" and I went back to my bedroom and packed my bags for when the police came...

When the police arrived, I was playing my classical guitar, and I forced them to interrupt me; I wanted them to know I was disciplined and in full control. It was dark out now. My mother was at the neighbors, and I'd previously gone to them to use their phone concerning my mother, so they had a head's-up about what was going on. Apparently, my mother went there to call the police and then started back toward the house, but the neighbor grabbed her authoritatively by the upper arm and detained her (for which my mother was furious). I was sitting down in the living room talking with the officers and of all the people to come, it was Joe Garrety, toting a notebook too heavy for him to handle! I had no longer been a client of Joe Garrety's and I told him in front of the officers that he had been breaching my confidentiality to my mother. But he simply said he was oblivious to it, and proceeded to try and take some haphazard, psychological assessment of the situation because the police were standing right there waiting for it. The "good-cop" sent me off in the back of another patrol car, "That book in your hand there is the strongest weapon you can ever have."...

They shot me so full of Haldol and Ativan at the hospital, after calling Dr. Conlon in the middle of the night for direction, that I shit my pants. I remember trying to flush my underwear down the toilet and then I must have fallen between the bathroom and my bed, because when I woke up, I had clean clothes on. One particular nurse, Marie, tried asking me if I remembered it the next day, but the nature of her question seemed less to do with medical examination as it was condescending, because it simply fizzled out. She was purporting, in effect, the trouble they had to go through, while I was standing my ground in case she had not considered the trouble I went through, which was like a

THE PART ABOUT THE SERPENT

light wind that pushed her face away – that maybe she shouldn't play that game with me.

No one had asked me my side of the story again. I knew what they had: a representative of God, threatening to kill his mother…

When I woke up the next morning, my brother, with deep lines all through his face, was sitting in my room. When he said, "Mom's down stairs" the Haldol and Ativan evacuated my bloodstream like the cockroaches where I used to live, to pervade into the baseboards where they could no longer be detected. Keep in mind that I have brain damage that I've been trying to hide for years and years. Lyn Conlon was now sitting in my room. I spoke only essential words; I didn't have time or energy to fool around. I began setting up for what I wanted to tell her. "Criminally psychotic people are capable of amazing strength..." She nodded emphatically. Then referring to my experience at the hotel, I said, "I think someone was reading my mind." To which she gave an emphatic, no, with her head swinging side to side." I said, "I saw my mother being sneaky with the telephone" (my mother was *always* sneaky with the telephone). And Lyn said loudly, "Well don't ya think she was a little scared!" I just shut up.

Now I had to rehearse a what I wanted to say to Lyn. I was going to expose my mother's violence. The strangest thing happened, however, the next time she came to talk to me. As soon as I began to tell on my mother, the muscles in my mouth seized up tight and

THE PART ABOUT THE SERPENT

wouldn't work! It was the strangest thing. Nothing like that has ever happened to me before, and nothing like that has ever happened since. I literally couldn't speak. I conveyed to her I would try to write it down...

A couple days had already passed with a heavy load of anti-psychotics reeking havoc in my system. They were diminishing my already-compromised ability to withstand - what I'd worked so hard to gain to keep from yielding to the enemy. I tried to explain to them my theory how the cars on the road would encroach across the double-yellow at me, et cetera., but they interpreted that as Satan sending cars out on the road to run me down.

The nurses asked me if I had been hearing things or seeing things, and when inspecting my medical records, I discovered that some of the nurses reported I was experiencing hallucinations and some of them reported I wasn't. Most interesting to me was that the particular nurses who said I had been experiencing hallucinations were consistent with those submissions throughout the course of my treatment; while the nurses who reported I wasn't experiencing hallucinations remained consistent in their submissions throughout the course of my treatments, as well. That meant, if I were having hallucinations, I was lying to some of the nurses about not having them while not lying to other nurses about having them, and sharp enough in a supposed delusional state to remember which nurses I had lied to and which ones I had not!

THE PART ABOUT THE SERPENT

My mother had been calling and calling the hospital. She talked at length with everyone she could though I requested <u>NO CONTACT.</u> All they saw of the situation was a sweet old woman whose son was being harsh and unreasonable, and would frown at me - having to resist repeated attempts from them to reconcile me to her.

Apparently, my mother informed them of a violent history of mine - that she had even wound up with broken bones on several occasions…

I requested a meeting between my mother and I with professionals present. It would be me, Don Jaquish, Lyn Conlon, and my mother. If my mother really wanted to see me, she could not refuse this appointment. The day the appointment came, a nurse negligently let my mother on to the unit, no questions asked, and my mother walked right up to my face, the way she did when she threatened to beat me with a 2x4, and growled, "Joe, don't you dare tear me down in front of those doctors, because I can't take it!"

I had notes at the meeting, but my testimony began to crumble…then eventually I said, "Maybe I just made this all up." My mother asked Lyn Conlon what her diagnosis was, and I remember Lyn's response: "Schizophrenia!" as if she had hit a bulls eye. Her response was inappropriate in that any compassionate doctor would say, "I hate to inform you but your son has… it's a life long disease…it is difficult to treat, et cetera..." but not Dr. Conlon. It was if her diagnosis somehow afforded her more attention than the supposed illness of the patient - like a form of aggrandizement by association... At that time, Lyn Conlon had been being scrutinized in an article featured in the Traverse City Record Eagle for employing that particular diagnosis followed by personal testimony submitted by the author. The article can be found at www.joyfulnoisedaycare.com/ben1.html posted by Ben Hansen of The Bonker's Institute. My friend Philip and others in his group informed me of the article and cautioned me no to accept Dr. Conlon's diagnosis.

Another particular therapist named Tony tried to tell Lyn Conlon that I had adjusted the blinds a number of times while group was in session which was not true. He saw me adjust them to suit the room before group began, and that was it. He also assumed that the arrangements of the books in the room were due to me at times when they weren't. My denial of adjusting the blinds insinuated to Lyn Conlon that I was having periodic black-outs and couldn't remember what I was doing. She thought it symptomatic of post traumatic stress disorder and was ready to treat me for it! I requested a meeting between me and Tony and Lyn, but after hearing me say I emphatically did not do as Tony was telling her, Lyn told me that she had to take the word of the "trained professional" over the patient.

The next day when Tony came to get me for group I told him it was my prayer time.

THE PART ABOUT THE SERPENT

Talking to Lyn Conlon about the devil was obviously not a good idea, but one day she had a professional resident of some kind accompanying her on her visits. When she asked me how things were going, with the resident there, I put her on the spot by saying, "I think the devil has been using weak people to try and crush me," to which she only gave a nod. Her nod could be interpreted as her either agreeing, or condescendingly consoling someone who's lost their mind - where it is less traumatic to agree with them than to disagree. But I knew her reaction would be different with someone else present nonetheless, and I knew in my heart all along I had been under demonic attack…

My mother would inappropriately bring me things to the hospital which I know was to try to convey to the staff what a good mother she was. She'd bring a gallon of milk, a large bunch of bananas, large bag of potato chips, and books (paranormal books, mind you) – things that she had never done before, and were out of character for her…

It was very difficult for me at this early stage in my Christianity to differentiate the professionals from being caring people - simply getting paid money at the expense of another's misfortune - and holiness. If you look at the story of the Good Samaritan in the Bible, you will see that not only was a Samaritan culturally despised in Bible times, but this particular gentleman came upon a <u>real</u> victim with <u>real</u> injuries and treated the man with <u>his own money</u>; he didn't charge him for it, and he certainly didn't make a living at it. Should you have an ambulance arrive because something like that happened to you today, you will be paying dearly!

Also on the unit, a poster entitled *I AM* commands the hall just outside the nurses' station. To read it - it contains all the rock-star selfishness I had finally abandoned for God, but from a victim's mentality – provoking one's right to entitlement – and is by no means the "I AM" of the Bible. It is an imposter; self-deification.

Another hypocritical peculiarity at the hospital to me was that they would hand out material to everyone in group to discuss ways to combat unwanted and persistent thoughts. And the antidote was to speak to them assertively, "No!" or, "Stop!" et cetera.,.. Much like Lois Hawley's advice. However, if you were to make known that you had an inner dialogue whatsoever (as every human being does) in a different setting just down the hall, you would be condemned for having hallucinations, most especially if you were caught speaking audibly to them. Mind you, these groups were of the general population of patients, and there were usually only one or two on the unit who actually complained of hearing voices.

Although I believe I remember every patient during that time - even praying for the ones I most disliked - I don't have time to touch on every character I've ever met in this book, either, but I will tell you briefly of some, and one in particular was a patient of Dr. Conlon's who I will call Rachel (Rachel Weeping), because I want people to know about her. Rachel was a tall, slender, self-restrained young lady; feeble-hearted and in need of loving guidance. I remember her actions spoke louder than her words which may have been due to the fact Rachel was catatonic under a constant assault of electro-shock treatments Dr. Conlon was giving her in the basement. I noticed in the cafeteria, when Rachel was done eating, she would clear her place and then stand attentively behind the weakest person in the cafeteria. Patiently she'd wait…if their was a dish that was finished, or if she could be of any assistance, she was on it.

When we would gather a group of us to go outside, I would always begin talking Rachel into it, because she wouldn't go otherwise. And because her gaze was always bent to the ground, I remember how leading her with my body-language had became second-nature to me, specifically because she watched the movement of my legs for queues. Plus I was the one who had to live up to the promise that going outside was a good idea.

Noticing Rachel's servant-hood in the cafeteria was consistent - I told one of the nurses that she must think she is a nurse - thinking at the time it must be symptomatic, to which the nurse put a finger to her lips, "shhh, Rachel *is* a nurse."

One evening, in the lounge, there were three of us watching the typical filth put out there on the TV. It was me, another older woman, and Rachel – who was probably only there for the comfort of being with other people. Her room was right next to the TV lounge and I remember her being so disoriented that night from Dr. Conlon's treatments that morning, she couldn't understand why the back of the open door in the TV lounge didn't open to *her* room – because she knew her room was on the other side... She would pull the door away from the wall and see a wall, confused. Then she would push the door back against the wall to recheck things (with her hand still on the handle) and then pull the door away from the wall revealing the wall again, confused. After she sat, a sexual assault-scene came over the television and Rachel moved her head side to side before starting to cry. The patient sitting next to her pulled her in and held her while speaking softly to her. And I think that may have been the definitive moment I determined never to watch television ever again.

During which treatment, I don't remember, but I caught up with Rachel at a respite home where they transition patients between hospital and home. She was speaking, and I remember sitting there with her before a meal when she clasped her hands and squinted her eyes tight and said a silent prayer followed by an audible murmur of gratitude; she meant it! We even went for a walk. If she only knew the impression she had on me...I'd never seen such amazing compassion... Munson Medical Center typically did not keep psychiatric patients more than 14 days; long-term cases were shipped out to the state hospital. And I didn't know this at the time, but apparently Rachel had been held on that unit for two months...

THE PART ABOUT THE SERPENT

Jumping ahead, I didn't see Rachel again until many years later. She had deteriorated. Her clothes didn't fit, her hair was dry and streaked with gray, and she was awaiting to be seen for another appointment. She was seated across from me with a lobby full of people but I had to speak up. I asked her if her name was Rachel and confirmed it was her I was hospitalized with before proceeding to tell her what I witnessed in her while she was in the state she was in – helping other people who may have been better off than she was – and what that said to me about her… After she was gone, I overheard some things about her in the room after that…losing her house…bad things… and that she was working in the cafeteria, downstairs.

I went down to the cafeteria after my appointment to see if I could catch her one more time. I had to tell her that she'd been on my prayer list all those years. She caught the first person who went by, the dishwasher – carrying a rack of glasses in his hands – and made him look at me… "I'm on his prayer list!" while the poor guy tipped his head back and peered at me as if he should know me. And being stuck on the song *Amazed* by Paul McCartney at the time, teaching myself to play it, I told her I thought she was an amazing person.

THE PART ABOUT THE SERPENT

"Will I see you again?"

"Well, do you work here?"

"Yes."

"Well, then maybe I'll stop in and see you sometime."

"I hope you do!"

...

In totality, Lyn Conlon treated as having: schizophrenia, major depression, hallucinations (auditory or visual, I don't know), benzodiazapine abuse issues, alcohol abuse issues, alcohol poisoning (B-vitamins), hearing loss, impropriety issues, delusions, and mental incompetence in general and then sent me back home to live with my mother. I told people, "it seemed like Dr. Conlon and my mother were on the same team!" My mother had asked Lyn Conlon how my brain injury factored into things, and Dr. Conlon said after resisting hesitation, "…it complicates things." As studious and analytical as I was I had submitted to the unit my neuropsychological examination. And as extensive and thorough as my neuropsychological examination was, I know they never looked at it. And neither did Neil Fellows, the admitting psychiatrist from Community Mental Health called into Munson who inappropriately pop-assessed me with some kind of intelligence quotient in the midst of a personal crises. Not to mention, I had supplied Neil's office with that neuropsychological examination years before, even having them copy it for me while I stood there, when I was temporarily seeing him for prescription management and Don Jaquish for therapy. But he didn't recognize me at Munson, and I know damn well none of them ever even looked at the thing.

Although none of my diagnosis stuck, between Lyn Conlon and my newly assigned outpatient doctor, Curtis Cummins of Northern Lakes Community Mental Health, I was assaulted with a host of sickening medications including: Paxil, Wellbutrin, Risperdal, Trazadone, Xanax, Atavan (5 mg. shot upon request if I wanted it), Elevil, Haldol, Geodon; and Benadryl to keep me from wringing my hands and dancing on my feet due to the side effects (of which there is no such thing, they are the direct effects).

While at my mother's, I surrendered to her machinations. I slept in the dark, lethargic, letting the enemy and his lies ravage me. Sometimes I would get jolted out of bed. I read *The Road Less Traveled*, *A Different Drum*, and had a subscription to *Psychology Today*. I leaned into dependence on my mother which had a reverse-psychology effect. Like when a young lion chases a gazelle and the gazelle suddenly stops; the lion doesn't know what to do, he's stumped. He likes the thrill of the hunt, he wants a victim who feels threatened by him. He paws at the hind legs…"Go!"

THE PART ABOUT THE SERPENT

However, experienced lions who have seen that trick before will mount the animal and subdue it.

On one hand, it confused my mother and she told me I had to find someplace else to live. But at the same time, I could nearly exert enough of my own energy to do it.

Philip Asplund had arranged for me to get rides to and from his "Christian" groups with a guy named Rex who came out of the closet to me after a few rides, and I wound up renting a room from him because I didn't have anywhere else to go. I also went to work for a cedar log builder down the road, Mark Miller, a "straight" acquaintance of Rex's. Rex told me one day, "Like I've told Mark, well, like I tell all my friends, 'any time you want a blow job, just let me know...'"

I shut myself in at night with a coffee-pot, my one-year study Bible, and a recliner in the lamp-lit atmosphere of my bedroom, in Rex's house, and started knocking out that vow I had made back in the End Motel Room - that I would read every word of that book from cover to cover...and sometimes while having to listen to Rex and his gay friends banging...

During that time, I started two books of collections; one entitled *Mapping the Mind* (because I loved anatomy and psych), and the other *Prayers of Hope.* I imagined the purpose of my leather brief bag to perhaps carry prescription medications to indigent people in undeveloped countries at one time, but as time went on, it took on Bible gear and prayers. My *Mapping the*

THE PART ABOUT THE SERPENT

Mind book, though I put hours of study, gathering, and contemplation into it, remained only a jacket with an introduction by Aldous Huxley, and a distorted homogination of matter and spirit I concocted. *Prayers of Hope,* on the other hand, I could barely contain, as became the biblical contents of my brief bag.

Rex was a sponsor in the Alcoholics Anonymous program, and today I give no credence to any counterfeit religion. You can find a great article on that entitled *AA: Christian or Occult Roots?* at Way of Life Literature www.wayoflife.org. But one of AA's suggestions is that you do not sponsor the opposite sex to prevent authoritarian and love relationships. Now, Rex had sponsored maybe hundreds of people, including me, because Philip Asplund turned me down. Rex never went asking to sponsor anyone - he was too torpid of a guy for that - it wasn't his temperament, he didn't want to be bothered. But when Rex found out that a young man I was treated with in the hospital was gay and had a problem with alcohol, and had told me that if he ever wanted a sponsor it would definitely be me, Rex very inappropriately stepped right up and said, "Tell him if he ever needs a sponsor, I'd be willing…no ulterior motive."

And I could tell by the skewed visual paths of Rex's sex partners that they were no less vulnerable...

THE PART ABOUT THE SERPENT

Now, Philip Asplund had a roommate he had met in treatment who I knew was a walking time-bomb. He was the embodiment of a lie and he frequently relapsed and went back to jail. I had asked Philip if I could rent that room from him but he refused. And not long after I moved out of Rex's and got an efficiency of my own, Philip's roommate went back to jail while Philip had the audacity to ask me if I was interested in renting his room - the same room he declined me before moving in with Rex who he set me up with at his "Christian" meeting, now left vacant by a drug-addict he took under his wing to sponsor, after declining to sponsor me...

"Ye shall know them by their fruits."

During my visit to the hospital, there was a young woman who was to my imagination, a club dancer. She was in a bad way, even screaming at the nurses' station because they wouldn't let her have Motrin for her migraines. Now we are not allowed in one another's rooms, but I broke the rules on this occasion. I asked her if I could come in and read to her one of the prayers Lois Hawley had given me (via Philip Asplund). I sat down on the end of her bed while she took the chair and I read it, commanding Satan this, and commanding Satan that...even kind of sensing the inappropriateness that it was supposed to be a prayer as I was reading it... Then I didn't see her on the unit for a few days, but then she returned with huge bandages on both wrists...

At home, I was being harassed in my sleep at night but I really didn't know what was happening. Sometimes

THE PART ABOUT THE SERPENT

I'd be laying half-under in bed at night with a light on. Suddenly I'd be jolted into a half-wake paralysis, trying to fight off who-knows-what, with no strength; things growling at me. My mind would be just awake enough to experience it, while my body was still asleep. By the time I got to coffee the next morning it would be rationalized. I started capitalizing on "crashes", but because I was up all night in bed.

On one occasion, while my mother was dying, I went to stay with her because her hospice workers were on an on-call basis and she was terribly sick. It was about a 24 mile drive, and once, my return trip was black ice. This night there was a major snow storm. My mother clearly had pneumonia and aggressive medical treatment was the only thing we could do for her in that situation, so I called the ambulance. I'd been on the phone making calls all night. My Cherokee was stuck in the end of the driveway and towing companies had set their answering machines to take calls; everyone of them were swamped and insurance companies were offering reimbursements. It was full daylight now and I was exhausted. I laid down in the bed next to my mother's room and as soon as I began to fall asleep I heard, "BOO!" right in my face, and it rocked me! But I was so tired and that kind of thing had become so frequent, that I told myself that that was what I get for drinking so much coffee while on prescription medications...

I've always been very particular about what I read, and the kinds of books I read - I read them again and again. Usually, I extract the titles from the bibliographies of another particular book I've read, and then go and order *them*. I myself began writing a large manuscript with the audience being all the people I had ever harmed. It was an amends-work. The title was *Wither or Not*, reflecting my bizarre theory at the time - that death is the primary purpose of life - and later became *Lacuna*, which was a psychoanalyses term used in Daniel Goleman's *Vital Lies, Simple Truths: the Psychology of Self-Deception,* which I had borrowed from the library over seven times until I bought my own reference copy. I was still trying to make sense of the power my mother had over me. But the manuscript flowed out fast and from the heart. Some people loved it. My friend Kevin and his wife told me I should offer people $100.00 at the public library just to read it and tell me what they thought of it (which was Kevin's was of saying he liked it).

The manuscript retained a sort of whimsical undertone which kind of equalized the shock of the contents, one of them being, what happened to Samantha… "Why in God's name was she at her parents' house trying to dig up dead babies!?…Screaming for sixteen hours in the hospital!?…" Some things we can't bear - was the theme of Daniel Goleman's book - and I know from personal experience, such as when I heard a judge tell me he had never seen a case as bad as mine…or hearing my mother tell me I caused her permanent hearing damage because I hit her while I was drunk down in Florida - those thoughts can't come in; something else can, but not them, not yet…

THE PART ABOUT THE SERPENT

But I remember hearing a case on the radio during a lucid break from drinking, some while after Samantha had been incarcerated. A man had gone to the police because his girlfriend had been disclosing bits of information to him concerning incest between her and her father when she was a young girl. Allegedly, the babies that resulted from the pregnancies – her father buried under the front porch of their house. He went to authorities against her wishes and an excavation was performed of the front porch of the house in question, revealing the remains of the babies.

Now, I had to take this in with personal testimony from Samantha and compare it to what I knew, and what others had witnessed: How I was told by Samantha that her mother, on one occasion, had to run to the store in the morning before school to buy paper bowls for the kids to eat breakfast out of, because her father had smashed everything in the house during a drunken rage in the middle of the night... How I remembered coming to work one day in the aftermath of a brawl between the oldest son, and the father who was still trying to bend his glasses back into wearable shape... How I saw the youngest son sucker-punch someone at a dance one night... The testimony from my old roommate explaining to me how spiteful a drunk the father would be when he drank... How my brother told me, after calling him to tell him that the older son shot himself, that he'd seen the guy beating up a girl on the back of the school bus, once... How there were no pictures of Samantha in her parents' house... How Samantha was the whistle-blower of her family, just like my mother

THE PART ABOUT THE SERPENT

was the whistle-blower of her's... How there had been reported criminal sexual child abuse in the family... How Samantha had told me she had gone to her mother to complain to her when the oldest son was sexually molesting her when she was little, but her mother's solution was simply to cut her hair... And if Samantha had in-fact witnessed anything, or knew of anything, she would have been at the wrong house, because I don't think she was at the house she grew up in when she was taken into custody; and although Samantha was mind-boggling smart, it was typical of her to miss the elephant in the living room from time to time because of her hot head...

Nevertheless, I was scared. I took what I wrote, coded as it was, to Grant Parsons. I would not hand it to his secretary, but I did hand it to his brother, Rob, who assured me he would get it to Grant, and we sat down a few minutes while I told him what to expect in it. It came back to me via U.S. mail with the word "issues" written on the title page, with a note:

> "Dear Joe, I do not practice any type of law that can help you. I do wish you well with your doctors and therapists."...

My next drive out to a friends involved a black car following me; I had no phone to tap. I played the car for miles, and led them up M-72, going slower and slower as I climbed the hills...The slower I went, the more they hung back. Just over the crest of a hill, where they couldn't see me, I pulled over to the right and stopped.

THE PART ABOUT THE SERPENT

When they came over the top of the hill and passed, they immediately braked, put their left signal on, but with cars approaching – unable to make a quick turn - they signaled right and pulled over on the side of the road in front of me... Black car sitting right in front of me on the side of a northern Michigan back road... As soon as the line of approaching cars cleared, they made a flashy U-turn and were gone.

I attributed my never being followed again to my diminishing credibility via the social degradation rituals I'd been getting used to at the hands of professionals...

...

Next to be revealed was that contract I made with the devil. That's what this was all about.

Now I was up all night, every night, writing frantically until 6:00AM before I'd chew a tranquilizer. I began praying at the hour of six PM every night through to seven. There was always some kind of threat at that hour – akin to how I used to set the hands of my clocks when I was practicing the occult; little hand on the six, big hand on the nine. Then by six AM, things were so hairy because of the revelations I was making in my writing, I would have to stop.

I took my manuscript to Don Jaquish and read it to him while standing, while he was on the phone trying to get me emergency help. He didn't listen to what the manuscript said, and any reference I made to these people concerning the devil was sought as symptomatic of some kind of illness.

During this time, I had very tactfully told my mother that I didn't want her in my life anymore, before getting into my Jeep and driving away from her home. And never had I felt whole until that day. Never had I begun to experience such breakthroughs, and on all fronts. But then the strangest thing happened! A couple days later, the parents of the little girl my mother was babysitting told me that my mother wanted me to know that her cat was run over by a car! I called her on the phone…she was crying… She then sent me a note in the mail:

"Dear Joe, Thank you for your concern for B.C. (Brat Cat), I know how you cared for her. Please do note that you were not raised to be that way by accident."…

I felt I had to go and emotionally rescue my mother, while that very attempt sprang like a trap on me in that I became more a captive of my mother's than I was before, where I was now made to feel guilty for hurting her with my assertiveness. Now it was, "Maybe you can visit me but I don't know if I can trust you."…

I was in touch with Philip Asplund, who although had tried to deter me from accepting Lyn Conlon's diagnosis, thought that re-admission to the hospital would be beneficial for the sake of rest and nutrition. It would be respite, right?

THE PART ABOUT THE SERPENT

One particular night during my writing, uncertain whether I had accepted Jesus properly or not, I did it again. With Lois Hawley's advice, I then rebuked the devil sharply in the writing, and even extenuated it by cursing him. Then I made arrangements with Rex in the middle of the night to get me to the hospital the next morning. I had tried to call the police in the event they might take me seriously and get me to the hospital, but I was told that I could call an ambulance. And I did not call an ambulance considering where me and Doug used to get our drugs from. I didn't want some stoner rolling an ambulance full of surgical needles and shit, with me in it.

I knew I was going to take a hit, and I had too much going on in my head to drive. On the way to the hospital I told Rex (accustomed to my eccentric language as he was) that before I die, my last meal would be a cucumber because the smell of a cucumber reminds me of summer…and I will be eaten by a pack of wolves – which is what I used to tell my band-mates in my rock and roll days...

I noticed a cross scratched in the wall of the waiting room of the hospital, and I explained to Rex how people who are delusional think that all things they experience refer to them. Now it seemed the cross on the wall was not accidental, but something I was supposed to see, so when they asked me if I was hearing things and seeing things I said matter-of-factly, "Yes!" Rex knew what I was talking about, I'm a deep

THE PART ABOUT THE SERPENT

person, but they of course interpreted it was auditory and visual hallucinations, like they did before.

Moreover, I really didn't care what they thought. I never even cared when people would presume I was gay, because I have been through things in life and the truth always prevails. Furthermore, even if it *was* auditory and visual hallucinations, it was the devil.

Being the onomatologist that I'd been since I was a kid (one who study names), I often explained to Rex how everyone lives up to their given-name. For instance: my mother's, Ruth, which means "companion." My mother's friends were not the high and mighty beautiful people that she probably could have associated with, it was the old woman with cancer next door…the poor old man down the street who's house burned down… the woman who's daughter was run over by the school bus…just like the Ruth of the Bible, and she remained loyal to those people. And so it is with my name, Joseph. Someone told me one time, "I've never met a Joe that wasn't tough." And one of Charles Spurgeon's sermons explains why you don't want to cross a Joseph of the Bible, for he said they have sinews and smiteth hard! I myself have endured terrible things at the hands of cruel people like the Joseph of Genesis, even being sold away by my family, in a figure, because I wasn't supposed to know what they were doing was wrong. Moreover, people have told me (and I have overheard women say) that I would make a good husband. …And this I know, it's in my temperament, and I liken that to the New Testament Joseph.

THE PART ABOUT THE SERPENT

Intake records upon arrival at Munson Medical Center revealed that both my pupils were the same size, which is an impossibility since my open head injury five years earlier, and a preview glimpse of what to expect in the ensuing pages...

Ruth Ann, the admitting nurse, subtly taunted me while Rex sat there observing, "Your name is Joseph? ... and you're a carpenter?"... When she asked me if I had had anything to eat that day, I thought about it before remembering, "I had a half a cucumber."...

They let me sleep till afternoon. That night, I began making huge investigations into the number six (for I had books, and notebooks, and my brain). I prayed at night with a sheet over my head for a prayer shawl, the way the Bible indicates (even owning my own, authentic wool Tallit from Israel, today), however, the nurses made written submissions that my behavior was bizarre...

The room next to me at the end of the hall was vacant. On my second day, while praying on my knees next to my bed in the dark silence of my room, I heard running footsteps coming down the hall. I thought, "no one runs around here! Everyone's on medications and too despondent! Not even the staff has that kind of energy; their not healthy enough!..." It was inappropriate, something wasn't right. The running stopped just outside my door and a female voice yelled back down to the nurses' station in mocking fashion, "Do you want me to set my alarm for SIX O'CLOCK?!" It was like my face burned, and the hair on my back stood up. "They admitted someone under the influence of a team of demons and the devil's gonna have some fun!..." And that's exactly what happened! What's more, there are no alarm clocks on this unit; no one even wants to live, let alone get up for some reason! In fact, an alarm clock would be too disturbing to be allowed on the unit.

And I have to mention, at this time Lyn Conlon was practicing at Petoskey, 67 miles north. This was following the write-ups in the Traverse City Record Eagle. But soon after my arrival, as it was happening, a particular nurse informed me - as she was so distraught - that Dr. Conlon was illegally trespassing on the unit and was going through people's files she had no business going through. It was as if she was crouching down in my room to hide from her...

Mysteriously, Lyn Conlon again became my treating physician at Munson Medical Center during my stay...

Nonetheless, they brought this girl into dinner after we were all served and getting ready to eat, and they sat her down with us. I did not realize it was the girl who shouted outside my door, because she brightened right up and said, "Oh it looks like I'm just in time, should we all say a prayer about Jesus Christ?" In an instant, as gullible as I was, I thought perhaps she was brought in from a church or something, to help, so I said, "Sure, I will!" And as I began to pray aloud she started moaning with her eyes rolling in the back of her head, then all you could see was the whites of her eyes and she started thrashing! They had to drag her away! I shouted indignantly at the nurses - that they could be so ignorant not know the condition of this girl before letting her in there with us like that, to which Ruth Ann stopped and dropped her jaw at me. But it was true, and that was the girl who was given the room next to me.

Now, they chemically restrained this girl, but she would stand like a gatekeeper outside a doorway, like she was passed out, and as I walked passed her I could tell that even though her eyes were closed and she looked out-of-it, she was full of demonic energy that could breach that medication in an instant and explode. And they seemed to threaten to do that. It was like, even though I was looking at closed eyelids – even imagining she was a corpse – I knew her spirits' eyes were fully attentive to me, and in-fact, it was no accident that they were there.

The staff saw that I was terrified of this girl and they did something more bizarre than my praying: They moved me, my room, all my belongings, bed, nightstand, chair, books, everything; a whole recruit of people, even my friend with down-syndrome helped - down to the opposing wing of the unit next to the TV lounge, and exchanged the items of that room back to the room next to the girl. I asked no questions. Nonetheless, one of the nurses told me, "Ya, know Joe, the very first thing they moved was your name from the door....They treated it with importance!" she said, trying to get me to smile, but I wouldn't. I was also told by this particular nurse in a private conversation that it

THE PART ABOUT THE SERPENT

was OK to cry, but which was so out of context to the nature of what we were talking about, that it had surpassed inappropriate to rude, that she might think I was that out of it.

Now the girl spent all her time in the TV lounge (next to my room!). She sat in there at all hours in the silence, sedated. One night during prayers, I read an *Our Daily Bread* passage about Stephen the Martyr who cried, "Lord, lay not this sin to their charge" while being stoned to death before "falling asleep." It reminded me of my brother, Steve, who'd recently had his break lines cut and said he could hear rocks whizzing by his head at work, because he was hired to travel for store closings for a lumber company, and the employees took it personal. And I imagined my brother - remembering how he was almost killed by a bunch of guys that bloodied him up and broke his glasses down in Lake Orion - saying something like that... So long I hadn't cried, but now my heart was broken. As soon as I began to cry the girl in the next room began to growl out and spit. I stopped... As soon as I began to cry again, she began to cough up something and spit out, almost like a growl. I tested it. I've been through this before. I waited for clearance and acknowledged that nothing was happening as long as I waited. I re-read the passage and evoked my emotions. As soon as a tear began to form in my eye, the girl in the next room began to vomit up something and spit. The harder I leaned into the cry, the more vile-sounding and violent she got. I simply got up, put the book down, and found something else to do.

THE PART ABOUT THE SERPENT

I never told a soul until about a year later.

...

New on the unit was a young Christian man who'd had more experience with the dark side that I had, at least as a combatant. As soon as he took in the situation between me and the girl, he spent all his time and energy on her. He absolutely overwhelmed her; I could see her shoulders surrender, she was backing down to him, he was shutting her down, but with love.

On one occasion, he wrote large letters on the dry-erase board in the cafeteria, "KNOW THE FUTURE, GOD WINS!" The girl try to hide her eyes from it, even holding a napkin up to her forehead while she tried to continue to eat. Seeing the distress it was causing her - having made his point with his graffiti - he got back up and erased it. But that is where he and I differed; *I* would have left it up there! But on the other hand, he didn't seem to have any fear of the devil, and he had ten times the power over it I had; while I was terrified out of my wits, and helpless against it. He taught me some valuable things after we re-occupied the TV lounge (with the TV off!) He said to me, "they're wolves, all wolves!"...

Back in the cafeteria, I remember keeping my feet planted flat on the floor in preparation of a wild physical assault. One morning, the girl walked by and said to me - as she swung her tray away to look at my feet - "keep your feet flat on the floor!" and then proceeded to her seat. It was like blacking-out in my mind...I couldn't take it...not with a bunch of professionals who were not only ignorant to their own negligence, but abusive to any thought that might suggest spiritual overtones were dictating these engagements.

Now, I witnessed this staff myself, scared with this girl on the unit, locking themselves in, and locking the nurses'-station door, which was a two-part door, usually left open at the top and unlocked at the bottom, bolted together and locked at all times! And I've seen these nurses at other times - unable to figure things out, suspicious - looking behind open doors... How do they think an unarmed Christian man feels being locked in with a bunch of authoritative women who treat his faith as if it were an illness, opening the door to someone completely under the influence of demonic spirits and giving them the room next to him!?...

The occupational therapist (who I had heard had been to Tibet) tried indirectly getting me to communicate with the girl. Here, they sit every type of person from every type of background and every type of faith - down at the same crowded table and expect them all to work together collectively in a peaceable manner. It is a condensed version of the same kind of abuse you find in the public education system - herding all types of learners, no matter the level, no matter the background, into the same classroom, as equals. And it's the same kind of abuse that results from pantheism - someone assuming all roads lead to the same god – of which individuals make such claims, but on what authority?

It is man's insatiable need to apprehend things (cats, dogs, kids, predicaments, whatever it may be that promises him freedom from feeling inferior), assuming he knows what is best for everything while he himself is under no authority, which in essence, is playing God, even if that means having to wrangling something under him. However, no one can be in authority unless he is under authority. And no one but a hypocrite can preach anything he himself can't practice. We don't take physical fitness advice from couch potatoes; we take it from someone who has the physical resume to back it... We don't go to divorcees and casually dating women for family and marital advice; we go to those who have strong families themselves. Anna Freud, the cocaine-advocating Sigmund Freud's daughter, lived as a celibate wretch her entire life while her most prized and long-term psychoanalytic subject committed suicide in her very own house, Sigmund Freud's old house! You only have to saved once! Carl Jung, Freud's prodigy, was a full-blown spiritist, contacting disembodied spirits as casually as little kids play with teddy bears, and incorporated the encounters as a higher intelligence in his writings!

When I was younger, I was prescribed by allopathic medical doctors a destructive amount of antibiotics for frequent bouts of bronchitis, because what doctors don't tell you is that antibiotics don't just kill the bad bacteria, they kill *all* the bacteria! The result was that my stool has been nearly water my entire life, suffering from severe dehydration, due to the fact I have no good anybodies anywhere to be found in my intestinal tract. And the amazing thing is, that even though Medicine created the problem, Medicine also failed to determine it's pathological origin despite hundreds, maybe thousands of dollars in medical tests – everything from Celiac disease testing (with stool samples) to gastrointestinal specialists... And it takes someone who has actually suffered themselves – forced by the malady to study the symptoms for years and years until they actually nail it. And the prerequisite of such discoveries is becoming acquainted with what health is *supposed* to look like.

Moreover, on one occasion, this particular therapist received a bloody nose for being too pushy with one of the clients in her group.

So, here's the girl, slumped over at the table. The therapist is trying to give us good examples of how to unwind at the end of a hard day or when our nerves are shot. She suggests rubbing some olive oil into our feet, and the girl retorted, "I think I'm gonna' puke." The therapist looked right at me and said brightly, "*That* was clear!" But all I could think was, "Ma'am, I'm sorry, I don't like this game, I want out of here!"...

Now, the nurses are assigned approximately three patients each. It has nothing to do with proximity, it is arranged by the severity of the client's condition and

THE PART ABOUT THE SERPENT

the temperament of the nurse. Now, I've seen on more than one occasion, where all of one nurse's clients begin acting up at the same time. They will all have their emergency call-lights on outside their room while the nurse runs from one hall to the next, sweating it. Everyone else is fine…Then they must have a code for this, because as soon as she admits she is getting overwhelmed, they bring in the big guns. One of the nurses admitted to me how relieved she was to finally ask for help; her face was red, and she was glowing with heat. But they don't understand the spiritual component; that is the devil playing games with them. I tell you, these nurses are craving the medications they are pedaling to their patients!

…

Upon returning home, my neighbors had informed me that there had been <u>men</u> in my apartment, and <u>people</u> going through the mail boxes while I was gone. And that's when I appallingly discovered Grant had sent his copy of my manuscript back to me, and that through the northern Michigan mail system!

And in the event anyone happened to have planted a bug – I gave them 24 hours of Jesus music and deliberately complicated my schedule for a while.

THE PART ABOUT THE SERPENT

This time following treatment, however, I smoked heavier than any man I had ever known. Huge, home-rolled menthol cigarettes; four to six of them just to wake up in the morning. I was still a sporadic runner and I went to the gym on occasion. My dentist and his technicians saw pre-cancerous formation in my mouth due to smoking and told me that even cutting back could reduce it. But that was a threat to my addiction, and I smoked even heavier because I wanted cancer. I hated myself: The false presumptions they made about me at the hospital… My mother… A nurse I trusted, or needed to trust, who I felt certain had feelings for me the way I did her, had also created a stir about me - that she thought I might be stalking her after I had made a desperate and formal pass at her – giving her a copy of *Lacuna*, - now turned love letter, which incited Dr. Conlon to contact Don Jaquish to try to determine if I might be dangerous, apparently with plans to possibly have me picked up. Don told Dr. Conlon that he thought she was making a big mistake, and called me to intervene for them. He told me the day he heard the news – it came to him from three different sources (in a building cross-town) while I still had to face these people for ongoing appointments, knowing the extent of their gossip, trying not to come across as The Lurker!

If I didn't want to die before, now I did.

If I was going to commit suicide, it was not going to be some freak explosion of emotion I couldn't contain; for years I thought I might climb the backside of the biggest hill on the water-side of the Sleeping Bear

THE PART ABOUT THE SERPENT

Dunes my brother and I once scaled while camping out there – with a fifth of whiskey and a bottle of pills. It seemed but a stumble for Janis Joplin, Jimmy Hendrix, Keith Moon, and Bon Scott… I'd simply watch my last sunset and expire next to a large concrete block having spray-painted, "I love my Bro" on it...

My brother talked me into going to a weekend gathering of his support-group friends the following day after I received Don's call, whom he met in an online chat-room, and the entire weekend I slept out in an atrium with their dogs.

My grandma died (the one I stole my Bible from). She was in a nursing home in Roscommon and was catching pneumonias from forgetting to swallow her food. The nursing home's answer; stop feeding her! I remember going to the bereavement room (to pick up my mother after the nursing home said my mother was causing problems) and seeing my grandmother - the poor woman who was beat down in life - starved to death with eyes that looked at you as if she were pleading with you, while we just went along with it as if we didn't notice…"Goodbye Grandma!…Have a nice Easter!"…

My grandmother (who loved people by feeding them when she barely had food enough for herself) lived 11 days deprived of food and water when both were plentifully available.

THE PART ABOUT THE SERPENT

I told myself in the ensuing years that even if I had to go to jail, I would do something different…"Hell, I could have gone and lived with her myself for Chris sake!"… But I wouldn't have, then…

Years later, I met a gentleman who had lived in the bush in Africa. He read books like I did – obtaining them from the bibliographies of other books - and he said his mother was a classical pianist. He told me that in Africa, because their level of survival is so great, their level of joy is that much greater. He said they sing while they work! He said, in this country (speaking of the U.S.) when there are three people and only one has food, the one with food might give a portion to the other two and keep all the rest to himself, and we think that's generous…that's normal. But he said, "In Africa, it doesn't matter who you are or where you come from; if anyone has food it is divided equally."

This gentleman went on to tell me how he would sleep under a tree, and every morning a black woman in a flowing dress with flower prints on it would ritualistically rock a basket of fruit back and forth in her arms before giving it to him while signing out loud. Then he exclaimed, "Can you believe in this country they put their parents out at the end of their life (meaning nursing homes)!" And unfortunately, until he said that, I thought that was normal, too...

The commandment to honor your father and mother is not to try and agree with everything they say or something; that is impossible. Honoring your father and mother in the Bible simply means to take care of your parent's financial needs as they are dying. That is why the Pharisees found a way to get out of it, calling it Corban. For, they said, what they would have given to their fathers and mothers, they gave to the church.

And I can't forget being up from downstate with my mother, when I was still little, stopping in a nursing home to see my uncle Roy. We passed someone in a wheelchair posted toward the front doors as we walked in. We were looking for a big tall man with an exaggerated chin. We looked everywhere, it was getting late and there was no one around. We may have even been planning to head back down state that night and this would be the only time we would get to see him (or he would get to see us, rather). Then as we were pushing our way out the glass doors, I looked back at the wheelchair and noticed a little, feeble old man reaching his hands out toward me. "Mom..." My mother realized it was uncle Roy and when we walked up to him, he uttered, "Jo Jo the Dog Faced Boy!"

...

Next, my cousin Jack died of a drug overdose. Surprisingly, Samantha was at his funeral, but I kept my distance from her. I was still responsible for who I was in the past, but who I was responsible to was now a different story...

THE PART ABOUT THE SERPENT

Then, my Aunt Pat left a most tactless message on my answering machine, that Samantha had died. It too was a drug overdose. Samantha was unrecognizable at the funeral. Her mom kept her back to the casket and diverted my attention to the pictures."That's the Samantha you *used* to know."

Next, my Aunt Pat died, a drug overdose, on her birthday... Samantha's mom and little sister were there. Samantha's mom sat to my right with her daughter to her right. Samantha's little sister had pictures to show me, taken by Samantha, and had questions for me about some of them. Her mom leaned into me, "She doesn't know it yet, but she's angry...she thinks she has to take over Samantha's work." Her sister told me, puzzled, "Samantha took *a lot* of pictures, but all I ever found were the negatives."...

Samantha had also been investigating the death of her brother. According to her older sister, the police had told Samantha it was of no use to anyone to keep the case open for her...

Samantha's younger sister also told me Samantha had gone back to school on a grant, and that her scores were exemplary, in other words. She said, "The mind..." and twiddled her fingertips around her temple area... Her little sister, sometime later, also entertained the possibility of beginning a website featuring Samantha in her glamour, while inquiring if I sold any of my music or my writings. I voiced my disapproval in a letter, for both: that although Samantha may have been

THE PART ABOUT THE SERPENT

very attractive and enviable, for those who actually have to live with having been endowed with such features, to them it is more of a curse. And that I myself had no business being involved in the entertainment industry (her father had even offered to manage my band at 20%, which is exactly the going rate) being that chasing that lifestyle almost killed me. And I have been relieved to see that as of this writing no such photographs of Samantha have hit the internet.

...

At home, after the hospital, I was kneeled down at my bedside with my face to the floor, wrenched in psychosomatic pain for months, begging God – that he perform a miracle or change their minds about me – that they would know the truth about me, or let me die… I knew from reading Karen Horney that I really didn't want to die, I never really did; I wanted to punish myself. My thoughts now while I lay in bed were of the splitting of bone and torn arteries…super painful stuff like sky-dropping through glass…

I would tell myself over and over I wanted to die until it made me feel sick. Then I would tell myself over and over I wanted to die until it made me feel better.

I lost the ability to salivate, and the garbage under my sink became wet-heavy garbage because I had to eat wetter, heavier foods in order to digest it. I remember

THE PART ABOUT THE SERPENT

lying in bed thinking that If I just lay there long enough without eating, without resisting, that whatever it was that wanted me to be that way would just come and ravage me till there wasn't anything left... and seeing that there wasn't anything left to destroy - that there wasn't anything profitable left in it for them - that there was no meat left on my bones – they would simply move on. But it doesn't work that way; I became increasingly aware of every moment my condition worsened.

I vividly remember watching what seemed like the last sunset of another summer wasted in bed, out the cloudy windows of my smoke-filled efficiency...

All along, I was having terrors at night and I sensed that I was still screaming my sleep. It even felt at times that something was trying to get down my throat at night but I couldn't wake up enough to fight it off. It was as spastic as a giant eel. Between its semblance and strength, it reminded me of the silvery color and might of a huge Musky. And sometimes I heard grumblings going on next to my bed while those kinds of things were happening. The harder I tried to force myself up into a wakeful position, the more intense the grumblings got. Then, with a burst of force, I would wake up to a room saturated with the absence my screaming. Any time I would call someone, a crises line, anybody, I would hear the same thing, "You just need to take your pills and go to bed." Or, "You just need to call your therapist", et cetera...

THE PART ABOUT THE SERPENT

As sick as I was, I had made a vow to study harder and improve because I thought perhaps to work at the hospital some day. My music had basically died. The guitar I had, which I purchased new (with a limited lifetime warranty) remained nearly unplayable the entire time I owned it. Every dream I had was a reduction of another... The cost of my books was getting into the hundreds. I disciplined myself and studied several subjects daily, for one hour intervals over the next several years. And I had to enforce the time-limit on each subject because I knew from retrospect that if I didn't, my brain damage would not permit me to stop, and I would be four weeks into a project – writing formal petitions to foreign government officials all night, every night. (And that's not a joke).

I remember telling my mother, to which she nodded, that I told myself if I was going to make it - I was going to have to live, and live very methodically.

I became computer literate, and taught myself to type from workbooks. I studied Susan K. Ferrett's *Peak Performance* which takes case studies of high achievers like Colon Powel and Mary Kay Ash and exemplifies them toward actualizing your goals. Her workbook, I found at a Salvation Army store, years before, and then I ordered the annotated instructor's addition when I needed more. I typed out every question, and then every answer, and formatted all my teachings on old Windows programs. It wasn't Machiavelli or Flavious Josephus, but it was self-improvement nonetheless, and that above any sacrifices any of my accusers were ever willing to make for themselves. Where once I had been a visual guy, I converted all that for words. The used space on my hard drives was all due to text, whereof if we had been using computers the way we were now, in my 20's, it would have been all visual (e.g. guitars and girls).

I learned of a therapy called The Same Way Every Day and I got so good at it that I out-shined any therapist who might have practiced it himself. I got scheduling down to making homemade time schedules that were better than the ones you buy at Staples, and I did the gym three times a week; and I ran three miles, three times a week. I would not allow myself to be late on a payment of any of my bills for a total of 12 years, and if one of them didn't come in the mail on time, I would track it down. I attended over 800 open-speaker and closed - crises meetings and conventions in a seven-year period. I taught myself to write in Hebrew (which, I may add, had no capital lettering or punctuation in Bible times). Between a combination of sleep and nicotine patches I was able to kick nicotine. But I still couldn't keep groceries in the house, I ate only because had to, and I was as hollow a being as Anna Freud...

I collected, one by one, a box set of all of Karen Horney's books; and at one point I set out to read every book M. Scott Peck ever wrote, coming shy of a collection of papers apparently written from his failed attempts at demonic exorcism. Curtis Cummins himself loaned me *The Road Less Traveled* because I saw it in his office. Despite the fact that anything I shared with

THE PART ABOUT THE SERPENT

Curt about Satan or demons was red-flagged as symptomatic, Scott Peck, a natural diagnostician and famous psychiatrist himself, stated that the DSM (Diagnostic & Statistical Manual used by every psychiatrist in the industry to make a psychiatric diagnosis) should include demonic possession.

When I shared with my Christian friends all the reasons why I wanted to write my own book, one of them noticed that writing it for God was not one of the reasons, and when I shared that with Don Jaquish, he said, "Do you really believe that?" Don was also performing EMDR (Rapid Eye Movement Desensitization) therapy on me, using left and right tapping methods, which is a regressed-memory form of hypnosis...

The staying power I had with the Bible - you would think my favorite part of it would be about Jesus being raised from the dead, or David taking down Goliath or something, but no. I kept going back; "the part about the serpent! the part about the serpent!..."
I ordered Malachi Martin's *Hostage to the Devil* and obtained three different transcripts of the Annalise Michal story after watching *The Exorcism of Emily Rose*. And the night I watched *The Exorcism of Emily Rose*, I was at my mother's house, using my brother's DVD player in the basement (where he now lived) when my mother fell with her walker upstairs, breaking her face. Then I recall having my Bible with me at Munson Medical Center when a technician made big eyes at me, then to my Bible, then to me, "Just in case,

huh? ...In case you need to bring in the big guns?!" But I was a fool to let him say that - as if my faith in God was secondary to medical procedures. Not to mention, the trained professionals sent my mother home with a stitch on her chin that night, failing to detect the broken bones in her face.

THE PART ABOUT THE SERPENT

Kindling

MY THOUGHTS HAD LONG TIME BEEN - when passing an old abandoned shack of some kind - specially those made of concrete and were semi-industrially structured likened to those in my poems of castles and queens (or more honestly, resembling the End Motel Room) that maybe I could live *there!*.... Most everything I owned was given to me, and not as charity mind you, but people naturally gave to me because I could never stoop to charge people for stuff; if I have food, you have food. I could not charge people for music I played for them; it was a gift. Nor could I charge for any inspiration I might have given anyone, nor has anyone ever accused me of being lazy; I herniated a disk in my back and the very reason was because of straining, and usually for the benefit of employers.

THE PART ABOUT THE SERPENT

There was a time, now, not so long ago, were all my senses were deleted, where I had no choice but to stay entangled in what I had been trying to disentangle from – just like the day before – just like every body else, but now with an impaired brain. And how it was that the demonic used to respond to me - now my only sight forward was through retrospect: "how did that work out?"… What did I learn?… Was it worse than before? ….Should I try that again?"… As I heard someone say, in other words, "God is in the business of giving: everything He gives freely. But man, on the other hand, is in the business of selling (and *that* what God freely gives!). He gives everyone oxygen freely; you don't have to ask for it. But walk into any hospital and you will pay for every breath."

The guy who had been skinny all his life was now 225 pounds - taking his doctors' advice. I was torpid, a dud, and on the rare occasion I might entertain sex, my semen was brown due to the toxic doses of psychiatric medication prescribed to me by Curtis Cummins. I had eight bottles of morphine stashed in a lock-box in my bedroom I'd inadvertently obtained from my mother's doctors (they asked me to make a sweep of her house during a narcotic overdose) that would serve as my suicide weapon.

I was screaming in my sleep at night. Something was always trying to get down my throat, and there were always two "somethings" arguing in some mumbled language, next to my bed.

THE PART ABOUT THE SERPENT

My bed was constantly soiled with my sheets rolled up in a ball in the middle of the mattress, while I would only allow myself to lie on a sliver of the bed in penitent shame...

Sometimes I was pinned down with all kinds of hands frantically frisking all across my body, while I said, "Jesus Jesus Jesus Jesus…!" in terror, but nothing ever happened... I presumed they would have been afraid of the name. Sometimes they would grab hold of my balls, and once I felt something go up my rectum. Other times, I would be shouting in my sleep while something was prying to get down my throat, "Jesus Christ lives in my heart and there is no room for anything else!" (which is not something I would typically say). Then with one burst of force, I would push myself up into the upright position and my throat would be raw from actually screaming - well aware that the neighbors in my apartment complex were probably listening. And after 10 minutes or so, I could hear my neighbors getting out of bed...

My old teacher had told me when explaining to him the fights between my mother and I, that I was probably fighting her demons. Moreover, her guilt-provoking techniques had become so flagrant in her later years that it was almost impossible to pretend to enjoy her company. For instance, she hired me to renovate her basement to make a money-generating apartment out of it for her. I went by building manuals from the library, therefore some of the codes were dated, such as how high my drill holes across the floor joist ought to be to string coax wire through them. The new code indicated a hole about two inches higher than the old, and the only purpose being – so people are less likely to drill into wire when they're hanging something from the ceiling. But this was getting a drop-ceiling and it would never be bothered. The house my mother purchased had a tremendous shake to it when you walked across the floor, and as it worsened, my mother told me it was because I drilled the holes in the joist too low when I was building her apartment...

I explained the symptoms of my mother's floor to my cousin, who happened to be a magazine-home builder, and asked him if my drilling the holes lower could have had anything to do with it, and I told him it was because my mother was blaming me for the shake in her floor. His forehead tightened up like he was disturbed at the absurdity of it, and shook his head and said, "no!"

Another was, my mother installed (with the help of someone else) a wood burner in the basement, but the flue on it often created a back draft and would smoke the house out now and then when trying to light a fire in it. I used the stove when I stayed there, as did her other tenants. A time came when my mother wanted me to paint her living room, and there was a yellow-dark on the walls around her chair from her chronic smoking. She voluntarily told me it got like that from me smoking the house out when I lived there, trying to use the wood burner...

THE PART ABOUT THE SERPENT

My mother also began telling people she was a widow, as a defense, and she even told some people she was a Christian when asked by Hospice, so she might gain some honor she might otherwise have missed...

My old teacher told me one day after inviting me over and asking me what I'd been studying lately, "Ya know Joe, you could be unrecognizable in 10 years to who you are today; who knows; maybe writing books, traveling the world, and giving lectures. And that doesn't mean I don't like who you are now!" When I tried to share that with my mother in my defense, she said, "Yeah, but does he know about your past?" After a day I called her back on it and asked her, "What does my past have to do with anything?" Then out came, "I just didn't know if he knew what you were dealing with. I didn't know if he knew what you were up against..." Subsequently, our communications seemed to fizzle out and it wasn't long after that she died.

"Who is he who accuses? it is God that justifies."
(Romans 8:33)

...

I could never forgive my mother until after she died. My brother, on the other hand, said she should have done time. Something my brother also told me was that he was told by my mother to beat Dinky when he did strange things when we lived down in Lake Orion. And by no means am I trying to exonerate myself from my own behavior.

I tried to keep in touch with my dad's second wife, who I presumed to be the author of the handwriting that came back with his Christmas gifts, "not at this address." And although I refused to speak even a word to her at my dad's showing (I did not go to his funeral), I had to say to myself, "Now, she was probably very good to my dad, why can't I just forgive her? I am supposed to be a Christian! I'm supposed to be forgiving people!"… I mailed her a Christmas card, to which she responded, and much to my surprise, her handwriting was nothing even close to the handwriting I remembered seeing on the returned packages. After sending a subsequent card on Christmas, however, her daughter contacted me to inform me that her mom had died.

Apparently, my unknown stepsister's daughter lost her father before she was a year old…my father (a genius in mechanics) promised her that he would build her a go-cart one day and lived up to his promise, even hand-painting the roll bars… And this concurs with a mini-bike frame I paid $20 bucks for as a kid – putting it on my Dad's van after asking him if he could put an engine in it. He did; though I didn't realize that meant he'd have to machine every part, count every sprocket tooth and align them with a proper chain, provide breaks, design a chain-guard, everything; but he did it. And I realize most divorced fathers would never do that for their kids...

THE PART ABOUT THE SERPENT

My Bible studies had become normal, meaning, you tend to lose the need to identify yourself by your endeavors after you've been at them awhile, and you're strength and confidence in them no longer depends on what other people think. I hosted weekly Bible studies at my home, and there came a point when it became easier to tell people all the churches I *hadn't* gone to in the area, than all I had.

The people I studied with were all strong family men in their 60's and 70's, had run their own churches, and studied the Word - sometimes 12 hours a day, and some studying the Word with the sole intention of teaching it. Looking back, all my acquaintances were in their 60's and 70's through my 30's and 40's, as is that discrepancy today. I ordered my own study books, sometimes 12 workbooks in an order, and I actually sat down and systematically did the work while everyone else was dreaming in front of the television, similar to the same way I learned to front a rock band by practicing every night while everyone else was dreaming in front of the television...

I studied the raw Bible, and 10 very specific ministries. In the throws of a particular issue – I once found myself surrounded with 11 open study books when returning from a bathroom break in the wee hours of the morning, and I loved it.

What needed to change was my priorities. The top drawer of my file cabinet next to my desk held all my business files: insurance papers, bank statements, bill copies, income reports, et cetera; all labeled, beautify filed, and taking all the respect. While the bottom drawer held my bible notes, my study notes, written prophecies, my own print jobs and original stories I had mailed out to publishers, and photographs, but which got the least respect. Then one day I switched them. I then starting setting the phone to a greeting when I was at my desk, working, and then that same file cabinet became top-heavy; loaded with all good, creative life-giving material in the top drawer, even fun to open and look at, while the bottom drawer had all the crap files in it such as lease contracts and insurance policies, and I still pull old garbage out of my bottom drawers for scrap printing jobs.

Standing alone in my apartment one day – the threat of my mother now gone - I heard a non-audible impression,

"Joe, if you feel you are strong enough, there *are* some things we need to take a look at."

I was scared. "What about all the horrible things I've done?…What do I have to do?" I rifled through the phone book… I talked to one of my Bible-study partners… In three days I was sitting before a group of deliverance ministers and prophets at Pine Grove Church of God, in Traverse City Michigan - a Pentecostal church. Julia Hoard, the pastor's wife told me, "Now Joe, appointments like this just don't happen, the Holy Spirit is telling you it's time." I said, "I know, I can tell" and I lowered my head. I was scared to death.

THE PART ABOUT THE SERPENT

Present was Lisa Duga and a woman they call Pastor Betty. Lisa and another, Elder Leslie, had gone through the same demonic attacks as me (they call them night visits). Leslie herself was a full-blown case of demonic possession in which they had to perform an exorcism. Lisa used to get bruises - she still does when it happens - and apparently that is not uncommon for girls. Julia told me, "Now, when you stick with us through this process, you are going to come out the other side of this unrecognizable. Your friends are going to know it. Your family is going to know it. Your doctors and therapists are going to know it. Everybody who knows you will know it. Even people who don't know you are going to know it! ...The last piece will be the medication, when you are certain you can walk out these doors and handle the situation anytime, anywhere."

Pastor Marc wanted me to make a list of all the demonic involvement I had in the past and bring it with me next visit. He also wanted me to make a list of all the people who had ever offended me, because it was time to forgive them.

My Dad's brother and his wife (my Aunt Cindy and Uncle Jim), had taken me to a Christian prophesying back in 2004, but I resisted the entire thing. For one, it was weird. At least that's what I was saying to God while standing up in front of everyone, with all kinds of different hands on me, speaking things I couldn't decipher. There was a woman there too - a cancer survivor - who played the tambourine so ecstatically, she would remove herself into a corner to shout, shaking the tambourine so violently with no bra on that her boobs were nearly jumping out of her shirt. This woman also asked my Uncle - who was standing to my left - if she could give him a prophecy that night before we left. She asked him if he had anything to do with fish...that she sees a vision of teeming fish... And it so happens to be that my Uncle was a sort of an aquatics expert; even being hired by an aquatics museum in the area, and fishing had been his life-long passion. They also gave to me nine written prophecies, all of which came true...

My Aunt hadn't taken into account that I might have been a serious Bible student. From the time I was a little boy to the time I was an adult we never saw each other. Their Christianity is the commercial Christianity; the God that's on TV. So she sent me some more invitations to her church along with some study materials that were loaded with non-scriptural mind-over-matter techniques, Health & Wealth gospel, and entertainment-oriented worship; all presented by women (who are not permitted scripturally to hold an office in the church {Exodus 28:41, 29:9} or usurping authority over a man {1 Timothy 2:12}). And being that my Aunt is a schoolteacher herself, she must have presumed I'd be game for anything...

The 13th chapter of Deuteronomy is very clear in that instance:

THE PART ABOUT THE SERPENT

> "If there arise among you a prophet, or a dreamer of dreams, and giveth thee a sign or a wonder, and the sign or wonder come to pass, whereof he spake unto thee, saying, 'Let us go after other gods, which thou hast not known, and let us serve them'; thou shalt not hearken unto the words of that prophet, or that dreamer of dreams: for the Lord your God proveth you, to know whether ye love the Lord your God with all your heart and with all your soul...That prophet, or that dreamer of dreams, shall be put to death; because he hath spoken to turn *you* away from the Lord your God...thou shalt put the evil away from the midst of thee"
> (Deuteronomy 13:1 – 3, 5)

So the order is precisely prescribed: If what they say to you comes true, and *then* they come to you asking you to follow other gods, get rid of them. This was congruent with other things I knew were going on at my Aunt and Uncle's church, such as "territorial mapping" which is a non-scriptural prayer-assault against demons of a particular region to bring more money into an area. It's the same as Lois Hawley's drawing-a-line-around-you-and-commanding-Satan-not-to-cross-it technique, but on a larger scale. Plus my uncle informed me of the miraculous healing of a young man who had internal bleeding, but when doctors went in to find it, they could not - attributing the miracle to those who laid hands on him and prayed for him before his surgery. Needless to say, every health and wellness-report of my Aunt and Uncle and their family was catastrophic and indicative that their faith was not working. If God were healing them so wonderfully, than why did they need to repeat unscriptural daily mantras borrowed from the occult world such as,

"The healing virtue of God is in my body and every day and in every way I am getting stronger and better!"?

I met with the Deliverance team at Pine Grove three times a week. What they would teach me – I would take home and practice on my own time, in my own way. Julia, a former psychiatric nurse herself, told me, "You being dragged through the hospital and being given the diagnosis of schizophrenia; Satan was just having some fun with you." The team asked me if there was anyone in particular I had any difficulty in forgiving, and I told them, "Dr. Conlon." I told them that she had a private practice called Wellspring Psychiatry, and that anytime I saw the word wellspring in the Bible, I got sick to my stomach… I told them about Rachel…I told them Dr. Conlon was abusing my friends… And I told them, "It seemed like Dr. Conlon and my mother were on the same team!" Julia consoled, "Now, I have worked in the ER along side Dr. Conlon, and have observed her… and I can *guarantee* you that *her* wellspring does not come from the Bible!…Just so you know, Joe, Dr. Conlon comes from the same place your mom did…she doesn't hate *you*, but she hates the Holy Spirit living in you…you will come to recognize her for her hurts and traumas…"

I knew it *all* along…

THE PART ABOUT THE SERPENT

Philip Asplund noticed; "Joseph, you look like you're ten years younger!...the first thing I noticed was the weight!" (I was back down my old thin self). Years before, Philip had introduced me to a pastor he knew by telling him, "...this is my friend Joseph; he's been through the mill and he's come thought it!" To which the pastor replied, "I know, I can see it in his eyes." Philip then told him, "When I first met Joseph, I asked God to help him, and God replied and told me, 'why don't *you* help him!' Now Joseph is helping *me*!"

Now Philip said to me, "Joseph, I think your wisdom has surpassed your doctors and therapists, maybe even that of your teachers!"

Then Philip invited me over one day. (It was probably 2009). "Joseph, I didn't want to show you this, but..." He had saved an article on Dr. Conlon. Philip was ministering to a client by the name of Christopher Morden via the jail ministry but died in 2002 while on medications administered by Dr. Conlon. Funny, I met Philip while I was in jail, too, following Dr. Conlon's treatment. I even remember meeting with Dr. Conlon for follow-up upon release and mentioning to her, against what would be considered ethical, that an old man (a Catholic) she had being treating in the hospital, who was now in jail, was doing terrible...

And it wasn't many days following my jail release - I was taken back to the hospital...

"Wherefore by their fruits ye shall know them."

THE PART ABOUT THE SERPENT

Apparently, me and Christopher Morden were both young men who were in Jail around the same time. We were both desperately seeking Christ as an answer to whatever it was that brought us to that place (and I can speak on Christopher's behalf in the desperation sense, because that's exactly what it took to resist the ridicule of the other inmates to go to a Christian group in the jail). But our faith-pursuits were intercepted by the sentimentalities of Philip Asplund, who never took the Bible serious enough to recognize false teaching (i.e. Christianized psychology, Lois Hawley's non-biblical antagonisms toward demonic spirits, involuntary speaking in tongues, et cetera), and both of us were being medicated by Dr. Conlon.

It works like this: Biblically, spirit is like wind. Anyone who has a sin-door open (which includes all non-saved people) are not only susceptible to being influenced by a demonic spirit at any given moment, but the greater the spiritual traffic through that sin-door – the more that path is beaten down and widened by demonic entities (thoughts being evidence of them) - the greater susceptibility that individual has to being used like a piece of meat.

> "I am the way, the truth and the life: no man cometh unto the Father, but by me."
> (John 14:6)

I saw this in the hospital. That is why I told Dr. Conlon, "I think the devil has been using weak people to try and crush me." Because that's all he *can* use. Given, many people have a "form of godliness" (2 Timothy 3:5) and may not appear weak or morally undisciplined, but what may appear to be a strength in some individuals is simply a better disguise. Someone sporting the disguise of a caring professional is less likely to jump out of nowhere to stick you with a shank than the streetwalker who's just got picked up. The difference is, the streetwalker's simply got less to lose. A "caring professional" cannot let hatred toward God or another human being be found out; it will be done subtly...

The late Dave Hunt of the Berean Call said this concerning the mind/brain connection:

"...So we began to realize that we have ideas that are not the result of some stimulus around. They are innate within man and you can't explain them physically. So, we realize that there is a ghost in the machine. Your brain is not running the show, you are running your brain. Now what happened in the drug movement, in an altered state of consciousness, (I often quote Sir John Eccles, Nobel Prize winner for his research on the brain) in an altered state of consciousness the normal connection between you, that is your spirit, and your brain is loosened and that allows another spirit to interpose itself and begin to tick off the neurons in the brain and create an entire universe of illusion."
– Courtesy of the Berean Call.

THE PART ABOUT THE SERPENT

This, I found in a 247 page (double spaced) deposition given by Lyn Conlon in the aftermath of Christopher Morden's death, posted online by the psychiatrist watch-group Psychrights. No commentary accompanied the submission:

"...On occasion they (human beings) can be medicated to the point and cross over to where they are much more voluntarily compliant with taking their medications on a regular basis." – Dr. Lyn Conlon (Parenthesis mine) - Courtesy of Psychrights

Recall if you will the crux of the Hippocratic oath - that no physician will prescribe such medicines as they would not prescribe themselves…at least that's the essence of the word hypocrisy. If you can't practice it, don't preach it. And if that's not the case, find another word for your oath! Now imagine taking a humanly concocted poison that your body and spirit vehemently rejects, only to have it forced on you till you can't tell whether you like it or not. And even if you still don't like it, you're still gonna get it...

One of the drugs Dr. Conlon was administering to both me and Christopher Morden was the drug Risperdal. One of the main ingredients in Risperdal is fluoride, same as many of your psychotropic drugs. Fluoride is a neuro-toxin which used to be used to kill coyotes, and was used by Hitler in the concentration camps to make his victims more docile:

THE PART ABOUT THE SERPENT

"The first occurrence of fluoridated drinking water on Earth was found in Germany's Nazi prison camps. The Gestapo had little concern about fluoride`s supposed effect on children`s teeth; their alleged reason for mass-medicating water with sodium fluoride was to sterilize humans and force the people in their concentration camps into calm submission. (Ref. book: "The Crime and Punishment of I.G. Farben" by Joseph Borkin.)" - Courtesy of: American Patriot Friends Network http://www.apfn.org

Now we'll take things one step deeper to look at the spiritual connotation of the original Hippocratic oath translated from Greek:

"I swear by Apollo the physician, and Aesculapius, and Hygieia and Panacea and all the gods and goddesses as my witnesses, that, according to my ability and judgement, I will keep this Oath and this contract:

"To hold him who taught me this art equally dear to me as my parents, to be a partner in life with him, and to fulfill his needs when required; to look upon his offspring as equals to my own siblings, and to teach them this art, if they shall wish to learn it, without fee or contract; and that by the set rules, lectures, and every other mode of instruction, I will impart a knowledge of the art to my own sons, and those of my teachers, and to students bound by this contract and having sworn this Oath to the law of medicine, but to no others.

THE PART ABOUT THE SERPENT

"I will use those dietary regimens which will benefit my patients according to my greatest ability and judgement, and I will do no harm or injustice to them.

"I will not give a lethal drug to anyone if I am asked, nor will I advise such a plan; and similarly I will not give a woman a pessary to cause an abortion.

"In purity and according to divine law will I carry out my life and my art.

"I will not use the knife, even upon those suffering from stones, but I will leave this to those who are trained in this craft.

"Into whatever homes I go, I will enter them for the benefit of the sick, avoiding any voluntary act of impropriety or corruption, including the seduction of women or men, whether they are free men or slaves.

"Whatever I see or hear in the lives of my patients, whether in connection with my professional practice or not, which ought not to be spoken of outside, I will keep secret, as considering all such things to be private.

"So long as I maintain this Oath faithfully and without corruption, may it be granted to me to partake of life fully and the practice of my art, gaining the respect of all men for all time. However, should I transgress this Oath and violate it, may the opposite be my fate."

THE PART ABOUT THE SERPENT

- Translated by Michael North, National Library of Medicine, 2002. Courtesy of: U.S. Library of Medicine.

For many years I hid the fact that I let so many people take me for such a fool, even from myself. I still have files on my prayer list from that time – I would simply brush aside when I saw them in years to come – consisting of 140 + people and every staff member that worked at Center One during that time were on it, including every patient. But through the Bible I could see in words what was happening:

"Every day they wrest my words..." (Psalm 56:5)

"False witnesses did rise up; they laid to my charge *things* I knew not. They rewarded me evil for good *to* the spoiling of my soul. But as for me, when they were sick, my clothing *was* sackcloth...I behaved myself as though *he had been* my friend *or* brother: I bowed down heavily, as one that mourneth *for his* mother.

"But in mine adversity they rejoiced, and gathered themselves together: yea, the abjects gathered themselves together against me, and I knew it not...with hypocritical mockers in feasts, they gnashed upon me with their teeth..."
(excerpted from Psalm 35)

THE PART ABOUT THE SERPENT

And:

"For my love they are my adversaries, because I follow good…they rewarded me evil for good…then I gave back that which I took not away…"

And further:

"Woe unto them who call good evil and evil good! Who put darkness for light and light for darkness!…"
(Isaiah 5:20)

…

I remember telling one of the nurses upon my arrival to the hospital, which was just following my self-deliverance attempt (which had been sabotaged by Lois Hawley's dangerous advice and returning to rescue my mother after finally breaking free from her), that Myasthenia Gravis (muscle grave), Asthma, and Lacuna (void) were all Latin. And I tapped my index finger to my temple with a raised eyebrow… Medical records revealed that this particular nurse quoted me exactly in her notes…

Ten years later, during deliverance, I drove out the other side of the lake where my mother used to live, with my guitar, to revisit the very place I had first made my commitment to God just prior to my involvement with jail and the hospital. I found something at that time someone had written which spoke to my particular situation. I cannot recall the source, and can only paraphrase:

"'Sometimes when people are younger the devil tries to get them between a rock and a hard place – a place of desperation where he might press them to make oaths of some kind which might vindicate them of their predicament. Later in life, having then forgotten all about the oaths, if they happen to take the call to become Christians, strange things suddenly begin to happen to them because the devil is trying to exact revenge for the pledge that was broken.'"

This is what was spoken by the prophet Isaiah:

"How art thou fallen from heaven, O Lucifer, son of the morning! *how* art thou cut down to the ground which didst weaken the nations! For thou hast said in thine heart, 'I will ascend into heaven, I will exalt my throne above the stars (angels/ministers) of God: I will sit also upon the mount of the congregation, in the sides of the north: I will ascend above the heights of the clouds; I will be like the most high…" (Isaiah 14: 12-14)

This vow Satan said before he fell. Eve was next. Now he is bent on getting people to fall exactly the way he did. That is why the Bible not only forbids oaths of any kind, but James, a brother of Jeshua, said anything above yes or no comes from the devil. But Lucifer doesn't quite get us to fall exactly the same way he did; he presses our face in the dirt to get us to make oaths like some kind of mercy game whereas Lucifer

THE PART ABOUT THE SERPENT

apparently had everything going for him before he fell…

I'll never forget driving away from that lake-scene that day, taking in all the abuse I had gone through since the day I knelt down by the water there, and I was sobbing and wailing and then staring back at the place, and then sobbing and wailing and then staring back at the place…I have never been so violated and I have never been so vindicated. It was the same kind of cry I cried after being kidnapped and entrapped by the bigger kids down in Lake Orion (which was years in the making) when I finally made it home and told my mother...

…

Back in deliverance, Marc Hoard had to challenge me: "You're a quick study… you know demonology, and brain chemistry, and everything…you know more than the doctors do…but you sell yourself short!"

Funny, just months before, I couldn't bare to get out of bed, while I was passive and neutral to everyone in my world, who were in turn, passive and neutral toward me. Now I was firing out of bed in the morning and hitting the dirt trails and hills while blind in one eye with double vision, running on sprained ankles - and it seems the moment that all started, the moment hope revived - everyone in my world began to hate me! Pastor Marc also told me that I would be breaking off all my dysfunctional relationships, only I was in denial that meant just about everyone I knew.

I told the Deliverance team at Pine Grove, "I don't know if this has anything to do with deliverance or not, but when I was a kid, me and my friends used to huff ether, and when I did ether I would be <u>ushered</u> into the presence of the devil!" Julia nodded emphatically, "*We* know what *that* is!" Julia was referring to the Spirit of Python (pharmakeia in Greek). They refer to the most prominent passage of the Bible on it, Acts 16:16, known as a spirit of divination. Then I had to educate myself on what that Python spirit was all about. I remembered Julia had also said, "the devil's not a very creative guy, so he works in patterns..." Now I recognized the pattern of the Python Spirit in that every time I had set a goal, as I described earlier, the new goal would be a reduction of the first, and so on and so on till I couldn't even get myself out of bed anymore... That's exactly how that thing works! It is thoughts, it is suggestions, it is defeating words spoken by the Spirit of Python through your inner dialogues and the sin-door of your acquaintances.

The Spirit of Python (or it's name) originated from Delphi, in Greece. In mythology, Apollo is said to have slain the Python at Mount Parnassus. According to tradition, a certain shepherd boy is said to have noticed that his goats acted strange around the site and he himself began to say things that would come true. The site was known as the Oracle of Delphi. It is where all your Latin medical terminology comes from. A shrine

THE PART ABOUT THE SERPENT

was constructed over a fissure in the rock which emanated intoxicating fumes (thought to be the stench of the slain Python) where a virgin priestess, known as the Pithia, would sit and give prophecy. The Pithia also smoked laurel leaves to enhance her connection to the demonic spirit-world (thought to be Apollo), and at times she became too intoxicated to speak sensibly - the magi would form their questions to a yes/no format which is where we get the ouiji board from, today.

The Oracle of Delphi became the hub of celestial knowledge; even emperors came seeking military intelligence, but most especially, people came seeking answers to their physical infirmities. The entire area became a sort of health-spa resort and at least one of the churches Jeshua rebuked in the book of Revelation was an offshoot of that.

So now I understood why I was so attracted to the Swan Song record label emblem which depicted Apollo with wings leaping into the sky. I used to draw it for all my friends during high school. You saw it on Led Zeppelin and Bad Company albums. Apollo was the very god of music and it is said that he had a chariot pulled by swans. And on the other hand, he was the god or a god of medicine. I was attracted to both.

So here, my mother who grew up so poor as to be too embarrassed to have anyone come over, but always spoke of how impressed she was by being invited in to a doctor's house in her neighborhood, wound up marrying my father who was a medic in the military, whose mother wanted him to become a surgeon, and whose father was a pharmacist, and wound up at the end of her life destitute and sick – having taken all her doctors' advice – dying at 66, ingesting and injecting both, about $2,000 dollars of prescription medicine a day ("But you don't have to worry we'll just bill your insurance!") all of which accelerated her death. Any accidents?...

One of the words to describe Python in Greek is "portal." The drugs act as a doorway for the demonic. Am I saying that everyone who takes a prescribed medication will be taken under by demons, of course not. The damsel in Acts 16:16 was probably deliberately ingesting something to see in the demonic. But keep in mind it is a spirit. And when your faith leads stronger and stronger into medicinal arts which have their roots in the occult, you should expect to be in grave danger.

"Cursed is the man who trusts in man...blessed is he whose hope in the Lord."

"...yet in his disease he sought not the Lord, but to the physicians. And Asa slept with his fathers, and died in the one and fortieth year of his reign."
(II Chronicles 16:12,13)

"And it came to pass, as we went to prayer, a certain damsel possessed with a spirit of divination [Python/Pharmakeia] met us, which brought her masters much gain by soothsaying:...." (Acts 16:16)

THE PART ABOUT THE SERPENT

"Consider the work of God: for who can make *that* straight which He hath made crooked?"
(Ecclesiastes 7:13)

Of recent, Delphi has been more carefully researched. Images from space now reveal two fissures crossing exactly at the point where the shrine of the Oracle of Delphi was located. The gas has been identified as ethylene...

Pastor Marc related to the deliverance team that there was a "generational piece", meaning, he knew my family had been under a curse.

These were, in a figure, the very things I only knew spiritually, but was trying to tell that nurse back in the hospital. I was convinced people practicing medicine and the mind were sharp and into these things...

So I spent the next several months - focusing as an exercise - on where particular pieces of knowledge come from. Informational Pathology. "Does this come from the bad well, or does this come from the good well?" Those are the kinds of things I will be teaching my kids to look for in their studies. I noticed a coffee-table book that Philip Asplund had recently given me, denoting a dove on the cover (supposedly the Holy Spirit) but was full of eastern mysticisms all wrapped up in fancy, swirling, sorceric designs. And every several pages would be a single line from Jesus - no artwork accompanying. The book was subtly mocking the words of Jesus, showing them to be cold and harsh, while the mysticisms were far more warm and easy to accept. And that is how I started seeing truth from lies. Lies have to dress themselves up - they have to sound rhetorical and doctrinaire. Like a sick fetus - my teacher once explained to me – it has to be given all sorts of special attention, and when it's born it has to be incubated and protected, whereas a healthy one never does; only lies have to be protected, never the truth.

And I knew this through art. Art is vain and puffed up; it says, "What do you think of me?" "How do you like me?" and if it doesn't get the attention it expects, it changes accordingly. Truth does not change.

Now, Julia Hoard told me that my testimony will speak to a particular type of person, and that became another reason that this book had to be written.

I also found that night visits were not that unheard of. A young lady practicing eastern spirituality at my gym had heard my testimony and proclaimed to me that she had a similar experience being pinned to the ceiling in her bedroom where she wound up with bruises from it but no one believed her. She said, "But I *knew* it was a demon!" The nights my grandmother lie in bed shouting, "Stop it!...Get away from me!" I am certain she was experiencing demonic attacks.

I was taught that one of the ways demons get in is through physical objects and made a witch hunt of my apartment, for months. Piled on the carpet in the corner of my living room was an estimated $2,000 of books and music headed for the dumpster, including a wall sized print of Michelangelo's Creation of Adam I so fondly adored. These were all new books, book series; the music I'd been hunting since I was a kid, and I knew the estimated value of it all by my renter's insurance application which my brother ridiculed me over because I was so anal about everything. Plus my brother always judged me that I was too good to go to the library to get books. But what my brother didn't understand was that I didn't have the luxury of taking things for granted - my education being one of them - and I didn't read books because I was bored. Not to mention, I employed the libraries more than anyone I ever knew, even handling the reference books and medical journals, and setting up one-on-ones with the librarians to familiarize me with the current colleague systems, and to show me where everything was. I checked out the *Scarlet Letter* (which I read to help enrich my vocabulary) so many times that the library was getting hot with me until I stepped up and told them I was reading it with brain damage. And still having to buy my own copy of the *Scarlet Letter,* it was two years altogether before I finished reading it; looking up words, absorbing what was being said; even having to dissect some of Hawthorne's sentences - one of them being 149 words - and then having to piece it all back together to make sense of it. And before finishing the first few chapters of the *Scarlet Letter,* I knew more about Nathaniel Hawthorne, the man, than if I had read his biography; what he looked like, things his wife had said, who his contemporaries were, and where he was gleaning his ideas from. And it wasn't from watching television!

I have six library cards in my wallet at present (and a copy of *Pioneer Girl; The Annotated Autobiography* and *These Happy Golden Years* by Laura Ingalls Wilder out on reserve), shy of one from a campus in Oregon, because having made arrangements with administrations to utilize one of their meeting rooms and to haul my gear in with their dolly, they'd failed to inform one of the front desk clerks who thought it his duty to interrogate me and inspect my totes (for a bomb, I suppose) to impress his colleague, so I clipped that one.

Of the books of mine headed for the dumpster were M. Scott Peck's works because what he was teaching was also a form of pantheism - using catchy terms such as "psycho-spiritual" - mingling psychology (science falsely so called [1 Timothy 6:20]) and religion, and the guy didn't know if God was a he or she! He was offering the road less traveled as a concept for his book that would be an alternative path to God, couched in Biblical-sounding language, but the Bible is clear again,

"Enter ye in at the straight gate: for wide *is* the gate, and broad *is* the way, that leadeth unto destruction, and many there be which go thereat; Because straight *is* the gate, and narrow *is* the way, which leadeth unto life, and few there be that find it." (Matthew 7:13-14)

THE PART ABOUT THE SERPENT

Remember,

> "...no man cometh to the Father, buy by me."
> (John 14:6)

And keep in mind that no alternative religion refers to their god as a father...

One of my Bible Study partners loaned me a book, *Vine's Expository Teaching of the Bible,* which she told me was compulsory reading in her formal Bible school, but because it was not exhaustive and could not answer even one question I could think of, I gave it back to her, which may have hurt her feelings. To me, it was a brochure on how to understand the Bible, just a brochure. It was simply incomplete. And I realized around that time that I could not just passively allow information into my mind without critically analyzing everything. And that was another reason I could not waste my time watching television, or give all my attention to external stimuli; I choose not to. I had to shield myself from the nonsense and enforce that as a way of life. I *was* impressed to discover, however, how my *Strong's Exhaustive Concordance of the Bible* took 40 years to complete...

I also learned how my brother's voice, which constantly belittled me because I didn't have a formal education - a man who did little more than watch cartoons in life - was from the Python Spirit. And I told myself (and the people I was teaching) I would much rather have a non-formal education and be able do something with it than have a formal education and piss it all away.

One particular demonic spirit, the one that had provoked me to take aggression out on myself, I called the Masochistic Spirit. Although the deliverance team cautioned me not to provoke the devil, when I revealed to my old teacher that I had actually been having physical encounters in the night with demons, he became indignant and told me to curse at them. The Masochistic Spirit I hated so bad I did curse, and still curse, and he doesn't come around anymore.

And it was like the next day my eight bottles of Morphine went down the toilet...

...

"Night visits" didn't only happen at night, they would happen just laying down in the afternoon. Just about the time you are ready to fall asleep and then, "party time!" One day, I could sense that the demons were getting ready to pounce. It was as if my fear was the antagonist – whether or not they would do it, and exactly when. So I said, "Go ahead, do it!" and they did. And while they were doing it, I said, "I'm not afraid of you. The more you do this the stronger I get." Then a few days later, when the same situation presented itself, I told them, "Don't even try it!" And they backed off...

I told Julia that saying the name Jesus repeatedly had no effect on the demons, but early on I would say, "I love you" repeatedly and they would all go soft. She told me that was because that was authoritative and they have to obey.

My music was coming back; I actually took my guitar in to have it serviced properly, and I bought myself a new twelve-string, and stands for them both. I told people; "four guitars, a grand piano, and a brunette, and I'm good!"... During that time, a few unlikely people contacted me. They were old friends and acquaintances, like my brother's old best friend, John, now suicidal, and apparently needing me. Packing up and driving 90 miles south to make sure John didn't take a gun to his head, I had a very pure and strong night visit on his couch while I was there. The demons, when certain my Christianity was making more of an influence upon John than his dark philosophies were upon me, were in essence saying, "GET OUT!" John, the following day was even puzzled that his dog had been barking the entire night. And anytime I had looked out at his dog, his dog's eyes had been fixed into the widows of the house. Remember, John used to be an ether-huffing partner of mine back when I saw shapes coming out of his speakers. Plus John had been like a music coach to me - generously sharing his guitar playing methods and furnishing me with instruments and miscellaneous gear at no charge; stuff no amount of money could ever touch...

Another was a roommate of my mother's. A sexy brunette who probably helped shape my taste in women, and suddenly we were having deep conversation in my living room; the first common denominator being ether again. She had been administered ether as a child from the dentist; and whether it was true or not, she told me that she herself had had night visits. The second common denominator: neither she nor John could keep from betraying their hatred toward the God of the Bible, and that same belittling spirit...

See, pythons can't see very good so they sound out with their tongue; similar to how they do in the natural. They probe and ask questions and when they hear you say something that might be sensitive to you, they lock on. Maybe not just yet, but they heard the sensitivity, and they'll remember it for future humiliations. You could test it, actually, if you were good enough a lair to fool demons. You might say to someone suspect of condescending to you, "Those days are over" regarding some insecurity you were at the same time conspicuously trying to conceal. Give them time, let that topic come round near the fire again, and should they strike that sensitive area in an ill-promoting way, you've got yourself a Python!

One of the definitions of discernment I remember learning in an in-home fellowship was:

THE PART ABOUT THE SERPENT

> "Distinguishing between that which promotes health and that which promotes illness."

Now I started getting good at profiling the python type. One in particular was at an in-home Bible Study. The pastor had already unwittingly betrayed himself to me with what the Bible refers to as "accursed" because he'd mentioned a particular author when I explained to the group my struggles with deliverance. I had attended a seminar of that particular author in the past, which said church had sponsored, later to discover he was using Biblical-sounding inner-healing techniques borrowed from the occult world, strictly forbidden by the Bible.

> "For there shall arise false Christs, and false prophets, and shall shew signs and wonders…Wherefore if they say unto you *he is* in the secret chambers; believe it not." (excerpted from Matthew 24)

> "But though we, or an angel from heaven, preach any other gospel unto you than that which we have preached unto you, let him be accursed." (Galatians 1:8)

But one particular young lady that night, a medical oddity like my mother; overweight, disabled, victim mentality - taking up the breadth of the couch - announced to the rest of the group during this prayer request session that her prayer was for me. That sympathetic reaching out was something the devil knew I could not be cold to, not at that time, and I wound up wasting all my time speaking with her after the group, rather than with the people I really wanted to speak with.

The devil, through that Python Spirit (and here was another individual whose core faith was given to medicine) played on my sympathies; the devil himself knowing that I would even pray for those I'd rather not before those I wanted to as a long-term disciple of mine. It was the same spirit as my mother...

One thing I observed studying real Pythons is that they are very, very long and have the same pattern again and again and again so that sometimes when you are looking at them you might not know if you are looking at a portion nearer the end or the middle or the beginning. I also learned that one of the physical symptoms of people under demonic attack from the Python Spirit is that their mouths will suddenly tighten shut when trying to speak...

Now, the deliverance team gave me their best answers as to why my brother's treatment toward me mimicked that of my mother's. They say it was learned. But he seemed to have picked up where my mother left off when she died to subtly treat me pathetically; the intention I might follow suit and become it, or remain it. It is an apprehending game - a perpetrator casting parameters upon a victim with the designs he will not rebel - and confine himself within the likeness and

THE PART ABOUT THE SERPENT

image perpetrated upon him, which sometimes comes disguised as a favor. If the victim can prove to the perpetrator that he won't rock the boat, he might also get strokes as a reward. As time goes on, and the resistance of the victim wears down, his dilemma is, that should he resist the increase in disparaging remarks at this point, not only does he face the threat of not getting the strokes (he doesn't want anyway), but he also knows he will face the punishment of an increase in insults.

In the case of serial killer, Ed Kemper, the victim goes from being portrayed as someone creepy and potentially dangerous (initiated by his mother in this case), to not only becoming creepy and dangerous, but even doing so out of spite, and will transpose his own name with the perceived label given him by his accusers to spare them from having to!

Napoleon Bonaparte said that men are what you want them to be...

It is a control game, and I noticed the closer the victim of this game gets to freedom, the more irrational the perpetrator will become. Their behavior will quickly escalate from inappropriate to bizarre; lashing out and condemning you, trying to antagonize you into over-reacting, sitting in front of a door so you can't get out, locking you in, running red lights, or maybe even illegally trespassing and going through files they have no business going through...

THE PART ABOUT THE SERPENT

They are losing their victim. They are losing what it is that makes them feel powerful. They are losing their toy...

As to paraphrase something one of my teachers taught me:

> "The devil has no power of his own...he cannot create. He only takes what God creates and destroys it, and calls that power."

And take the case of The Heckler. I can tell you from being a life-long runner that you have to deal with hecklers. I've had to deal with everything from weirdo perverts chasing me down in the Detroit area to having to deal with people's Pit bulls (which simply betray the mentality of their owners). Now, the heckler hates himself. Rather than to take the initiative to appreciate what he's been given - to better himself and discipline himself - to make good use of his time by investing in worthwhile pursuits to improve the quality of his life, it might be easier for him, driving by in his fifth luxury automobile, exerting no more energy than ankle vs. gas pedal (and to flick his cigarette) to mock someone going by, who is. Perhaps if he is successful, this runner might internalize the Heckler's insults and maybe he won't be out there striving with a cause the next time he has to drive to the cigarette store. It the same concept as Cain and Abel:

THE PART ABOUT THE SERPENT

> "And whyfore did Cain kill his brother Abel? Because his own works were wicked while his brother Abel's were righteous."

And I will guarantee you, if you have the spirit of God living in you and you are living godly, you will be dealing with this on all fronts. I will tell you, this Python, or at least any tearing-down spirit, hates sharp things. And I'm talking about your tongue. We are called to be the salt and light of the earth, and that doesn't necessarily mean God' people are to make everything palatable for everybody so it tastes good, nor does blessing those who curse you necessarily mean you ought to bake a birthday cake for everybody who offends you. But salt stings in wounds, "He who is without sin cast the first stone" and it cleanses wounds. Furthermore, light exposes. Lift up a rock and watch what happens to all the little creatures that were hiding under it...

> "Jeshua came to save man from the power of darkness,
> But man loved the darkness more than the light."

Bottom line: the Python has to be offended.

Sadly, I have to admit, while a big part of deliverance is warring against other peoples' abuses, I started realizing how I myself had been subtly treating my mother and my brother in that when they would buy me gifts, I had a way of letting them how the gifts weren't good enough... I was, on the one hand, forbidden from saying what I meant to them; and on the other hand, I forfeited years and years to game-playing rather than to step up and tell them I knew their gifts were only a way of trying to appease me in a subtle attempt to offset their hidden abuses, and that I didn't want them.

I often wondered too, having vowed never to let my mother see me smiling ever again - that we didn't go camping year after year, recalling the only memory I had of my whole family being together and laughing while up in Munising - because it was as memorable an experience for my mother and brother as it was for me; and if we were not somehow hopelessly trying to recreate that point in time...

...

Concerning the excessive fright of evil and preoccupation with the devil people under demonic attack experience is actually the result of internal demons in them corresponding to the demons without. I believe this is where a lot of conspiracy theory comes from. Point blank: You rewind footage of me coming into a post office or public library and watch how differently secular-humanists treat me than they do their other patrons. And I am not saying every librarian and mailman is ungodly, nor am I saying no one in the government ever tries to cover things up. I know personally of a postal worker in Roosevelt Arizona who prays for her patrons, who had even gone to her own Post Master because she couldn't understand why getting my mail forwarded from Munising Michigan was so impossible. But I understood it; it's a compliment, actually.

Conspiracy theory is like this: You are Christian (a Believer), you've suddenly become convicted of all the reasons why celebrating the demonic pagan holiday of Halloween is wrong...You come home to find your wife has carved a pumpkin on the patio to greet you... You get Halloween cards in the mail...You are invited to a Halloween party... Conspiracy theory is like this: Once, court-appointed to attend the counterfeit religion of Alcoholics Anonymous, I heard a story of a man at my meeting-place who was also sentenced to attend but because of vehicular manslaughter, though no one up until this time knew it...Upon closing another selfish litany of how life is better in the "program" that night, one of the members said, "At least I ain't killed nobody!"...

Now, cut through the irony and distinguish between that which promotes health and that which promotes illness in the preceding scenarios... Are they coincidence? Is the way a particular nurse at Center One - who are sometimes frantic, suspicious, looking behind opened doors, suddenly flushed with emergencies from all three of her drugged-out psychiatric patients at the same time while everyone else be so at rest as to be amused by the commotion - simply due to her having been assigned the three bad ones? Where there really patients of Dr. Adams conspiring against him and his staff while I was there because someone found it was easier to talk to me than the gossipy nurses? Well then maybe this book is for them!

> "But he that is spiritual judgeth all things, yet he himself is judged of no man."
> (1 Corinthians 2:15)

> "For God hath not given us the spirit of fear; but of power, and of love, and of a sound mind"
> (2 Timothy 1:7)

I was still having periodic night visits until one day I remembered my nunchakus laying over the headboard of my bed. I had simply kept them there that way so long they'd become a fixture. They were high quality, lead-filled speed chucks with elaborately painted dragons on them. When I got rid of them, the frequency of my night visits all but stopped.

When it came time to breaking off the professionals who had been practicing occultic arts at my expense, Don Jaquish was the first to go. Don had seen the changes in me through the ministry of deliverance, and was amazed. He said, "You're not nervous!" He wrote something in his progress notes to the effect of, "I have never seen Joe so…" During that time I had given him a copy of a letter I wrote to Philip Asplund, just about the time deliverance began for me, which was my way (in addition to all the other ways) of telling these people that my condition was spiritual, like I'd been trying to tell them for years.

THE PART ABOUT THE SERPENT

I'd gone back to Don Jaquish at his private practice, paying him cash, at the request of Curtis Cummins. But seeing Don in previous years, when I was laying in bed committing a form of living suicide, Don stated that he didn't think I was benefiting from therapy and cut me loose. It was the same scenario as when my mother asked me to find another place to live; my hyper-compliance was repulsing them. I'd even sensed that Don was going to do it and I'd brought us both a gourmet coffee to my last appointment as a way to try and appease him. On the one hand, I was subtly doing this all out of spite: "225 pounds, torpid, can't get out of bed…but if you say so!…" having become more disciplined in the therapies they were teaching me, while emulating their lifestyles (i.e. reading their books, tanning, health club memberships, self-indulgence, et cetera) than they were willing to do for themselves. And on the other hand, I was also too dependent to leave…

So I know it was a blow to Don's world to have me come back to him. I know he hated my guts behind his coffee-stained smile. And I know Don only agreed to it as either to make an impression upon Curtis Cummins, or to cover a bad impression made upon him in that he terminated our relationship to begin with. Moreover, Don knew things about Dr. Cummin's personal medical condition and its prognosis that only a close acquaintance would know...

Don prided himself on never missing a meal in his life, "only once", he said, "because I had to have emergency surgery, but then I made up for it." His temperament made him the closest semblance a man could have to a powdery old woman though I somehow used to feel inferior while sitting in his office, watching him use real tissues from a tissue box, and hand lotion for his hands... He told me he had hated his brother before he died, ridiculing him for the fact he used to have to peek at his mail through slits in the side – too afraid to open it – and used to have to iron his blue jeans before going fishing. And what I know about that type of behavior personally, and observing it in others, is perfectionism. And behind perfectionism, anger issues. And behind those anger issues, a mother who's kids will never be good enough...

Any inquiry Don Jaquish made of my Christianity, like Curtis Cummins, were done so as if my faith was problematic. There was a time when Don asked me how much I was praying, and I said, "All the time." He sat back in his seat and repeated to himself, "all the time…" his eyes searching from one side to the other. And I'll never forget, when I told Don during another visit that I could see red flags going up when I'd told him I prayed all the time, he said - eyes wide open and distancing themselves from me - "Oh, no, I didn't see red flags going up!..." Then would come the lip biting and rigidly pushing himself sideways up into his chair as if he were trying to get away from a biting dog, betraying himself with his own behavior, too complaisant that the type of people that sit in his office were aware enough to actually see it...

THE PART ABOUT THE SERPENT

Furthermore, at the time I began breaking ties with Curtis Cummins, I called Don to ask him for that letter back (because I didn't want to help them twist things they could use against me). I made a special trip to Don's office that day to get it and when he handed it to me, I noticed it was a copy in a brownish ink (Don is colorblind) and I ran though my mind what might happen if I said something...that perhaps technically he couldn't give me the original, but I also doubted it... When I went to leave, Don offered me his hand from a seated position while I was still standing, something he had never done...

Dr. Cummins was another story. Though I (as a pathetic attempt of a fluoride-poisoned Christian Passivist to defend himself) had asked him in the past how he felt about me getting a second opinion concerning his treatment, he too had become complaisant that I never would, and had relaxed by the time I was paying hard-earned cash to be seen by Wedgwood Christian Services whose doctor and therapist refuted Conlon's and Cummin's diagnosis. Cummin's had once told me, compared with his typical clients, that I was someone "in tune" with my treatment. He also admired my ability to control myself, and said I was convincing in person; that I was "Zen-like."

Now, however, when I visited his office I was prepared to watch for deceptions. And it worked like this: He greets himself cordially like a little timid schoolboy (though he is well over 6 ft.) and then he sits down on egg shells and opens a massively overloaded notebook of multiple colored files upon his lap. (Kind of like the one I saw falling out of Joe Garrety's hands as he was trying to make it up the steps of my mother's house). Should I question an order he has given or a change that he has made, both hands flip the note book this way and that way before he conjures an answer… Should I question a move of his he is considering making, the notebook goes back and forth, even making distinct flopping sounds; the contents of the notebook obviously having nothing to do with his answers. To me it was Krishna, it was eastern… Krishna running and hiding behind a veil of entertaining shows…Then I would take the experiences back to Bible study and explore them with my group.

Pastor Marc noticed something else. He told me that he could tell by my attacks he was dealing with an intercessory anointing (intercessors pray for people). He said they are rare, and out of a crowd of 50 worshipers he might see three (I've been told less). Not to mention, I had not disclosed to Pastor Marc anything about my prayer-life, or my list of 140 + people….

"The devil's smart" he said, "and he knows if he can take out an intercessor, he can take out many…"

Now things were really making sense: My dad throwing me off the dock when I was a little boy… The harassing treatment from people everywhere I went, the asthma attacks and being rushed to the hospital, the near-death stuff, the deplorable living conditions I constantly settled for - all facilitated a solitary life and empathy for hurting people befitting for an intercessor...

My brother had also noticed a pattern – that it seemed like every time I had a good day I had be punished for it... And I told my brother early on in my conversion that I didn't want to bring him down, but that I had been suffering, to which he said, "I know..." My brother also pointed out to me that my asthma attacks stopped when I moved away from home...

I asked Dr. Cummins for a written basis of his diagnosis of me for the nine years he had been treating me and he suddenly stalled. I pressured him with another letter carbon copied to the staff in his office, and politely told them it had been a pleasure working with them over the years, and that I will not be needing their services anymore. But Dr. Cummins went back and used the Munson Medical records as the basis of his own diagnosis of me, careful to call them "impressions" rather than "diagnosis" as I asked for. He also mentioned "multiple doctors" at Munson Medical Center shared those "impressions" and he reminded me that I complained of Satan putting cars in my path... Below are two letters I sent to Dr. Cummins. He was advised before receiving the last that I would not be speaking with him again without witnesses present:

THE PART ABOUT THE SERPENT

Thursday April 16, 2009
Dear Dr. Cummins,

Interesting talk we had during our appointment yesterday. We do not have the time allotted during an appointment for me to explain to you what you call my optimism. My hopes were to leave your office without the words, "Against medical advice" put in my file but it looks like that's unavoidable. When you try to motivate me with fear you are talking to the wrong person. You said that not only am I at risk where I am with medication reduction but that people like me have a 98% chance of relapse when they stop taking it. You asked, "Do you where seat belt?" And I said, "Always." Then you said, "See." I told you that I do not fear that I am going to be a victim of a fatal crash toodling around town at 25MPR, not even 35 or 40. I told you that I wear it because it is the law and that I've made it a habit. Like I said, "When I am going 55MPR I want it on. Sometimes because of seatbelts you will break your collarbone, fine. You can be in traction for months and have three lumbar fused together if your lucky and then doctors will scare you and tell you that you cannot lift over 25 pounds for the rest of your life. Sometimes you will get your hips crushed and you will moan everywhere you go. Sometimes they cause you to drown. That is called permanent damage and death because of precautionary advice.

If I ran on shear optimism I would expect to hit a wall. It is called faith and it is more than hope, it is a practice and a way of life. In the last 9 years that doctors and

THE PART ABOUT THE SERPENT

therapists have been treating me I studied the Bible whether they told me to or not, and it was leaning toward not with every one of them. My condition was spiritual. The rest of my family died horrible premature deaths. It is not rocket science. I got into the ministry of deliverance and I told them my symptoms; nightmares, schizophrenia, suicidal thoughts, treatment resistant depression, living in bed, and night visits where I get held down in bed and molested. They knew exactly what I was talking about. The pastor's wife was a psychiatric nurse and she told me everything that will happen; When I come out the other side everyone is going to know it; your doctors, your therapists, everyone who knows you, and people that don't even know you are going to know it. She said the medication will be the very last piece, only when I am certain that I can walk out the door and handle the situation anytime, anywhere.

If you are going to help people and understand the mind you need to be aware of it's capabilities and strengths. Focusing only on the physical aspect of the brain is a very limited practice in its overall function. You cannot help someone with their weaknesses unless you are aware of what their strength are. You might as well kick them square in the balls. You said that you were not the only doctor who diagnosed me with schizophrenia. First, you are going to have to prove to me that the temporary delusions I had were not real and I had no reason to be scared and then you'll have to prove to me that Dr. Conlon had enough information to make that diagnosis. Then you'll have to prove to me that Dr.

THE PART ABOUT THE SERPENT

Conlon was not written up in the Record Eagle during the time of her diagnosis of me for throwing around the diagnosis of schizophrenia for people who where psychotic and nothing else, and that she did not move away to practice at Petoskey and then I heard an auditory and visual hallucination when one of the nurses at Center One I trusted told me the day after I readmitted myself (could have been the same day) because of fear, that Dr. Conlon was illegally trespassing and going through patient's files she had no business going through. Then I will tell you whether or not I will ever trust her or you again.

I told you that I've never heard or seen things and you said that there is also delusional thinking and that is what you were basing your diagnosis on so I said, "Ok what"? And you looked in your book and saw that in 2001 I was emotionally upset and had confused thinking. You will have to do better than that. Emotionally upset and confused thinking is not grounds for the diagnosis of schizophrenia. And those were temporary conditions that somehow warranted lifelong medications. If you want to try and find disorganized or chaotic behavior or thoughts in my life I dare you to try. Not in my life, not in my relationships, not among my belongings, and medication did not do that for me. Now let me tell you about the medication. In 2001 I went through the hospital and respite two times back to back before the medicine even fazed me and I began taking it days before I checked in. I remember sitting at my dining room table and I could feel it start to blanket out the thoughts. I almost cried in relief. I said to myself, "What I do not know, cannot hurt me, let it be!" See, back then I got myself into some trouble. Actually it started when I was 20 because I was occult dabbling. But I was playing with fire. I didn't know the Bible and I didn't have a church family to help me. But I have control of my thoughts today. I have a gift of discerning spirits and I know how to use it. I used to know them by symptoms and now I know them by name. When they come I kick em out. That's not medicine. The medicine you maxed me out on disabled my ability to discern and then the spirits had free reign for 8 years plus it made it humanly impossible to identify God and worship Him. Exactly what I was created to do. I was a sick ticket for a long time. I almost killed myself and I am lucky to be alive.

Dr. Cummins, we have been working together for 9 years. I don't think it would be too much to ask for a written statement from you on what you base your diagnosis of me on. Now I would like to know. It would be helpful to share it with people like the doctor and therapist at Wedgwood Christian Services who refuted that diagnosis. Then I could share it with every person I know who has known me in the last 9 years and even those who knew me before, who refuted that diagnosis. I can share it with those who told me I could be free from schizophrenia. Then I could take it with me when I go crawling back to Center One on my belly for more abuse. Or am I just going to be one of the lucky 2%? The DSM 4 does not list the diagnosis of demonic possession or demonic oppression. I, and others I know, including a famous Christian diagnostician I learned from, believes it should. I believe it should at least have the terms, "We do not know" or, "We do not practice this type of medicine" with a referral to someone who may be able to help, rather than conquer everything that walks through the door and shove pills down its throat till it dies.

BTW: Inspiration is superior as a motivator as opposed to fear, regret, and guilt.

Take Care,
Joseph Kacin

Friday May 15, 2009

Dear Dr. Cummins,

It was interesting for me to find that auditory hallucinations never had anything to do with your diagnosis of me in the past. They were never mentioned because they didn't exist. I asked you for a basis of your diagnosis of me between the dates of 2000 and April 15th 2009, the last day I sat in your office. But instead, in my opinion, you either disrespected what I said like you always have, or you went back, and upon researching the Munson Medical Center records, found that I complained of hearing things and decided to add it to the diagnosis you made of me a long time ago (the one that required 8 years of abusive medications that clearly caused severe suffering) to give it validity in order to better cover your ass.

THE PART ABOUT THE SERPENT

For a man who values false pretenses like yourself, you probably thought nothing of it, but it is called: lying, falsifying information, and treating your clients like human pieces of garbage.

When I told you that Dr. Riddle thanked me for working so hard in the hospital, while you said I had "negative symptoms", "affective flattening", "disorganized thoughts", and "depression", he said it in front of someone I truly admired and have all compassion for to this day. I almost couldn't accept it, it meant everything to me, and it almost makes me cry to think about it. As a result, you can bet your ass that I worked even harder and I came to admire Dr. Riddle who calls his patients his "good friends." Those are the types of inspirational techniques that motivate people that I showed you, you are lacking in. When I told you how inappropriate your fear tactics were you did it again in your letter with words like "decompensation" and "hospitalization" because you are bent on treating people with abusive psychiatric medications that clearly cause harm whether or not the diagnosis is correct or your clients got the help they needed from the proper sources, rather than admit that you had no idea what you were doing. On the 15th of April, I was trying to pay you a compliment for never giving me the diagnosis of schizophrenia until you asked me if I wanted to know why you did.

See, Dr. Cummins, I was properly diagnosed and treated successfully for my condition and it was not schizophrenia. The reason why you cannot accept and believe that is because of a void in reality called denial. It is a lie. It is a thought that is accepted, agreed upon in the mind, and contrived. It is a covering like I told you about. That is exactly what happens before crimes are committed. First it is contrived in the mind, then the act is carried out. I do not need *you* to grow up and accept the truth: every mature, gifted, intelligent, competent, respected, credible, stable, person, friend, acquaintance, pastor, teacher, group, neighbor, and professional that I know, knows it, can see the change, are amazed, compliments me, and rejoices with me. Like they promised me in deliverance, "everyone is going to know it." Unfortunately, you choose to learn things the hard way. I hope that you do not think that the correspondence and transactions between us are, or will remain, some big secret between us, because they're not.

Sincerely,

Joseph Kacin

I never saw Curtis Cummins again until seven years later, entering a coffee shop with his bicycle helmet still on his head while I was inside sitting at my computer. I hadn't lifted my head to see who it was until he had already made it to the service counter. He remained pressed in the direction of the counter, ordered a drink on his wife's tab, using only her first name, and exited.

THE PART ABOUT THE SERPENT

Fire-breathing

"YOU'RE PLAYING DIRTY POOL DEBORAH, GOODBYE!" Debbie (I will call her) and her live-in boyfriend were two of my Bible-study partners who would come to my group, and were among one the dysfunctional relationships I desperately needed to break off. I cleaned my apartment every Wednesday for studies, supplied all the baked goods, the coffee, the study criteria, and I even played the praise music live – and sometimes with songs I wrote myself. But every night it turned into politics. They would apologize to me while I sat there – the only one left with his Bible open. I began making rules for them but my old teacher called me after group one night to caution me that if I begin making rules, it might become un-fun for Debbie's live-in (a non-believer), and he might not want to come. But I could only take a few more weeks of it until I quit calling any of them back but continued my weekly studies with another in-home fellowship.

THE PART ABOUT THE SERPENT

My thoughts were, "I don't clean my house every week for Bible study, supply all the refreshments, gather the study material throughout the week, provide the music - even making reminder calls about the event - so you can talk politics. If you just want to play checkers and socialize, go somewhere else!"...

About a year after that, Debbie asked me if we could have studies again. I mentioned to her that the group only wanted to talk politics while everyone's Bibles remained closed. She said, "Well then maybe we can make rules!"...

I learned through a combination of psychology and Biblical mandates that it is wiser to let the dysfunctional party to the parting. You let them be the aggressor. For instance: it is known in behavioral psychology that when a member of a dysfunctional relationship seeks to better himself - say he's decided to quit drinking where the other has not - the member left remaining in his dysfunction is usually the one who breaks off the relationship because they cannot handle the new light coming in. Add to that, personal experience: if they sense you are going to walk, or even if you've formally and politely told them so, they cannot just let you leave knowing what you know about them - and so must sabotage your exodus to make you out to be the bad guy before you get there. They know that once you experience some distance from them you will also experience freedom and will probably find support, and that you will realize the gravity of the situation you couldn't see while up close to them.

THE PART ABOUT THE SERPENT

Debbie was scary in that she was powerful. The day she told me that one of her family members were responsible for designing the way to measure the laser beam for the military I said to myself, "Oh shit!" She was native American, unwilling to give up her heritage for her Christianity (by her own admission, and my antagonisms), and I would get heeby geebies at their house which was decked out with all kinds of dream catchers and Indian art. In fact, one Christmas eve they invited me over and while one of them was talking I looked up on the wall and saw a hand-painted Indian drum. The painting on the skin depicted something akin to bear-paw prints or something benign like that, but in the spiritual sense – something I could tell the artist had no idea he was doing – was painted a demonic face that absolutely freaked me out! I remained calm and recalled something I thought I read in the Bible (which I've not been able to confirm) which was to recognize the design of the devil, and that's all I knew. While they continued talking I looked up again to be certain I saw what I saw and that thing was alive! I went home that night and slept with the light on in my haunted bedroom, and continued to sleep with it on for weeks...

One characteristic of Debbie was her excessive use of the words "you need" and "you should" in a controlling way. Rex had taught me that those words were used to control, and thought I should mention it to her at a time when she wasn't doing it, to make her aware of it. When I did tell her, she was amazed at it (still not realizing her own involvement), and even asked me to repeat it because she knew people she wanted to share it with. She'd been encroaching and advancing on me for a long time. The funny thing was, she was the individual who suggested that I might need deliverance, but then came to regret that she advised me of it when I began discovering the deliverance ministry itself was practicing non-scriptural techniques that were dangerous, and could prove it Biblically. And funnier still, when I told Pastor Marc and Julia that I intended to bring Debbie to a service (which I did) they didn't want to have anything to do with her, and said, "well, we don't know Debbie, and we'll have to judge her by her fruits."...

Along the lines of characteristics: Debbie and her live-in would often re-neg on Bible studies at the last minute, and on one occasion – deliberately being proactive with people to try and commend their good behavior rather than condemn their bad – I told her live-in after coming to my door at five minutes to study-time to tell me they weren't coming, "Well, I appreciate you letting me know!" To which he said, "We'll, we wouldn't want to tell you at the last minute or anything…"! And unfortunately that's just typical behavior; you give people an inch and they'll take a mile!

Debbie also explained to me she had astro-projection-like experiences, and that when she was a little girl, something like a lighting bolt hit her in the kitchen and she began speaking out in tongues <u>uncontrollably</u>, having no idea what had come over her. And sometimes she would do that on the phone when I'd give her a praise report on my deliverance. After she saw I began exposing the hypocrisies and dangerous teachings of Pine Grove, she called one day and told me that she hoped I didn't mind, but she'd been telling people she ministers to on the internet that she knows someone who knows the true and living God because he can recognize false teaching...

For the record: speaking in tongues is a voluntary form of prayer. If something overtakes you and forces you to pray to it, that ain't God! Only a sick God would overtake people to direct adoration and worship back to himself! What's the point!

"By their fruits ye shall know them."

"But the fruit of the Spirit is love, joy, peace, longsuffering, gentleness, goodness, faith, meekness, temperance (self-control)..."
(Galatians 5:22,23[parenthesis mine])

Debbie had given me items - insulting to me - like rubber band exercise bands (being I am seasoned weight lifter) and some new, micro-fiber cleaning rags I never used – crap like that. But they were encroaching gifts I knew were bad – just like those from my mother. I could sense they were dry, hollow appeasements that they were going to use against me on a rainy day. Furthermore, I had genuinely loaned Debbie a $20 hardcover I sent away for about the manners and customs of Bible times...

THE PART ABOUT THE SERPENT

I started to break things off with Debbie formally over the phone. I explained to her that her politics had ruined Bible studies and that I quit calling her back, and that I had to go and study elsewhere. I told her my thoughts about her live-in boyfriend situation, and that I knew the only reason he ever came to studies was to use what he learned about the Bible in his arguments *against* God. She called me back and told me that she wanted to come over, to give me my book back (which she had only had for a couple days) which is a maneuver likely known in the art of self-defense as "Sucker!" She wanted to intimidate me with her presence. I told her I was leaving and she kept me on the line and told me she was offended at what I'd said… She wanted to argue and was working to confuse me, she said, "Your flip-flopping!…your going back and forth on your teaching!…" similar to Dr. Cummin's gigantic book of many colors. I also told her how uncomfortable I felt at a church they invited me to (and one they did not know my relatives attended) with a non-married couple yelling hallelujah during the service – and obviously parading me around with them to introduce me to people to bolster their image.

Debbie then informed me that a song from the Zac Brown band I had sent her over the computer at one time she deleted because the lyrics were too dirty (which romantic intent on my part had never been a factor), and that the reason why she would bring her live-in boyfriend with her to Bible studies was because she didn't feel comfortable being alone with me. But for the record: this was an overweight woman, well into her 50's, who rode shotgun with me to church, talked endlessly with me on the telephone; a grown mother who sat at my kitchen table *alone* with me and told me how guys used to want to "nail" her…a grown "Christian" woman who'd also tried warming me up to her live-in's idea of having a third party in bed with them. Not to mention, I found it so disturbing that she'd shared her masturbation preferences with me over the telephone on one occasion that I had to tell Don Jaquish about it! But now, all of the sudden *I* had become some perverted monster that couldn't be stopped because I asserted myself.

Debbie told me I was angry at everybody and asked me what I was really angry at (another blame-shifting antagonist) and I didn't know what to say but I still kind of fell for it and started filling in the blanks (still keeping it focused and objective) and then she said, "You need to get back on your meds!" and that's when I ended it, permanently. Not to mention, Debbie had also asserted herself that I was wrongly diagnosed with schizophrenia for the simple fact I had beautiful house-plants, because she said she had been around the mentally ill, and no schizophrenic could keep house with beautiful house-plants like that.

I mailed Debbie's insulting gifts back to her in a formal manner, and one day came home and discovered my beautiful hard-back hanging from my doorknob in one of those plastic grocery store bags...

THE PART ABOUT THE SERPENT

Philip, the still-registered social worker, told me that in his line of work, whenever someone tries to use bad things against you or try to dig up dirt to hurt you because you've addressed them on something, that at that point termination of that relationship was always mandatory.

Philip also shared with me a letter from Lois Hawley that stated in the letter she was so excited by something her daughter had taken part of she was overtaken with tongues. When I drew attention to the matter by asking him who it was that was overtaken with tongues, Lois or her daughter, to be sure; Philip said Lois, while inflecting attention from the issue, sensing I was suspicious...

I still remember the day Rex was sitting at my kitchen table when I explained to him all that I was experiencing through deliverance. There are times when people are in a place to hear and other times when they're eyes just aren't going to open. But I can assure you when I told Rex (who I am certain at times probably thought I was Belleview material) what Julia Hoard told me concerning Dr. Conlon - that she doesn't hate me, but she hates the holy spirit living in me, that at that moment Rex's eyes were opened. In fact, I saw him quake, and likely because he himself had been guilty of ridiculing my faith and wondered if he too had lost his cover... But he'd already had. He also treated me as an extremist (of which I will admit any day) because I told him I thought I should fill up on some worship music before going to bed on one occasion to

THE PART ABOUT THE SERPENT

help prevent having a night visit, until I told him that Julia had even suggested the same thing some time after I began doing it. I also said to him concerning it all, "An attitude? yeah, I have one! I just fought my way out of the kingdom of the devil...40 years of it...who's next?!"

Rex was next...

I'd been cleaning Rex's house in exchange for letting me record there during the week while he was working down-state. Every transaction of ours started becoming increasingly confusing, like it was deliberate. I sent him a formal note in the mail – that due to differences in our spiritual practices, I felt it was best that we disassociate at that time. A couple days later, a shaking Rex showed up at my front door to give me some money he owed me, and said to me, "I got your note...I'm sorry that you feel that way...If you still ever need my help, I'm not going anywhere."

I could also now recognize "I'm sorry that you feel that way" as another subtle blame-shifting technique which puts the focus back on "you" - people used that is at the same time supposed to pass as some kind of apology. Rex was also saying, in effect, that all he's ever done for me was helped me. And that was the very reason he was at Philip's "Christian" group in the first place. He was saying, in effect, to the Christian community, "If I tolerate Christians and do service work by giving them rides to their meetings, then they should be tolerant of my homosexual lifestyle."...

THE PART ABOUT THE SERPENT

I saw strange things in deliverance, and could back it up scripturally. For starters, it was abusive. Pastor Marc kept telling me that people usually run and never come back. He would tell me that he never tells people how tough he is, but then proceeded to tell me how he broke some guy's back wrestling one time, and other things like that. He kind of taunted me with the fear of the Python Spirit – that one of the girls, a seer, had told him she saw several heads around me… He said, "If you don't stick with us through this process, slowly, you'll be back to these doors." He told me, "Ask God if He loves you." I said, "Hhhhe doesn't have to answer that!" meaning, to me. "He says that over and over in…" "Oh yes he does! Ask Him!" What pastor Marc was trying to demonstrate was that if I didn't get a noticeable reply from God on demand like that, I wasn't hearing from Him properly. But the Bible is clear,

"Thou shalt not tempt the Lord Thy God."

One day, when I told Pastor Marc of an actual vision I had – a re-confirmation of a prophesy I all but bailed on back in 2001 – he tried to ridicule me for it even though it was so strong it gave me fearless power over the demons that still stands to this day.

One of the books they gave me, David Seamunds *Healing Damaged Emotions* had me hooked the first time I read out of it. I said to myself, "What an excellent, excellent therapist!" The therapy takes the individual into a memory of a traumatic experience that caused damage; or let demons in, to be more specific.

THE PART ABOUT THE SERPENT

They also deal with PTSD cases. Keep in mind, not everything they were teaching me was wrong; the results could not be hidden, and their sincerity was right even when their teaching was out of line with scripture. For Paul wrote:

"For I bear them that they have a zeal for God, but not according to knowledge." (Romans 10:2)

But the teachings were non-scriptural inner-healing memory techniques couched in Biblical language. My main home-fellowship church (that Pastor Marc nor Julia were aware of) told me that anything contrived is garbage, and that the word of God comes simply. But through the Memory Healing exercise the victim is walked through the traumatic memory (by the pastors) where they are told to try and notice something they never noticed before in the memory and focus on it; a beam of light, anything, and then miraculously Jesus will appear, and apparently he often rebukes you, and if he does – the victim's are told to obey what he said.

Pastor Marc told me (the day he tried to shame me for the conformation-vision I saw) "Now, you are going to have a full blown, face to face encounter with God that's literally going to rock your world!"

I was all for it and submitted myself to them, the memory: the day my dad meanly pushed me to the floor when I tried to grab his beer...

THE PART ABOUT THE SERPENT

A small team of people chanting stuff assisted while they walked me through. I never did see anything, and when I rose my head and opened my eyes, Leslie was looking into each one of my eyes individually, as if she would notice if a trace of anything had gotten in. We had to reschedule for another session.

Leslie had also had a vision she asked me about, early on – if I had anything to do with trees – because she saw trees. It wasn't until sometime later that I recalled the giant elm tree outside my apartment that displayed moss on its north side when it rained. I used to tell people that I drew strength from it, even writing about it in a story I sent out to publishers…

Another peculiarity to me, however, was that the members of the church, and those who had gone through the Memory Healing process – who had met "God" face to face – were shabby looking and dispirited. "A bunch of slobs" Debbie called them. Plus I gave up asking them how long deliverance might take in my case because each answer was so vague and hopeless. "Stay…" "Stick around…" was all I would hear…

One night, Pastor Marc invited me to a "Mendings" night. I was to assist by giving written prophecies to the victims and then Pastor Marc employed me to stand behind a woman he was going to "slay in the spirit" to help catch her when she fell. A young professional by the name of Donald was there that night, who they called Don because the tear people down. But Donald

THE PART ABOUT THE SERPENT

was so on fire for God that he would stand up before a service with a praise report on how God had found he and his fiancé a van for $200, even though it still needed heavy work! And Donald was so engaging and alive that I would have to look away from him when he was talking; his eye contact was too stimulating for someone like me. But this night he was to undergo a "Mending" though he didn't appear to me to be a victim of serious trauma, not the demonic type.

At the end of the night, one of the more shabby looking individuals who had just gone though a "Mending" walked up near the alter where me and Pastor Marc were stationed and Pastor Marc asked with enthusiasm, "Did you see Him?" … We'll what did he say?!" To which this dispirited individual only gave a half-audible murmur while diverting his eyes away with a shrug! Apparently this man had just seen the God of the universe but all he could muster was a little whimper!

I was feeling tough that night because I too was fighting the good fight. I remember having my black leather jacket on with my black leather gloves and I stopped to shake Donald's hand who was now seated in the submissive position and could barely lift his eyes to me, when I grabbed his hand and said, "See ya round Donald!"

I started pulling away from Pine Grove in written emails on their inconsistencies and their abusive ways. Julia told me that the devil was subtly trying to twist my thoughts - that I couldn't recognize, and haunted me with more "stay" and "stick with us" words. The "Mendings" teaching was an obvious form of witchcraft, emphasis on the word "craft."

I saw the cover of a book that had a picture of a church with a cross coming 3D out of one window, and some kind of face coming 3D out of another entitled, *Neo-Pentecostilism: Witchcraft*, by Stephen Lambert. I told people, "I *know* what's in that book!"

These were shamanistic techniques borrowed from the occult world to turn people on to dialoging with spirit-guides (claiming to be Jesus) who would then come in and lead them on their spiritual paths. Pastor Marc also told me that once I have that encounter – I would be able to look back upon my life and know when it was when God was speaking to me, and when it was He wasn't…

The Bible says that no man has seen God at any time, nor can see God. This also means that Jesus is not God, and I said it. I said it because the Bible says it.

I took my emails and my testimony to the leader of my home church to ask him if I could report Pine Grove to higher authorizes and have their license to practice taken away. But he told me that the only reason a church has a license is to keep them tax exempt. His advice was, "run!" I asked the group, "Then how is it that these people are seeing God?" "They're not." they said…

THE PART ABOUT THE SERPENT

Remembering my last encounter with Donald - why it was the guy who had been too engaging and stimulating for me to talk to - was now deflated and in the submissive position, barely able to left his eyes up at me – was because on a subtle level Donald knew he just had the rug pulled out from under him and was helpless. I might have well have said, "Goodbye Donald."…

I talked with authors who expose this kind of teaching before running a special announcement in the local newspaper:

"If you feel you have been the victim of authoritarian abuse and witchcraft concerning the Inner-healing/deliverance ministry being taught in the local church, call me, I may be able to help…"

Shortly thereafter I began Isaiah 14 Ministries - a non-profit discernment ministry at the public-awareness and administrative level, based upon my testimony of coming from an abandoned motel room when I was a kid, and stealing my grandmother's Bible while focusing on that very chapter. And I can probably convince you that my grandmother never forgave me. Soon I went underground and moved out of town to try and finish this book.

THE PART ABOUT THE SERPENT

I placed a picture on my desk the way people do in their offices – who have loved-ones on their desk - only this was simply a painting of a woman. One night, however, I moved the picture to my nightstand, and that very night I had a very pure night visit. It was just as if something had walked right out of that picture and proceeded to assault me. It was in fact a demonic object that I gave too much power to; I had been idolizing it...

I started running between 10 and 17 milers, six days a week; and when it rained, the end of my brown trail shoes would turn pink from my toes bleeding; while my toes remained blue, red, and white so long I just quit caring about it. I started hitting my desk every morning at five AM, and when I ran, I'd bring home a handful of leeks, or a T-shirt full of wild apples; and not because I prefer the taste of wild apples as some people stated they didn't, it was because I didn't have a choice.

Sometimes I would run the Sleeping Bear National Lakeshore at four AM in a blizzard with ¼ inch hex screws in my shoes and a LED light strapped to my head, when all I could see was an animal track staggering down the road... I saw a cougar, an emu (probably lost from someone's farm), a bobcat, arctic whited owls, and I saw other people out running unlikely places I had run, knowing I was inspiring people... When I took my escapades to the Upper Peninsula, in the remotest part of it I saw 15 bald eagles in one sighting, meaning, all in one frame. Then eventually I ran the mountains out west with a machete on my back.

THE PART ABOUT THE SERPENT

The freedom I now had was immense, but anyone linked to me from my past such as my MSHDA caseworker, would deliberately throw wrenches in my growth and would sweep any discrimination I was contending with from my landlords under the rug; and I wound up homeless - putting my things in storage and living in a tent across the U.S. for four years on $661.00 a month of Disability - while I continued to write this book, having tried to run from one bad landlord-situation to the next with MSHDA still tethered to me. Because of that discrimination, I cut all state assistance, period (which had accrued from the steady decline in my health during the years I was under psychiatric treatment), before taking my complaint to the executive office of Governor Snyder, who had delegated the matter back to MSHDA. What fooled me was the name, MSHDA (Michigan State Housing Development Authority), but MSHDA is federal i.e. HUD. One of the discriminating landlords happen to be Mary Ann Shutz - professing to be an elder in the Faith Reformed Church; Calvin College...

I reported Mary Ann and her business partners in a 16 paged witnessed statement; along with 17 enclosures, including dialogue, photographs, and statements from witnesses to the leaders at Calvin College, including Professor Gaylin Byker; and to the leaders at Degage Ministries (a housing ministry in Grand Rapids where I discovered Mary Ann was on the board) for being in the business of buying junk houses and renting them to support their tropical-vacation lifestyle to the exclusion of the rights and welfare of their occupants, and blatant discrimination, to no avail. And if you are interested in those documents, God willing, I will mail them to you.

> "Against an elder receive not an accusation, but before two or three witnesses. Them that sin rebuke before all, that others also may fear." (1 Timothy 5:19-20)

I operated my own cleaning service and was working part-time as a gardener for a multimillionaire (also a Faith Reformer) in the area who brought me in to do other things when the summer ended because he liked my work. He told me, "Things are looking good!..." One day, however, my car broke down on my way home and I needed his assistance... He came to help and while we were sitting in his car, in the dark, making plans for my car, a patrol car passed by in front of us and he said, "Get in the driver's seat!" We switched seats, and after a few moments I asked him, "Now, why did we do the switcheroo?" "*Your* driving!" He said.

He was expecting me, his gardener, to lie for him if the police turned around...

Shortly thereafter this gentleman made a proposal to me. "I want a resume from you!" He said. "I want to see where I can best use you...where the best placement for you is. Here's the deal: In your first year you make 24 million. In your second year you lose two million. In your third year you make 26 million..." Typically, I love making resumes, but I had to think, "if this gentleman thinks so little of me that he is going to expect me to lie

THE PART ABOUT THE SERPENT

for him in small ways (which standing before a court and lying for him on the stand that I was driving his vehicle when I was not, is by no means a small way!) then he is also going to expect me to lie for him in very big ways..." His best employee is someone who will pull a dirty when there's 60 million dollars at stake. ... that's his best employee, not someone committed to upholding their integrity, desperately trying to live a life honoring to God. Therefore I could not bring myself to even begin making that resume and I mailed some money back to him with a formal letter, telling him I could not longer afford to work for him. He called again, but I simply backed away from the telephone and let the answering machine take it.

When I was a kid, all I cared about was fame and fortune and I didn't care how I got it - when it was the farthest thing from me - even selling my soul to the devil to get it. Now that that contract with devil had been disannulled, then extraordinary offers began presenting themselves, even girls half my age. Furthermore, I wasn't doing a good job for myself, or for the praise of some sneaky multimillionaire (a gem-manufacturer, by the way) I was doing it for God's glory.

I was on the docket to appear before Judge Michael Steptka in Leelanau County (1 Timothy 5:19-20) for eviction from Mary Ann Shutz's property just days subsequent to my formal resignation from the multimillionaire, when Mary Ann had her attorney (who couldn't get any of our names right) try to offer me $1,000 for my troubles with the understanding I vacate their property, in attempt to try to keep it from going to court.

But I refused to acknowledge any of them, and I forced Mary Ann to follow through and evict me, to teach these people that you can't just buy your way out of corruption.

THE PART ABOUT THE SERPENT

Hindsight

I THINK THE MOST PROFOUND effect brain damage had on me was in mental fatigue, but which no one else could see. And I say the words "was" and "could" in past-tense to keep with the story-form of my testimony, but which is every bit as real while I write this as it was 30 years ago.

People didn't understand what it actually takes me to process information. Essentially, I could not stop working. I couldn't watch TV, I couldn't let myself relax and be entertained; I had to reduce and enforce the amount of irons I had in the fire, which is still above and beyond the norm. The more tired I get, the more vague my vocabulary becomes - and coupled with coming from a family with a very dry sense of humor - I know I often come across as a prick.

THE PART ABOUT THE SERPENT

And I don't think people realize how shallow it is to try and console someone with brain damage by telling them they look fine. As if perhaps as long as I make the outer shell look good and pretty – what's on the inside won't matter... Assuring a brain damage survivor they look fine, or that you would never suspect them of having brain damage, also conspires with the victim's tendency to hide it. And there on the other hand, by not hiding it, he is left vulnerable in that it will be the first place people go for when they want to try and discredit him, because, unfortunately, that's the kind of deviance and depravity to be expected from people in this world.

As my old teacher once told me,

"If you're in a fight with an evil man, and you give him one chance, he's going to kick you right in the balls each and every time. That's why cops don't give people chances."...

I remember seeing another client while undergoing neuropsychological testing, putting his hand to a doorknob in the facility, but then freezing in a paralysis of questions. And I understand that. I could fill pages of what could be going through someone's head in such a moment, because as soon as he opens that door, everything is going to change: "Should I knock?... Oh my God I want to die!... Am I on time?... Will they be able to tell I've been crying?... Did my taxi driver understand that I don't want to pay for him to wait – but

THE PART ABOUT THE SERPENT

to come back? et cetera et cetera…" Similarly, I sometimes come across people in the grocery store - especially the big thrift stores – temporarily lost while gazing at their calculator, standing before a display of fruit; internalizing all the idle words and chatter around them - their peripheral vision taking note of everything going on… And I know to treat them in a loving spirit (which is simply treating them no differently than anybody else) rather than to grope them up and down with my eyes as some kind of conformity gesture people often try on me.

Victims of severe trauma can have a photographic memory due to the fact the brain records events around trauma, plus they can have 40% more visual acuity than a normal person...

On my quest to learn what was behind things, what people really meant, what they were really up to, I will share a couple of illustrations: I'm drinking spinach and blueberry smoothies because someone's turned me on to the health benefits, and you have to purchase spinach fairy often if you want it fresh. A woman working at the grocery store who used to live by my mother, and a bit of a downer to talk to, asked me one day, "So, what do you do with the spinach? you boil it?..." And I said, "No, I put it in a blender with blueberries and drink it. It isn't very good, though. But I do it because it's good for you." And what I am actually saying is,"Your not my first choice of friend, but I'm being nice to you because it's good for business..." Because speaking in metaphor has become the colloquial currency in a world of deception. And it is not always to deceive, mind you, but also to protect.

> "Behold, I send you forth as sheep in the midst of wolves: be ye therefore wise as serpents, and harmless as doves." (Matthew 10:16)

On one occasion, me and my mother overheard a man asking a woman out to eat across a parking lot (as she was wide-steppedly walking away). "We'll get together sometime! We'll do Chinese!" "I don't like Chinese!" she shouted back. "Then we'll do Sheldon's! We'll do Sheldon's!" he said. I said to my mom, "Did you hear that?" My mom tipped her head down to try to remember. It's because the woman said no and the man didn't want to hear it. And I will guarantee you they never did Sheldon's, or any other restaurant, for that matter...

But what may be more difficult than brain damage itself is self-deception, and that may have been the reason I took such interest in Daniel Goleman's work when I was younger, after filling up on Alice Miller. I didn't want to believe things were as bad as they were, and I cannot admit when and if I am tired. I saw a nature video of Saba, an elephant specialist, who actually grew up with elephants and favored a certain elephant by the name of Babel. Babel had a broken back leg and used her front legs like crutches for so long that it had actually twisted her back. As Babel works to stay behind the herd, the other elephants have already reached their destination and are playing in the water, throwing their trunks around and being silly while Babel may still have to face the current of a river... She is constantly in motion and she won't call on the rest of the herd for help, though they would drop everything to do so should she. Babel would die without the group, and I personally believe the reason she does not ever reach for help is because she knows she poses a risk to the herd to begin with, and may already have endangered them in places Saba is not aware of. But when Saba said what made Babel different - that she didn't get down-time like the other elephants - I positively identified with Babel the elephant.

I don't care for relaxation, it's uncomfortable; I've got a job to do and exposing the works of darkness and registering the victory of Jeshua in all territories of the devil during the short time I have left in this world is imperative.

Now whether you are legitimately trying to shield yourself or someone else, or you are trying to cover up something bad you did, denial is still volitional. Denial may seem automatic, and now we're getting back into spirit: You yourself know how quickly a lie can come out of your mouth; it's like mercury, bang, it's there. And if you have a hard time seeing that in yourself, certainly you know how it happens when other people do it to you, right?! Being a Believer who has come to Elohim (God) through Jeshua does not automatically assign them to some quarantined holy place were no one ever lies. As my old teacher used to say, "When someone is saved, they're still the filthy old man they were the day before; it takes time to shed the old filthy man off." And so as a man gets in the habit of telling the truth, lies are not so automatic to him anymore. And the greater the degree that individual can admit the truth about himself – which pars with the very brokenness that brings people to Elohim – the greater control that individual has over his own thoughts, and the greater discernment he will have of others.

"For the weapons that we fight with *are* not carnal, but mighty through God to the pulling down of strongholds (lies); casting down imaginations, and every high thing that exulteth itself against the knowledge of God, and bringing into captivity every thought to the obedience of Christ; And having in a readiness to revenge all disobedience, when your obedience is fulfilled."
(11 Corinthians 10:4-6 [parenthesis mine])

Now, when I was younger, dabbling in the occult, lies came out of my mouth with fluidity; I was the biggest liar that ever walked the planet. And when I was performing, especially while intoxicated or on drugs – when I would enter into that third mirror that held no image – it was actually a form of channeling for the demonic spirits. They were doing the work that was fascinating everybody while harnessing my leadership qualities to the end I lead them to where I was/they were. I sometimes recognize automatic channeling in other musicians today and it sends the hair up on the back of my neck!

THE PART ABOUT THE SERPENT

I didn't learn it from my neuropsychological testing but I knew I could see double words back to back in sentences where normal people who are deliberately tested to see them don't. And the answer didn't come until many, many years later after reading somewhere - that when someone who has survived a traumatic brain injury can find those double words – they do so because they have suffered loss to a degree that they can never again allow themselves to take anything for granted. And if you didn't notice, the very first line of this book following the dedication has a double word in it deliberately hidden to stress to you the power of subtlety.

I told myself during the years I lived in bed that I wouldn't pursue a romantic relationship with anyone because I wouldn't want someone who might care about me watch me suffer like that; I couldn't do that to someone. And I told myself I would not have a pet for the same reason. But when I heard what I heard shortly after my mother died (whether it was of an angel or Jeshua), it was a <u>compassionate</u> voice of someone who knew me <u>intimately</u> and <u>suffered</u> with me, and they had suffered with me through all those days of me lying in bed wanting to die (fruits of the Spirit the devil would never endure to fake; neither would he ever die for any of his subjects), even during the times I had rejected Elohim. And I flag at the ability to comprehend that kind of compassion. I am a living testimony that

THE PART ABOUT THE SERPENT

Elohim brings souls up out of the grave (Psalm 30:3) and there is no way in hell I am going back!

I believe very much Elohim has taken what has been a crippling in my life by putting it to work as a gift for recognizing deception, imperfect as I am. I've heard it said that the only way to spot a counterfeit is by knowing the genuine article, and the Bible says that only through much tribulation do we enter into the kingdom of God (Acts 14:22). And if Elohim asked me today if I wanted Him to heal me of my brain damage, after all these years, after all it's taken, after all I've endured, after all the struggling, after all the ridicule, after all the presumptions, after all the maltreatment, and after all the overcoming - I would have to say no. And I think that means He already has...

Joseph John Kacin III
Isaiah14ministries@outlook.com

Made in the USA
Columbia, SC
13 February 2023